W9-DBB-786

THE
ARMED
YACHTS
OF CANADA

Canadian Cataloguing in Publication Data

McKee, Fraser, 1925 -
Armed Yachts of Canada

Bibliography: p.
Includes index.
ISBN 0-919822-55-X

1. Yachts and yachting - Canada - History - 20th century. 2. Canada. Royal Canadian Navy - Boats - History - 20th century. 3. Canada. Royal Canadian Navy - History - World War, 1914-1918. 4. Canada. Royal Canadian Navy - History - World War, 1939-1945. I. Title.

VA400.M44 1983 359.3'258'0971 C83-099227-8

THE ARMED YACHTS OF CANADA

Published in Canada by,
THE BOSTON MILLS PRESS,
98 Main St.,
Erin, Ontario, N0B 1T0

Typeset by Speed River Graphics, Guelph, Ont.
Printed by Bramalea Printing, Bramalea, Ont.

The Boston Mills Press gratefully acknowledges the assistance of the Canada Council, the Ontario Arts Council, and the Office of the Secretary of State.

The author wishes to acknowledge the Ontario Heritage Foundation, Ministry of Citizenship and Culture, whose grant-in-aid of publication made this book possible.

Halonia, owned by R.A. Van Clief of the New York jewelry firm, and purchased by Oakville stockbroker A. Montye McCrae. She became HMCS *Raccoon*, and was lost.

DEDICATION

To all those who served in the armed yachts from 1939 to 1945 as their contribution to the freedom of the seas that we fought for;

and to my daughter Allison, who never saw a luxury yacht such as these, but who should know what the Navy managed to do in times of deep duress, as should all Canadians.

HMCS *Raccoon*

CONTENTS

Painting by Arthur Lismer in 1920 at Halifax
from a sketch made in 1916
"CONVOY AT SEA"

THE ARMED YACHTS OF CANADA

Fraser McKee

FOREWORD

I am honoured to have been asked to write a foreword to Fraser McKee's *The Armed Yachts*. The author has worked his meticulous and complete research into an extremely readable book.

This book is not only "a good read", it provides a fascinating and timely account of one aspect of Canadian efforts to respond to the onset of both the First and Second World Wars from a state of woeful unpreparedness.

What a splendid story it is! It shows we Canadians at our best: inventive, flexible, and responsive to the crises; the extraordinary willingness, drive, and spirit of our people to respond when the need arises.

It also illustrates that there is more needed than spirit, to be ready to cope with national emergencies. With the best will in the world, it took six months to bring the first of the armed yachts, *Sans Peur*, into shaky service, and over a year to bring in the last, *Vison*.

The yachts covered a gap, or rather a yawning chasm: it was a very considerable time before new equipment was able to be brought into service, and the expansion of the Navy could be said to have started to take place.

From the book, we get a clear picture of the enormous variety of tasks needed to be performed at sea in the event of a war, and the importance of being able to draw on our resources to perform them. Anything that could float and carry armament became an important component of our total naval force. Not glamorous work, in the yachts, but mostly rough, miserable, and thankless, risky enough without the onslaughts of the enemy. They suffered their losses both to enemy and to environment, but the cheerful nature of the Canadian sailor comes through loud and clear.

May we all ponder, as well as chuckle, over this excellent book. I wonder what was in *Otter's* medical kit (in Chapter 9)!

Vice-Admiral D. N. Mainguy
Deputy Chief of the Defence Staff,
Canadian Armed Forces
January 25, 1983

Solomon R. Guggenheim's *Trillora ex-HMCS Grilse* in the First War.

AUTHOR'S PREFACE

Apart from the normal difficulties of tracing and verifying history extending back in time some eighty-two years, the story of these twenty-one very large motor yachts is harder than usual to put down in a rational manner. One could follow each ship throughout its career, but by the time the reader had attained the halfway point, many stories would have been told three and four times over, for they often operated together. So I have elected to separate the story into time segments, telling the tale of the five First World War yachts to their completion, although that carries us right up to 1946. I then return to pick up the prewar origins of the sixteen Second World War Yachts, followed by their wartime exploits, successes and losses, and their postwar histories. The yachts themselves are the dramatis personae, and the index will help those with a technical bent to locate their particular ship throughout its career.

The primary sources of basic information for this study were the files in the Directorate of History of the Department of National Defence, and Lloyd's Registers of Shipping, and of American and Canadian Yachts. For the utmost in help at the former I am greatly indebted to the Director, Dr. W.A.B. Douglas, CD, and in particular to the erudite and always willing senior naval historian on the staff, Phillip A.C. Chaplin, and to Winston MacIntosh. They produced an endless series of ships' files, photographs by the score, and continuing guidance as to further research sources. For the Registers, I appreciate the help of Mrs. Joiner of the Royal Canadian Yacht Club, and Mr. K.R. Macpherson of Toronto, and of the Toronto Public Library. For his most helpful initial guidance through the excellent and very efficiently kept and produced records in the Public Archives and in the National Photographic Collection, I appreciate the assistance offered so freely by Mr. Carl Vincent. Ken Macpherson has provided me over the years of this book's gestation with a continuous stream of yacht photographs from his voluminous files of naval miscellanea, collected in the preparation of his own books on the Canadian Navy.

Apart from these basic and continuing sources, which by no means contained all the required details (and which did not always agree!), I have heard from over fifty sailors, from seaman and stoker to rear admiral, who knew and served in the yachts in both wars. They were contacted primarily through notices placed in the Royal Canadian Legion's house magazine *Legion*; in *Sentinel*, the Canadian Armed Forces magazine; in the Royal Canadian Naval Association's newsletter; and the quarterly *Starshell* of the Naval Officers' Associations of Canada. For tracing the civilian lives of the yachts between and after the wars, the Liverpool-published *Sea Breezes* produced world-wide contacts from the merchant shipping world.

From all the correspondents it would be invidious to mention particular names, but Herb Miller of Durham, Ontario, John C. Fritz of Dartmouth, Nova Scotia, Ben Seager of Hamilton, and Steve Gatensbury of Burnaby, British Columbia were all in touch with me on several occasions, loaned me valuable and personal material, and actively pursued other ex-naval yachtsmen on my behalf. Of the original Canadian purchasers of the yachts for the Navy, I was most fortunate in contacting four of the surviving gentlemen, who spent many hours with me retelling a tale of over 40 years before: the late Tom H.P. Molson, Pearson McCurdy, Clarence Wallace, and Frederick H.M. Jones. In the case of the late Stuart Playfair of Toronto, his daughter, Mary Stuart Lorriman, loaned me an invaluable carton of material Mr. Playfair had wisely (but partly illegally at the time!) retained concerning the secret purchase of his yacht *Arcadia*. Their tales were basic to the story, as were the memories of those days by members of the families of many other purchasers.

Perhaps not too surprisingly, none of the prewar owners of the ships could be contacted, it usually being found that they had died long before. So those sections of this history have been compiled from contemporary records, old yacht club yearbooks, and the memories of the golden days of large yacht cruising by contemporaries. Rather more surprising was the difficulty in contacting the post-Second War buyers of the surviving yachts. Again records and memories, always fallible, have had to be used. This is where *Sea Breezes* was most useful.

Maybe service in these yachts lead to a toughness in their naval seamen, man and officer alike, that has stood them in good stead in their later years. In retrospect, ships are rarely hated by those who served in them, after the days of sail had passed. Faded are the immediate memories of cold, seasickness, boredom and the terror of violent North Atlantic gales. Nearly all those who contacted me spoke with considerable humour and affection of their days in "their" armed yacht. So this approach by those who served, like the author, in these "luxury" yachts has allowed the story to be told with some guarantee that it is a genuine and significant portion not only of the Canadian Navy's heritage, but of the United State's Navy's too, for five of them served in that Navy as well.

I must also thank my wife Rosalind, who has put up with this project for many years, and who indeed became as much a lookout for stories of these ships as any contributor, and the John Spears family who for more than one summer provided a cottage at Owen Sound where I could work in peace.

F.M.M.
Battle of the Atlantic Sunday, May, 1983
Toronto, Ontario

As a yacht again. Joseph Simard's yacht *Fraternité* in the St. Lawrence in the 1950's. She was HMCS *Moose*.

CHAPTER 1

LUXURY YACHTS AS A WAY OF LIFE

Ever since man developed settled communities and evolved a system of trading with his neighbours, ships have played a major part in the economies of all nations whose shores touch salt water. Once fleets of merchantmen set forth to roam the oceans, it was only a short time before the rulers of those countries, and then their leading courtiers and merchants, developed more personal vessels, to oversee their enterprises abroad or even for a day's pleasure at sea.

The Doges of Venice travelled in the most elaborate of gilded and oar-powered galleys. Some of the earliest of Royal Navy ships were really the Kings's and Queen's personal transport for passages to Dunquerque and their properties across the Channel in France. One of Tsar Peter the Great's first home-built vessels, after his year of dockyard apprenticeship in Europe in the late 1600's, was a small open boat, not much larger than that which we would now call a dinghy, for his personal use on the rivers near his palaces at Moscow and St. Petersburg. By the time steam and engines were introduced in commercial vessels, there was hardly a monarch of a marine state that did not have a personal ship held in readiness for his instant use.

The first steam yachts simply had engines added to existing sail outfits; but they were inclined to roll heavily when not under the steadying influence of the sails. The problem was always the complicated relationship between hull shape, engine power, speed and weight. This led to some highly unusual and unorthodox designs such as the Russian *Livadia* of Czar Alexander II, 266 feet overall, with the huge beam of 153 feet across, an almost round ship. Paddle wheels were also often tried.

Some ships were only minor sail-powered vessels designed to cross a local river in comfort, or take a king to his country palace up or down the Seine, the Rhone or the Tiber. Others were for passages across open stretches of sea, or at least water more subject to storms, such as the Zuider Zee, the Adriatic, or the Sea of Marmora. As the sizes increased, so was introduced the yen for creature comforts on even modest passages of an afternoon, with soft armchairs, couches, good food and attentive servants. As royalty required these perogatives, so too did their immediate followers and high-ranking courtiers. Then, too, successful merchants, with a personal wealth often greater than the monarch's, had ships built suitable to their position in the world. The term "yacht" comes from the Dutch *jaghtship* or chase-ship, a light, fast sailing vessel. The Dutch presented such a ship to Charles II in 1660, the first of the royal yachts. She was the *Mary*, of 100 tons, and only 52 feet.

Queen Victoria and the Prince Consort were keen users of sailing yachts. In 1842 Victoria had the first *Victoria and Albert* built, a paddle steamer, the first of seven specifically built for her. In Germany the Kaiser had built the *Hohenzollern*, the size of a modest liner, and which was pictured on the country's stamps for two generations.

As the life on the ocean wave evolved from strictly business to a more comfortable pleasure, so membership grew in what came to be called "Yacht Clubs," where the well-to-do kept their vessels when not in use. The introduction of steam to the yachting world, after its slow commerical development at the beginning of the nineteenth century, was not without its setbacks. To this day there are many sailing yachtsmen who refer to those owning motor-driven yachts, no matter how grand, as "stinkpot sailors." In May, 1827, the Royal Yacht Club of England passed a resolution:

"The object of this club is to promote seamanship, to which the application of steam is inimicable, and any member applying steam to his yacht shall be disqualified hereby and shall cease to be a member."

However, by the late 1880's, steam-driven personal ships became the ultimate in luxury; by that time there were seven hundred in Britain alone. They were designed by the best of shipbuilders, and often, in the larger ships, developed for world cruising to distant properties in the colonies. Some of the senior officers, bound for the Crimean War, arranged to travel out in their own yachts. These floating residences were often equipped with extensive libraries, complete with a circular iron staircase, nurseries for the children and their nannies, and even ice to keep cool the necessities of life. In the United States Joseph Pulitzer's *Liberty*, with a crew of sixty-two, had a gymnasium and a dozen great staterooms.

The yacht crews were a breed apart, for although not necessarily well-paid, they were certainly well provided for, compared to the harsh discipline, squalid living and hard sailing under brutal mates of the commercial "square riggers" of Britain, Germany, Finland and the United States. Life in most navies was equally rough. Their crews were often in rags, barely provided with anything but the roughest of clothing, and only late in the century even with a common uniform in most navies. In the pleasure yachts nothing so unsightly was to be seen. Decent clothing — often quite resplendent uniforms — was the order of the day. To secure a berth as a seaman, engineroom hand or steward in a royal or personal yacht was a sinecure greatly sought after.

In the United States the steam and motor yachts were not as frequently designed for world cruising use by the leisure class, although there were some who did own such vessels. As the heyday of sail was still in force, the idle rich tended more to own large sailing schooners, and more for afternoon cruising off harbour mouths, in Chesapeake Bay, or on Long Island Sound than for ocean passages to distant colonial holdings. The motor-driven craft tended to be owned by wealthy busy businessmen, intent on creating major internal railways, or steelmaking complexes, or raising financial or real estate empires within their own country.

The first significant American steam yacht was owned by the famous railroader Cornelius Vanderbilt. His *North Star*, at 270 feet, was built in the 1850's at a cost of $500,000 by Jeremiah Simonson of New York. She had two 34-foot paddle wheels and two funnels, in addition to two masts and the rig of a brigantine, and the owner used her for world cruising.

But usually these tycoons used their steam yachts for commuting on the rivers of the eastern States — the Hudson and others around New York, the Potomac at Washington, and the Mississippi in the south — or on the Sound and other protected waters. Often these entepreneurs lived in grand houses on the banks of these rivers, or up Long Island Sound or Chesapeake Bay. They were only interested in a vessel that was comfortable and fast (the way we now use the family car or the subway) as a means of getting from their own dockside to offices in the Battery or Wall Street, or to the Navy Yard at Washington. Here, speed was of the essence. In Peter Rouss's *Winchester*, 65 per cent of the internal space was given over to engines and fuel tanks. This urge for speed tended to produce destroyer-like, high-speed hull designs in the larger yachts, often not too stable in a seaway. But except for the once-a-year almost compulsory attendance at the America's Cup races, the owners were not too interested in being at sea in boisterous weather anyway. Their engines were often the latest in steam turbine and oil engine (diesel) design, sometimes noisy, nearly always expensive, but producing a high speed-for-weight ratio.

The engineroom was often a polished showplace, so even the stokers and oilers had to be decently clothed. Double and triple-expansion steam engines developed from the side-lever and steeple engines driving paddle wheels, often encased in mahogany and brass. These were succeeded by high-speed turbines, and by oil engines and diesels, developed in Germany. In 1902, a French firm introduced the first marine diesel which had the advantage of instant readiness, rather than the prolonged wait while steam was raised.

In Britain and in most European countries, by contrast, the large yachts continued to be powered by the much slower coal-fired steam triple-expansion engine, producing speeds in the neighbourhood of 12 to 14 knots, but with quiet long-range reliability, and not subject to much wear, easily repaired on the spot by the ship's almost invariably Scottish engineer. One of the early large steam yachts is still in use today as a training vessel, the Egyptian *El Horria* (ex-*Mahroussa*), built in Scotland in 1865.

And so there arose hundreds of large steam-fired motor yachts, of many designs, from a multitutde of yards, all with different purposes and uses. A few of them were to be used for a purpose their designers had never suspected. For Canada, they were to save the day.

Albert Burrage's beautifully appointed, but elderly, yacht *Aztec*, that became HMCS *Beaver*.

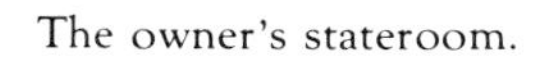

The owner's stateroom.

The music room.

CHAPTER 2

THE YACHTS OF 1915: JOHN EATON AND JOHN ROSS

After some years of political argument and a history of non-interest in naval matters in Canada, on May 14, 1910, Canada's first Naval Service Act was passed. From the time of the French Wars of 1756 and the American Revolutionary War of 1776, Canada had relied solely on the Royal Navy for her sea defences. Admittedly, from time to time, local marine forces were recruited. In the Great Lakes at the end of the eighteenth and beginning of the nineteenth century, there was a Provincial Marine, under control of the local Quartermaster General; but after the Revolutionary War its' ships were largely used for coastguard patrols, and it became little more than a government shipping company and transport service. When the War of 1812 broke out along the east coast and on the lakes, the Royal Navy provided the Altlantic safeguard (with only moderate success and, to their considerable surprise, losing several individual ship battles with the upstart United States Navy). On the lakes, a hurriedly rearmed Provincial Marine held the sea routes open for a year for the army, until the officers and seamen of the Royal Navy at the coast could be passed inland to take over.

Thereafter, during the long years of relative peace along Canada's borders, the Canadian "Navy" rarely appeared on anything more than paper, except on a very local and emergency basis. But by 1910 Canada was being forced to look more closely at her seaward defences. The advent of steam-driven warships meant that potential enemies were more mobile, more powerful and more wide-ranging than before. The new German Navy of Kaiser Wilhelm II was an obvious threat to Britain, and it was by no means certain that in an emergency the mother country could keep its commitment to guard the extensive and distant coasts of Canada. Submarines were a brand new and unassessed threat, and Germany had a head start in developing them. The tremendous costs of the naval construction race between Britain and Germany were straining the financial fabrics of both countries. Canada had already been asked to provide cash for the building, in Britain, of two or more battleships of the newest Dreadnought class as her contribution to Empire defence. Not a navy, not people, but cash.

This proposal, in fact, caused most of the political turmoil that surrounded the passage of the first Canadian Naval Bill, but pass it finally did, and Canada promptly acquired two warships by the transfer of two somewhat elderly cruisers from the Royal Navy. And that was where it stopped for the next four and a half years. The Liberals argued for a larger navy, quite rightly growing slowly. And the Conservatives, also quite rightly, argued that two ships were nonsense, that we should get out of the navy business, and provide money to the United Kingdom for shipbuilding for mutual defence.

However, neither of these policies were hard-and-fast and even R.L. Borden, newly-elected Prime Minister in September, 1911, was by 1912 expressing the desirability of at least encouraging some Naval shipbuilding in Canadian yards, over the long term. But in general, the Conservatives tried to drive forward their Naval Aid Bill, supporting the donation of funds for the building of RN ships, while the Liberals supported an even stronger RCN. Neither policy carried successfully, so the Navy grew not at all.

Of the two RN cruisers, *Rainbow* was allocated to the west coast (supported by the ancient RN steam-and-sail sloop *Shearwater*), and the larger *Niobe* to the east coast, at Halifax. There were no destroyers or small ships. In fact the two large ships only occasionally ventured out on training courses.

Thus, as usual, the unexpected onslaught of hostilities found the democracies unprepared for a naval war. True, Britain had the largest fleet of battleships and battle cruisers in the world, with Germany somewhat behind, and the newly emerging U.S. Navy was making every effort to overhaul the gap between her capital ship strength and that of the two major protagonists. In minor vessels Britain again had a majority, but by no means an overwhelming one. The requirements of having to provide for the totally new concept of anti-submarine patrols and escorts for merchantmen were little appreciated. These needs very soon stretched her resources beyond their capacities, which turned out to be far too modest to meet the world-wide demands on them. The ships of the Royal Navy were hard-pressed to provide any but the most meagre protection for her far-flung colonies and dominions. That protection may have been promised, but the practicalities of harsh warfare soon spelled out some home truths to the staff at the Admiralty and at Ottawa alike.

When the war began, the German Navy was already at sea, with a strong and modern cruiser force roaming the Pacific. In the last days of November 1914 it caught a much older and weaker British squadron off Coronel, Chile, and all but annihilated it, to prove that after four months of war Britain was by no means master of the seas. It was a tremendous blow to colonial confidence in the Royal Navy's ability to defend distant dominions and colonies, such as Canada. On Canada's west coast there was considerable panic when the authorities at the dockyard at Victoria realised that there was a very good chance that one or more of Germany's powerful new cruisers could quite easily appear in the Straits of Juan de Fuca and shell the port and harbour, almost with impunity, in the face of the small, elderly *Rainbow*. For them, the battle off Coronel, if an RN disaster, was somewhat of a relief! It at least meant that the German Far East Squadron was busy 6,600 miles away.

In the Atlantic, with two major fleets facing each other across the narrow North Sea, the German Kriegsmarine held one major advantage that the Royal Navy, even with the help of their allies, the French, could not match. The Germans had a significant preponderance of submarines. This was an arm of the service that the British still considered not very proper. "A damned un-English weapon," Rear Admiral Wilson, the Third Sea Lord, called it. It was accorded little encouragement even within the Navy except among a dedicated few. Even the nickname of the submarine service, known among its members as "The Trade," had a sarcastic ring to it. In August 1914 the Germans had a fleet of some twenty U-boats. Belatedly, the RN realized that these could be a major threat to the security of the seas, even if the German surface fleet never put out from Kiel and Wilhelmshaven.

True, the rules of war, still to be tested, required that any U-boat attacking an unarmed merchantman or liner must first surface, stop the ship, determine that she was indeed an enemy by examining her papers, and give the crew and passengers time to get away in their boats in safety. Only then could the vessel be sunk. Ludicrous? Maybe, but most of the public and politicians, and even the armed forces, thought that wars were still to be fought under some agreed-upon rules of behaviour. The Russo-Japanese War of 1904-1905 was an unfortunate case of the uneducated Japanese dashing off in a rather scurrilous manner to attack the inept Russians without a declaration of war, and was regarded by many as being rather too clever and gauche to be an acceptable norm for 1914. German "frightfulness" came as an immense shock, as did their professional skill in using their new U-boats, for which a counter-weapon had not even been developed, let alone tested and put in service.

But those twenty U-boats were obviously a threat to the patrolling warships blockading Germany. (By no means all recognized the threat however, including squadron commanders at sea, for three large cruisers, the *Hogue*, *Cressey*, and *Aboukir*, were sunk in a few minutes on quiet up-and-down patrol in submarine waters on September 22, 1914.) They were also a potential menace to the troop convoys from Canada, or to the individual ships about to sail from Halifax, Quebec and Montreal for England, and which would now need protection of some sort in the Atlantic. So where was Canada's new "do-it-ourselves" Navy at the start of the conflagration? What would be her contribution?

Canada entered the war with no anti-submarine patrol vessels, no useful destroyers, or better yet, no battleships to augment the Royal Navy. She had only the two original cruisers, the venerable *Rainbow* on the west coast, and the larger and bit newer (fifteen years old) *Niobe* at Halifax. Both were rather under-manned, their crews made up in part and hastily by the new recruits of the Royal Navy Canadian Volunteer Reserves, (RNCVR), formed only the year before. On the west coast *Rainbow* was joined by two ancient RN ships, the sloop *Shearwater*, and the even smaller sail-and-steam corvette-gunboat, HMS *Algerine*. *Rainbow* was sent south to meet them as they scurried up the U.S. coast (at something like 10 knots), hoping to keep out of the clutches of the marauding German Far East Squadron, if it turned north. On arrival they were taken into the Canadian Navy as HMC ships. Some protection! Fortunately they were not called upon to actively defend that coast, for the Germans never attempted to pass any other warships or submarines into the Pacific, and by December the Far East Squadron's cruisers had been caught and sunk in the battle off the Falkland Islands in the southwest Atlantic. All but one, which lead a fugitive existence for another few months.

At Halifax *Niobe* was under repair, and had to be hurriedly put back into service and manned partly by green reserves. As well, several very small craft were transferred from other government departments — Fisheries, Marine Services, Surveying, and the Coast Guard. But in reality the west coast was almost entirely dependent on the Royal Navy for any protection in depth; and that turned out to be a rather weak reed upon which to lean. When a troopship or group of them were to sail, a capital ship, and maybe one or two armed merchant liners, would be provided, and sometimes an occasional destroyer. But the trouble was that these destroyers were, as the term is, "short-legged." That is, they could barely cross the Atlantic with the fuel they could carry, with nothing remaining for hunting or searching about, being originally designed for North Sea service to face the Germans there, with bases never more than a day or two away.

While the U-boats were not really expected to cross the Atlantic to the Canadian east coast (one British Admiral in command stated flatly that they could never even reach the west coast of Britain), patrols were instituted early on as a precaution against the possibility of a German cruiser or U-boat appearing. With only the requisitioned small vessels from the other departments, the Canadian Navy soon realized that standing patrols could not be maintained with so few ships. And new trawlers or patrol vessels would take the best part of a year to design and build at the most optimistic. Where to acquire some interim vessels became a source of investigation, and there were few ready answers. There were practically no small Canadian steamers suitable for conversion that could be spared from their usual tasks. The larger fishing vessels were still needed to provide the nourishment from the sea; in any case, almost none was large enough to mount the required gun, and the risk of attack was not yet so demanding that those vessels could be requisitioned. Canadian yachtsmen were still, on the whole, using sailing schooners, albeit some large ones, and they rarely had engines. A schooner yacht was still the epitome of a gentleman's method of transporation on the water. However, one large steam yacht had already been drawn to the Navy's attention.

John Craig Eaton, by 1914, had built an enviable reputation and fortune in Toronto as the owner of a large department store. His father had started in a small way as a dry goods haberdasher on the city's main street. Timothy Eaton's unique policy of "Goods satisfactory or money refunded" drew an ever-increasing clientele to his shop, and by the war's start, the small store had been replaced with an enormous multi-storied, integrated department store. As the business was entirely family owned (and still largely is), the fortune of John Eaton, the dynasty's head, had prospered. Among other appurtenances of wealth, he had bought a steam yacht, the *Florence*, for cruising on the Great Lakes. Being an innovator, Eaton had installed in her the first ship-to-shore radio on the lakes, so that his store executives could reach him in an emergency from the transmitter on the roof of the store itself.

Being perhaps wiser than the naval authorities responsible for the safety of the country's coasts, Eaton offered *Florence* for naval service in August of 1914 to Sir Sam Hughes, the Minister of Militia and Defence. He was advised that she was not required at the time, being of dubious size. Although she was not a good anti-submarine ship, size was hardly a problem.

The yacht had been built in 1903 as the *Czarina* for Charles S. Bryan of New York by Crescent Shipyards, of Elizabeth, New Jersey. She was 166 feet long overall, and of some 237 tons, with a speed of about 13 knots, and a reported potential of 17 knots — very fast for a ship of that era. She was an all steel-hulled vessel, designed to the express order of Bryan, who, in the spirit of the day of "Remember the Maine" had ordered a craft capable of being used for Coast Guard duty in the case of war. John Eaton, looking for a craft adequate for extended lake cruising, bought her in 1908, and renovated her fittings, replacing curtains and upholstery to Mrs. Eaton's tastes, for she was to be renamed after his wife, Florence McRae Eaton. When purchased, the whole family went to the coast to pick her up, including their two small children, Timothy and John David. The seas were rough, as they often are crossing the Gulf of St. Lawrence, so one of the crew of eighteen made up a small seaman's hammock for baby John David to alleviate his seasickness, from which all suffered! They received a gala welcome on arrival at the Royal Canadian Yacht Club in Toronto.

Florence, owned by Sir John Eaton of Toronto, about 1912. She became HMCS *Florence*.

When the Navy refused Eaton's offer of his ship in the fall of 1914, she was covered over for the winter by her master (the full-time captain employed by the owner), and the Eaton energies were turned to other matters aimed at helping the Empire in its hour of need. Jack Eaton was later to equip the Eaton Machinegun Battalion with its guns and armoured cars at his own expense as one contribution. Ever in advance of the times, he also announced that for all Eaton's employees who joined the colours, their pay would be continued, at full pay for married men and half pay for bachelors. At the same time, he offered his shore radio station equipment to the Armed Forces. For these personal contributions throughout the war, he received a knighthood.

As the war deepened and the requirement for additional patrol vessels became more obvious, the Navy realized that even modest patrol ships were better than none. So on June 15, 1915, Admiral Kingsmill telegraphed W.K. McNaught, who was acting for John Eaton, to ask if *Florence* was still available. On June 22, after contacting Eaton in the United States, McNaught replied by telegram that the offer still held good. On July 8 he was informed that the vessel had been requisitioned, on payment of $1. She was handed over by her master at Montreal, and at once placed in the hands of the shipbuilders, Canadian Vickers Limited, for conversion into a warship. Alterations and some strengthening were carried out quickly, and a 3-pounder Hotchkiss gun and mounting provided, at a cost of only $4,626, plus another $1,143 for docking and running repairs. She was commissioned as HMCS *Florence* on July 19, 1915, under command of Acting Lieutenant Herbert Denyer, RNCVR. Naval headquarters suggested that the old crew, particularly for the engineroom, should be recruited into the RNCVR and remain with the vessel. Charles Benggrem, a U.S. Swede, was taken on again as chief engineer, with five of the ship's previous engineroom hands — two engineroom articifers (ERA's) and three stokers. They were to be in the RNCVR, and "... such ratings given them as will give them the same pay as they were receiving from the owner. In view of the fact that they take additional risks, they will probably have to be paid a little higher." By July 8, the first mate, Whynot, had turned up, and Captain Gott had returned from Montreal where he had been employed by J.K.L. Ross, of whom we will hear more later.

On July 15 Captain Gott telegraphed directly to the Director of the Naval Service, illustrating the ad hoc conditions and situations that arose in such a small naval service:

> "A. Shall he hire on the cook?
> B. Do seamen make application to be taken on direct to Admiral Kingsmill?
> C. Sir John had taken the linen out. What does he do about replacement?
> (Noted in the margin by Kingsmill: "The Eaton Co. should be given the order"!)
> D. One motor launch had been removed. Should we acquire another?"

As *Florence* was too small to warrant a paymaster carried on board, she was borne on the books of HMCS *Margaret*, the titular "Depot Ship" at Halifax. (In fact, *Margaret* was a motor launch herself, but to conform with legal requirements of the day, all bases had to have a real ship, no matter how small, as the vessel in which the bases' flag was presumed to fly. Ships could be "commissioned," making the services Discipline Act applicable, but buildings could not! This requirement only disappeared in the period between the wars.)

By July 22 *Florence* was on passage from Montreal to Sydney, Nova Scotia. But already she had been the subject of problems. During her trials above Montreal in the Soulange Canal, at 7:35 p.m. on July 22, she was involved in a collision with the steamer S/S *Iroquois* of the St. Lawrence and Chicago Steam Navigation Company. On October 20, the Navy's chief accountant wrote the St. Lawrence Company requesting payment of $602.62 for repairs to *Florence*, as a result of reports rendered by Lt. Denyer and Francis Gott, the master. (The master in these vessels was in effect the navigator, and the last vestige of the old ship-of-the-line sailing master, who was responsible for the ship's progress, while the captain was responsible for her tactical use and fighting.) The solicitors for the *Iroquois* denied responsibility and refused payment. The matter was allowed to drop, and Admiral Kingsmill wrote to the deputy minister in late October: "With regard to this matter, Lieutenant Denyer's services have now been dispensed with and it would cost the Department more to fight the question than the repairs have cost us."

On arrival at the coast, *Florence* was put under command of the Senior Officer, St. Lawrence Patrols, Captain Fred C.C. Pasco, RN (Retired), who had volunteered for service with Canada on war's outbreak. *Florence* operated out of Sydney and in the Gulf of St. Lawrence, patrolling to the north shore of Quebec, over to Newfoundland's west shore, and up into the Gulf. She arrived at Georgetown, Prince Edward Island, in mid-October 1915. There, the unfortunate Denyer became embroiled in an argument with, of all people, the Chief of the Naval Service himself. Admiral Kingsmill reported on October 26 to his minister:

> On the 11th October I inspected the steam yacht *Florence*, now acting as a patrol boat, under command of Lieut Denyer, RNCVR, at Georgetown. On her arrival at Georgetown I found that this vessel had one ton of coal and pointed out to the Commanding Officer that it was an unseamanlike proceeding to risk his vessel (running out of coal) in the Gulf of St. Lawrence unless it was absolutely necessary. This officer objected to my commenting on the way he carried out his duty and said that if I was not satisfied he should like to tender his resignation. As his work has not been satisfactory I accepted this offhand, and allowed him to return to British Columbia, whence he came. Lieut. Denyer is an officer who had resigned from the Royal Naval Reserve, and as he was not holding any commission it was necessary to give him an appointment to the *Florence*, an acting commission in the RNCVR, which should now be cancelled.

So poor Denyer passed from the naval scene, having held his acting commission from July 19 to October 15. But on closer examination, perhaps Denyer was not entirely at fault for allowing his coal supplies to run so low, although he certainly would have been wise to curb his annoyance when discussing the matter with his Admiral!

Lieutenant H.S. Matthews became the new commanding officer and he soon was reporting to Halifax on defects needing repair:

> - Move W/T (wireless telegraphy equipment), as location causes too much creaking and noise and rolling in bad weather to hear.
> - Re-caulk decks. In wet weather, water running down onto C.O.'s bunk and settee causes them to become saturated.
> - Deck house needs attention, otherwise it will collapse, as cracks open and close in walls at least an inch when in a seaway.
> - The fresh water tanks become contaminated with sea water.

In fact, a report to Ottawa recommended that she be laid up during the winter months, as being unsuitable even for patrols in the Gulf of St. Lawrence because she rolled so much and should have bilge keels fitted. Thus on December 22, the S.O. Patrols was ordered to lay her up in Saint John, New Brunswick, for the winter and for a refit, after a short spell as harbour entrance guard ship.

By the spring of 1916 she was repaired, and at the end of April was reported as clean, and her ship's company smart. It had been intended to make her one of the Saint John guard ships again; but before she could be recommissioned, it was decided to pay her off, return her gun and ammunition to Halifax, and turn her back to Sir John Eaton at Toronto, "after repairs." Plans changed again, firstly to turn her over to Sir John's representative at Halifax, then to sell her, presumably on Sir John's behalf.

Florence then lay around Saint John and Halifax harbours for the next five months, unattended due to the press of other and more urgent events, only manned by a few naval ratings. On September 21 she was ordered paid off once and for all, all her seamen sent to the cruiser *Niobe*, and the ship's books closed. Even so it was not all clear sailing for the crew:

> Mr. Irving, Mate, having asked to be allowed to resign on account of ill health is to be examined, and a report made. If he is considered fit he is to be sent to *Margaret* immediately to take up his appointment.
>
> Signed: Captain Superintendent, HMC Dockyard

Ill health, my eye! Tough luck, Mr. Irving.

Florence was then sold to a Martinique trading company, and she sailed for Fort-de-France, Martinique, in early January 1917. She was later lost in the West Indies, apparently from a mine or a U-boat torpedo. There is no record of any survivors.

The St. Lawrence patrols were made up of a miscellaneous collection of vessels, ex-Dominion Marine fisheries patrol ships, others like *Florence*, purchased or donated, or others chartered, the charter price to include the crews and their food, and the seamen not recruited into the Navy. Actually most of them were later to become members of the RNCVR. In addition to searching for submarines, they were "to ascertain if any small craft could be of use by the enemy as submarine bases in isolated harbours and inlets." They were also required to perform fishery protection duties. One patrolling ship would be covering the Cabot Strait between Cape Breton and Newfoundland, seven days out in all weathers, then seven days in; and two ships alternating in investigating the south and west coasts of Newfoundland.

HMCS *Florence* was the only Canadian large yacht to be taken up and armed for patrol work. But even before she was belatedly requisitioned, several rather interesting and unusual developments had occurred, destined to place four more rather better suited ex-yachts in naval hands. We must therefore now retrace our steps to the early fall of 1914 to pick up the tale of the first two, which were to become HMC ships *Grilse* and *Tuna*, both purchased in the United States by John Kenneth Leveson Ross of Montreal.

Born in Lindsay, Ontario, in 1876, by the outbreak of war Jack Ross was one of the wealthiest men in Canada. His father, James Ross, had been one of the syndicate who built the Canadian Pacific Railway, and on his death in 1913, his large fortune passed to his son. Jack Ross proceeded to spend it lavishly. It had been estimated that between 1913 and 1928, when he was declared bankrupt, Ross got through some $16 million.

One of Jack Ross's passions was horse racing, and by 1915 he had built up a very respectable thoroughbred racing stable. In 1919 his horse Sir Barton won the U.S. Triple Crown of the Derby, the Preakness and the Belmont Stakes.

In addition to having a consuming interest in horses, Ross was a yachtsman of considerable note. From 1913 on he retained his father's large steam yacht *Glencairn*, which had been the *New York World* publisher Joseph Pulitzer's *Liberty*, and he had an only slightly smaller motor yacht *Albacore* which he gave to the Navy for training purposes.

Ross had been an ardent supporter of the Conservative government's plan to contribute $35 million to the U.K. government toward the building of dreadnoughts to counter the growing German menace. The measure was defeated in Parliament, but Ross approached the prime minister, Robert Borden and suggested the money might be raised by private subscription. To start the ball rolling he himself offered to give $500,000. When war broke out, Ross again visited Borden and placed in his hand the $500,000 "to be used by the Govenment in any manner that might seem best for the defence of Canada and the Empire, without reservation or accounting."

Before the war, Ross had become a captain in the Black Watch, the Montreal Militia kilted regiment. But on examination for active service on the outbreak of war, he was judged medically unfit, a considerable disappointment for an ardent patriot. Looking about for an avenue which would give him the opportunity to personally serve his country, and, through friends knowing the state of the infant Canadian Navy, Jack Ross went down to New York early in August 1914, and there purchased the very fast steam turbine yacht *Tarantula* from the millionaire railroad magnate William K. Vanderbilt.

W.K. was a grandson of the first and famous Commodore Cornelius Vanderbilt, and a son of William Henry, probably best known for his reply to a Chicago newspaperman who once asked him, in relation to the operation of the New York Central Railroad's 'Chicago Limited', "But don't you run it for the public benefit?". W.H., intending to indicate that the railroad was in business to make money for its shareholders, replied "The public be damned!" Like J.K.L. Ross, while his fortune was derived principally from railroading, he was also a notable racehorse owner, winning most of his major prizes from an elegant and extensive stable in France, where on several occasions he was the leading money winner. He had already been the owner of two of the largest yachts in the world. He had bought the *Alva*, at 285 feet, in 1886. When she was sunk in a collision six years later, he had built the huge ocean-going sail and steam yacht *Valiant*, at 312 feet. She had required a crew of seventy-two, including a French chef, and the upkeep was estimated at $10,000 per month.

Tarantula was a unique vessel, being one of the very first high-speed turbine-engined ships built, modelled after the smaller *Turbinia*, which Sir Charles Parsons had conducted his first trials with marine turbine propulsion for the Royal Navy. The only other turbine-powered ships in the world at that time were the Cunard Line's *Lusitania* and *Mauretania*. *Tarantula* was notorious for her heavy wake. The damage it caused as she tore down the

John Craig Eaton loaned the Navy his *Florence* for one dollar.

Lt. "Jack" Ross, who gave two torpedoboat destroyers to the Navy, and commanded them.

East River at New York, carrying Vanderbilt to his railway offices in lower Manhattan resulted in litigation. It was the first time a ship's owner had been held liable for damages to shore facilities and vessels moored thereto, due to the wash of a ship's wake.

Tarantula had been built in England to a design of Cox and King of London, by Messrs. Yarrow & Company for Colonel Harry L.B. McCalmont, a very wealthy British M.P. and army officer, who was also a racehorse owner. When he died in 1902, the vessel had been promptly bought by Vanderbilt, strictly to provide speed for his commuting trips, and visits on Long Island Sound, although his house was on Fifth Avenue in New York. At 25 knots, she was then the fastest vessel on that coast. Her unusual design of three small propellors on each of three shafts was still very much experimental, and her poor manoeuvring qualities except at speed, and the expense to run her, mitigated against her and others that copied her. It didn't help much that many of her engineers were unfamiliar with the equipment as well; it being experimental too. The machinery of *Tarantula* consisted of three Parsons Marine Steam Turbines, connected in series. Steam from the boilers being first led into the high-pressure turbine on the starboard side, then passed to the intermediate-pressure turbine on the port side, next to the centrally disposed low-pressure turbine, from which it was exhausted to the condensers and the water returned to the boilers. Each turbine was directly coupled to its propellor shaft. In addition, a cruising turbine was provided to allow for some economy at speeds below 15 knots. The hull design was on the lines of the contemporary First Class Torpedo Boats designed by Yarrows for the Royal Navy, but with somewhat heavier framing. She drew 8.7 feet of water.

Ross's purchase of this vessel, and bringing it out of the United States, involved considerable risk as the U.S. government had prohibited the sale of any vessel likely to be used for belligerent purposes by either warring nation. There were stiff fines and even jail sentences, for both seller and purchaser, if detected.

Due to Ross's stature in both the business and yachting communities, the ship was obtained and fitted out, more or less secretly, at considerable expense, all out of Ross's pocket, except for armament. He brought her up to Halifax himself, and then applied for transfer from the Militia to the naval service, on the condition that the Navy would accept his ship for patrol duties and that they would commission him in the RNCVR. This offer of, in effect, a purchased commission was accepted without misgiving and with alacrity by the Navy. They purchased *Tarantula* from her owner for one dollar and Ross was sent off on a course of gunnery and torpedo while the ship was armed at Halifax. A course in seamanship, naval regulations, and so forth was evidently considered unnecessary!

On arrival in Halifax on September 10, Ross had reported that his civilian crew were all prepared to join the RNCVR. The captain-in-charge suggested that Ross be appointed a lieutenant, William Ross (a Nova Scotian and no relative) as second-in-command and sailing master, and C. Mitchel as seaman chief petty officer. J.A. Patterson was to become chief engineroom artificer, and two others as assistant ERA's, as well as one able seaman, five stokers, two stewards and one cook and one "cook's boy".

Only a week after arriving in Halifax, Ross was already writing to J.D. Hazen, the Minister of the Naval Service in Ottawa:

> "Martin [captain-in-charge of the dockyard] has wired you recommending work be done on yacht. Hope you can immediately authorise him to put this in hand at once. I will pay all expense, as I consider no more time should be lost in getting her ready for useful work.

Obviously Ross's pending appointment as a lieutenant in the Naval Reserve did not inhibit him from writing directly to the Naval Minister, and in referring to the C-in-C of the dockyard as "Martin", despite that he was Captain E.H. Martin, RN! At the same time

Ross advised that he would make up the difference in pay between his acting ERAs' naval pay and that which thay had received as engineers in *Tarantula*.

In September the ship's name was changed to HMCS *Tuna*, to make the tracing of her American parentage less obvious. She was commissioned for "scout and patrol service" off Halifax in early December 1914; Lieutenant J.K.L. Ross, RNCVR in command. During the winter, *Tuna* patrolled off Halifax, fair weather or foul, ostensibly on the lookout for U-boats and raiders, "which service was much appreciated by the Commander-In-Chief, as Canada had no vessels whatever for patrol work." While this was not exactly true, it was close enough, and she did at least lend a semblance of visible protection for the Army troops going to sea in vulnerable troopships, and for the Nova Scotia citizens, closest to the German Navy's potential attentions. While she would have been of not much value against a well-handled U-boat except for her speed, she would have been a very difficult target to hit if attacking a suface raider.

As HMCS *Tuna*, her unusual design and appearance caused some consternation and worry along the Nova Scotia coast, when she appeared off a rural village. A telegram sent from Whitehead on April 18, 1915 read:

> G.J. Desbarats,
>
> Deputy Minister, Naval, Ottawa
>
> There is now lying off Cole Harbour, Guysborough County, a ship of strange appearance. I have just come from on board. Her Commander gives his name as Lieut. J.K.L. Ross, RCNVR [sic], and says his vessel is the torpedo boat HMCS *Tuna*, but refuses to show his ship's papers. Ship has no name or number. Showing is a steel ship painted grey. Has two smoke stacks and more than one hundred and fifty feet in length. Very narrow, sitting low in the water.
>
> Clarence V. Wells,
>
> Preventive Officer.

Fortunately Ottawa was able to telegraph a reply the same day to the nervous and apprehensive Wells, confirming that the suspicious ship was indeed *Tuna*.

In the spring of 1915, after an arduous winter, Lieutenant Ross obtained permission to be relieved of his command, and once again proceeded to the United States, where he

Tarantula, owned by Wm. K. Vanderbilt, and to become HMCS *Tuna*. About 1910.

HMCS *Tuna* fitting out at Quebec in 1915, at Lieutenant Ross's cost.

HMCS *Tuna*, ex-*Tarantula*, in November 1915. Lt. J.K.L. Ross in command.

succeeded in buying and bringing up yet another large steam yacht, the *Winchester*, owned by Peter W. Rouss. This vessel was newer than *Tarantula*, having been built in 1912, again by Yarrows, but to Rouss's order and from a similar design by Cox and Stevens of New York. She looked very similar to *Tarantula*, but was longer by 47 feet. A simpler but more powerful turbine arrangement on only two shafts produced the tremendous trial speed of 34 knots, a detail which considerably piqued Rouss's commuting compatriots, whose yachts were thus left far behind. Since speed was the criterion, accommodation was certainly not of high priority. *Winchester* had below decks, apart from crew space for fourteen men, one small owner's cabin and bath, a tiny hall or dining saloon, a small double and two single cabins with a shared bath — all most unusual in a gentleman's yacht of that time. The rest was given over almost entirely to engines and fuel.

Peter Rouss even more annoyed the New York 500 by being the son of Charles Broadway Rouss, a dealer in dry goods and job lot materials, and a minor publisher, who had built up a huge business and had become a millionaire. Charles was an expert on the American Civil War, in which he had participated, building statues to its heroes, and contributing vast sums to commemorative museums concerned with that struggle. Contrary to Timothy Eaton, his business motto was "Cash before delivery"! Peter Rouss had owned two previous *Winchesters*, which tends to confuse the records. The first was built for him in 1907 and was later owned by A.G. Vanderbilt and others, lasting until worn out in 1914. The second was built in 1909, again for Rouss and for more speed, and on destroyer lines, steam driven. It was this *Winchester* that caused M.C.D. Borden, owner of the handsome but somewhat slower *Little Sovereign*, when passed by Rouss one morning, to say to his captain: "Don't go to my pier in New York. Go to C.L. Seabury's yard" There he ordered the yacht that was to be known as "the fast *Sovereign*," driven by three steam turbines. The second *Winchester* eventually became the *Mariscal Sucre* of the Columbian Navy, from 1938 to 1955. The third *Winchester* was Jack Ross's purchase as *Grilse*.

Rouss's third *Winchester* was a rather more successful design than *Tarantula*. An engineering paper of the day gives some idea of what it was like to travel in her in reasonable weather: "While running at high speed there is an absolute absence of vibration in the boat, and she moves through the water without creating any appreciable disturbance, so far as can be seen from the boat itself, the wake being perfectly flat and the diverging wave system being scarcely noticeable."

Although no records say so, there are indications that Ross went south to buy this second yacht for Canada with the blessings of the Navy, if not their money. While no price was recorded for the purchase of *Tarantula*, that being entirely a private matter, *Winchester* cost Ross $100,000. Ross prepared the ship for her passage up to Canada, again very secretly, the sale being confirmed on June 29th, 1915, when Americans were still being quite notably neutral.

On July 2, the Halifax "Report of Ship Movements" recorded: "*Suffolk*, *Berwick*, *Cumberland* (three RN cruisers) in wireless communications with Barrington. Lieutenant Ross arrived in *Winchester*."

From this it would appear that the Navy was fully aware of the purpose of his request for leave, although it understood that Ross would again pay for the vessel out of his own resources. Admiral Kingsmill recorded later when recommending Ross for promotion to Commander in 1917:

> "Getting the *Winchester* out was a still more difficult job than that of *Tuna*, and cost Mr. Ross some considerable sum of money before the vessel was brought to our port of Halifax. The purchase money, one hundred thousand dollars, was paid by the Dominion Government for this vessel; Mr. Ross made no charge for the refit or transportation.

Ross had, in fact, intended to make no charge at all, but found himself short of funds after buying the ship, and asked naval headquarters for a loan equal to her price to tide him over for nine months. The reply to this unique proposal was that the department had no authority to lend money, but that it would be happy to buy the ship from him at the price he had paid, and to give him first refusal of her at the same price when she was to be disposed of. Ross agreed to this proposal and the purchase was authorised by the Privy Council on August 12, 1915.

Meanwhile Ross had paid off his civilian crew who had brought the ship up to Halifax, and commissioned her as HMCS *Grilse* on July 15, himself in command. He sailed for Montreal on the 23rd to fit her out for war service in Canadian Vickers' yard. She brought from Halifax, a 12-pounder (3″) gun and a 14″ torpedo tube to be mounted on her deck. The gun was mounted on her forecastle, and later another 12-pounder was added on the quarterdeck aft. The after deckhouse, on the plans called a "social hall" which gave access to the owner's and guest's cabins below, was removed to make way for the torpedo tube. This structure had been chiefly made of wood and glass and would have added nothing to the stability and fighting efficiency of the ship. She was 202 feet long, with two squat, flat-sided funnels and a tall mast amidships. She had a nearly vertical bow, and very little flare forward, so was a wet boat in heavy weather. It was experience such as this with First War ships that encouraged the naval constructors to copy the trawler builders. By giving small ships the widely flaring bows that became typical of the later destroyers between the wars, the seas were thrown off rather than coming aboard.

At Vickers in Montreal her mast was moved aft and another added between the compass platform and the fore funnel. These vessels, like the true naval torpedo boats, had no bridge as such, simply having an extension aft of the raised forecastle deck, surrounded by a canvas dodger, behind which stood the officer-of-the-watch, the helmsman and, if necessary, the gunnery officer and captain if in action. The second mast was to give a high horizontal radio antenna to improve the reception of the elementary spark-type radio equipment. Alterations were made below to allow for two mess decks for seamen, and for a radio room, as well as officer accommodation. On August 13 an inclining trial was carried out in Vickers' yard to test her stability: "The vessel was completely equipped with gun, torpedo tube, three torpedoes on deck, ammunition on board, searchlight, masts, etc., forty men distributed, stores and fresh water on board, boilers at normal working height, no oil fuel or feed water on board". In other words, more or less as she might be on return from a war patrol. Despite her breadth of only 18

HMCS *Grilse*, ex-*Winchester* (II), which had been owned by Peter W. Rouss of New York. Almost identical with HMCS *Renard* ex-*Winchester* (III) of the Second War.

feet, it was deduced that with oil and feed water she would have "stability greater than many vessels of a similar class in the British Navy." That did not mean to say that she was necessarily all that stable in a North Atlantic gale off Halifax, whence she was destined!

Shortly afterward she left Montreal under Lieutenant Ross's command and returned to Halifax for war patrols there and in the Gulf. We will leave these two vessels for now, to pick up the thread of the last two armed yachts that were taken into naval service during the First World War.

HMCS *Grilse* alongside at Halifax.

CHAPTER 3

TWO JARVIS YACHTS AND WAR SERVICE

With the naval policy of providing anti-submarine and anti-raider defence by area patrols, and thus the very real need for more patrol vessels off the east coast finally tested and realized by mid-1915, the Navy became aware clearly enough that *Florence*, *Tuna* and a miscellaneous collection of little ex-Dominion Marine and fisheries vessels were not enough to allow all the routes to be patrolled. Among the several Dominion Marine vessels available as well were *Canada* and *Vigilant*. They were the size of large destroyers but lightly armed, and so left large gaps in the patrolling commitments. Also, ships were always out of service for repairs, stores, rest periods for the crews, and off on other fisheries and searching duties.

While the Canadian Navy had been assigned the task of patrols off the mainland coast and in the Gulf of St. Lawrence and over to Newfoundland, even as late as mid-1916 there were only twelve vessels in all, five at Halifax, and seven under Captain Pasco in the Gulf. The Canadian government suggested to Britain that in line with prewar policy agreements that, protection from the apprehended danger from submarines should be provided by the British Navy. But the Admiralty already had tremendous and unanticipated responsibilities in waters where submarines were not merely feared but already swarming. It therefore declined to provide any help with Canadian east coast patrols. If Canada was seriously concerned, she was going to have to provide her own solutions.

With the example of *Florence* and *Tarantula* already digested, the Navy began to inquire discreetly among American east coast yacht brokers if any other large steam yachts would likely be available. This was done without reference to the law that specifically prevented their being sold for any foreign naval purposes. The history of the last two armed yachts opens with a letter from Cox and Stevens of New York to the consulting naval engineer in Ottawa, on July 9, 1915, saying: "The following can be purchased or chartered, but not fitted out for war in the U.S.: *Virginia*, *Alcedo*, *Surf* and *Florence*." Prices were quoted for each. Obviously Cox and Stevens were either supportive of the Empire's dire needs, or were more interested in the handsome commissions they would receive for selling several expensive yachts than they were concerned about the spirit of the American neutrality laws. On the same day the Navy replied that they already had *Florence* (they were probably talking about two different vessels), but were interested in *Columbia* as well, "althought the rates seemed too high". At the same time a cable was sent to Canada House in London in the hopes of better bargains, saying they wanted small ships: "Any available? For immediate service on the Atlantic coast." On July 17 the Admiralty replied directly, not too surprisingly, "No."

So on July 16 Admiral Kingsmill advised AEmilius Jarvis in Toronto that American ships would have to be bought. Obviously there had been some confidential discussions taking place between the two, although due to the delicacy of circumventing the U.S. laws, there is nothing in the files as evidence as to how these discussions originally opened.

Edward AEmilius Jarvis was, in 1915, a fifty-five-year-old successful banker and broker in Toronto. After being employed as a young man in several banks, he had founded the banking and stockbroking firm of AEmilius Jarvis & Co., and had made quite a comfortable fortune, being at the same time a director of several large companies. He was a descendant of one of the most powerful and influential families in Upper Canada, and one of the principal streets in Toronto is still called Jarvis Street after his forebears. He was also a deservedly famous and skilful yachtsman of long standing, having won the Canada's Cup, the premier race on the Great Lakes, in 1896 and again in 1901. He was to be a commodore or vice-commodore of the prestigious Royal Canadian Yacht Club no less than seventeen times, as well as being a master of fox hounds for the Toronto and North York Hunt Club.

AEmilius Jarvis was of a very dominant character, often the centre of controversy. At one stage he was found guilty of improper bond trading on behalf of the Ontario government and spent time, quite unfairly many local business and social acquaintances felt, at a local jail farm. Some years later, when out hunting, a dubious character made a too pointed remark about this affair, and Jarvis leaned over from his horse alongside and knocked the other man out of his saddle with a single blow! He was a thrusting rider. One day when hunting with his second and quite young bride, the girl's horse stumbled and being relatively inexperienced, Mrs. Jarvis fell off. Jarvis rode up alongside the standing girl and simply advised her to grasp hold of his stirrup leather and set off across the field at a brisk pace to catch up with her horse! It was not hard to see whey he was a leader in the old style.

He had been one of the founding members of the National Council of the Navy League of Canada, when that organization gathered into a single Canadian operation all the separate branches across the country then reporting to the British Navy League. This was a body to which Jarvis actively dedicated considerable effort and money, as a pressure body to influence the government on naval affairs. Like J.K.L. Ross in Montreal, he was dedicated to the idea of the Dominion helping the mother country with naval support, or with cash for naval purposes. When war was declared in 1914, Jarvis turned his office premises on Bay Street in Toronto's business section into a recruiting office, specifically for the Royal and Canadian navies, and in some publications he was even referred to as the RN's "Chief Recruiting Officer". The police had to be called to control the stalwarts thronging the street to join the newly formed Royal Navy Canadian Volunteer Reserve.

It is not recorded who initially opened the correspondence or talks with Ottawa on the matter of buying more yachts in the United States for offshore patrol work, but by July 21, the Director of the Naval Service was reporting to his minister that the prices reported by Cox and Stevens New York were $78,000 for J. Harvey Ladew's *Columbia*, and $80,000 for Randal Morgan's *Waturus*, and that AEmilius Jarvis could make the purchases if necessary. Admiral Kingsmill submitted that the ships should be bought. Cox and Stephens offered several other vessels, but no further action was taken to buy more, for by early 1916, the need was less urgent, and new construction trawlers were starting to arrive from the builders.

So on July 29, 1915, the Deputy Minister for Marine and Fisheries wrote to Mr. Jarvis asking him to act for the Canadian government in closing the deal for *Columbia* and *Waturus*. The consulting naval engineer had visited the United States and seen the yachts, for there is a letter in the files from another broker referring to the visit, and quoting prices and particulars of six yachts, including the two negotiated through Cox and Stevens. So much for the secrecy and penalties attached to selling vessels for naval purposes. But the pretense of buying them for civilian purposes was maintained through Jarvis, and the deal was promptly closed. On July 29 Jarvis wrote Ottawa saying he had made an offer of $70,000 for each ship, adding that the bid for *Columbia* had already been accepted. On July 31 the deputy minister sent a cheque to the Bank of Montreal in Ottawa for $155,968.75, asking that A. Jarvis & Co. be credited with $155,000 in their New York branch. Thus *Waturus* cost $70,000 as well, and the extra $15,968 went to Cox and Stevens as commission and transfer of ownership costs for *Columbia*, and to Tams, Lemoine & Crane as agents in the purchase of *Waturus*. Jarvis had meanwhile forwarded letters to the two brokers authorising the purchases in his name. On August 6 he advised the deputy minister: "Everything arranged and expect I will leave Tuesday for New York to see the ships."

Waturus, owned by Randal Morgan of Philadelphia, whose daughter married Lord Fisher's son. Became HMCS *Hochelaga*.

HMCS *Hochelaga*, during the First War.

Columbia, the second of that name owned by J. Harvey Ladew, of New York. Became HMCS *Stadacona*.

HMCS *Stadacona*, at Sydney, N.S. in 1917, Lt. Wm. ("Cargo Bill") Barber, RCNR in command.

Just to keep up the secrecy, the following day headquarters sent a message to the naval dockyard at Halifax warning that the ships were coming, but that their origins were not to be discussed, nor were they to be contacted. Jarvis then wrote to Admiral Kingsmill reporting that in accordance with phoned instructions, he had written to both ships' captains that they were to clear and sail for Quebec immediately on arrival at Halifax. The ships' names had been painted out as soon as they had temporary British registry at New York. *Columbia* was renamed *Stadacona*, *Waturus* renamed *Hochelaga*.

Columbia/Stadacona was a steam yacht built in 1899 at Crescent Shipyard, Elizabethport, New Jersey, of Swedish iron below the waterline and steel above, as a wedding present for a member of the Le Duc family of New York. She became the New York Yacht Club commodore's yacht in 1899, but by the time of her sale to Jarvis, she was owned by J. Harvey Ladew, an executive of the Singer Sewing Machine Company. She was his second *Columbia*, and often confused with Ladew's first, which was taken into the U.S. Navy at the time of the Spanish American War as the USS *Wasp*. Our *Columbia* was just over 200 feet long, if one counted her long clipper bow and bowsprit, was of 682 tons, and could do about 13 knots. Unlike *Winchester* and *Tarantula*, she had ample accommodation and had been designed more for comfort on longer trips than for high-speed commuting. Her coal-fired steam reciprocating engine was of but 99 horsepower. She was commissioned into the Royal Canadian Navy on August 13, 1915 at Halifax, and left at once for Montreal and Canadian Vickers to be fitted out as a patrol vessel, sailing under Lieutenant H.G. Jarvis, no relation to AEmilius Jarvis.

Even after her refit and strengthening and a coat of grey paint, the owner's cabin still had its mahogany panelling and a large brass bed. There was a passage from the after living quarters to the dining saloon under the bridge amidships, and this passage was completely glassed in where it went through the engineroom, so one could watch the engines at work as one walked along . On board, even the lowly midshipmen (such as the later noted Canadian marine and landscape artist Harold Beament, RCA) who in most warships had to sling hammocks and keep all their belongings in sea chests, were accommodated in double cabins with bunks, lockers and mahogany chests of drawers for their possessions. She had a rather high freeboard, and was not a weighty ship, so tended to roll badly, a fact remembered long after by those officers and men inclined to seasickness.

On arrival from the United States, it had been intended for the passage crew to take *Columbia* up to Montreal, but they refused to do this; now that the ship was one of Her Majesty's Canadian warships, this made them in theory, if not in practice, naval seaman, which they did not necessarily want. So Furness Withy, Jarvis's agent at Halifax, turned the vessel over to the Navy for manning for the trip up-river. For patrols she was armed with a 4″ gun on a small raised platform forward (another was added aft later in the war, when supplies allowed), an 18″ searchlight on the mast immediately forward of her diminutive bridge, and a coat of grey paint. She was based at once on Sydney, Cape Breton, where at first the Commander of Patrols had his headquarters, although these were moved later to Halifax, and under command of Captain Walter Hose. *Stadacona* patrolled the Gulf, the Nova Scotia and the Newfoundland coasts in a rather tiresome and boring routine, but at least she gave the impression of keeping the foe at bay, and lent heart to the merchantmen under protection.

Waturus/Hochelaga was a similar ship, also coal-fired steam-reciprocal engined, of some 196 feet, 682 registered tons, and also capable of about 13 knots. She had been built in Scotland by Hawthorn Leslie & Company for the Archduke of Austria, but after a few years was bought by Randall Morgan of Philadelphia for $150,000, who spent another $100,000 fitting her out to his requirements. She too sailed to Montreal after commissioning on August 15 at Halifax, and was back again by mid-September, serving on Captain Pasco's patrols. These ships were often referred to as Armed Patrol Vessels, or APVs for short.

The manning of this patrol flotilla was a matter of considerable difficulty, since practically all the trained naval personnel and merchant seamen in Canada had been preempted long before. As usual, no adequate steps had been taken before the war to train complements for the growing auxiliary fleet. The Regular Force was miniscule, a few hundred all found. Until 1913 there were no Volunteer Reserves, those that were in existence were due to public spiritedness in a couple of locations. Only in Newfoundland had any merchant seamen and fishermen been given even the slightest naval training. Officers were often but ex-yachtsmen, with a passable knowledge of pleasure sailing and ship handling, now given the briefest of courses in naval matters; or even young enthusiasts right out of the universities. There was a leavening of retired naval petty officers, even a few retired officers discovered living in Canada on pension after their time in the Royal Navy. Some Canadian officers and petty officers were returned eventually from England where they had been serving in trawlers off the British coasts, but there were never enough to go around. For the most part the crews were inexperienced recruits, "untrained not only in technical knowledge required to handle weapons and offensive appliances, but also in Service discipline." They were fortunate that the U-boats did not arrive early off the Canadian coast, with their well-trained, regular force naval crews. It would have been a massacre, the way it was to be in early 1942 off the American coast under almost identical conditions.

Some idea of the problems can be gained from the notes of a later court of inquiry when *Hochelaga* was accidentally run aground in overcast weather, by confusing "magnetic" courses with "true" courses. Evidence was given by Mr. Butt, *Hochelaga's* mate and her navigator at the time:

Q: How long have you been Navigating Officer of *Hochelaga*?
A: Since the 19th of August, 1917.
Q: Can you take astronomical observations?
A: No.
Q: Can you find out the error of your compass bearing on the sun?
A: No.
Q: You say that you took the distance by the log on the first day. Does your log run correctly?
A: No, not when the vessel is going slow.
Q: What certificates have you got?
A: None.
Q: What have you done before this?
A: I sailed a schooner for ten years on the coast.

The court found "that the OOW took little if any interest in the navigation of the ship ... and that the Commanding Officer, although aware that the Navigating Officer was not qualified, did not take extra precautions to check him. Also that no written orders were given pointing out the necessity of checking the course steered with the course laid down on the chart."

Having already seen how *Florence* was used very briefly, then laid up at Saint John, and finally sold off, we can now complete the First War histories of the other four yachts by tracing each vessel until they too were sold out of naval service after the war. HMCS *Tuna* performed her most useful duties off Halifax after commissioning under Lieutenant Ross in December 1914. His commission was back-dated to September 25 for pay and record purposes while he had been on the technical courses. For a while she was the only "warship" available for patrolling off the harbour, indicating the paucity of resources the infant Canadian Navy was able to muster. Nonetheless, she provided the protection deemed necessary for the merchant ships at their point of departure for the United

Kingdom with troops and supplies. In those days merchantmen were only provided with escort protection as they left port, and at "concentration points" when they arrived at the other side. All ships sailed independently, without escort of any kind, except for the most valuable of trooping passenger liners, who might have a heavy warship for surface defence escort. Even the rare anti-submarine patrol vessels had no submarine detection devices until 1916 at the earliest. Even if a submarine were detected, there was nothing to drop on it, only their deck guns to be fired if it was on the surface. It was not until the spring of 1917 that any convoys were established to protect merchant vessels against U-boats, despite the most appalling losses during 1916 and early 1917. And not until then that accoustic microphones for detecting underwater sound became practical, and depth charges were issued in sufficient numbers for most warships to have several.

Tuna continued her patrols without interruption for the rest of 1915. Due to her age and hard use, by December she was laid up at the Halifax naval dockyard, awaiting a chance to be repaired and refitted for continuing duties. It was then decided that this refit could be better handled at the civilian shipyard at Sorel, Quebec, so she was towed up the St. Lawrence after the ice was out in the spring of 1916. After considerable delay, due to the pressures of other ship-building to replace sunken merchant ship tonnage, her refit was finished and she left Sorel for downriver on December 4, 1916. But it had been left too late, and *Tuna* was caught in the winter ice between Sorel and Trois Rivières, after having been broken out twice by local icebreakers. Even at that she suffered boiler and engine room fan breakdowns due to strains when battling the ice flows, and had to be towed to Rimouski, on the Gaspé coast. Then it was decided that her problems could be resolved at Halifax, where at least she would be at hand, ready for duty when they were repaired. So a tug was despatched to tow her the rest of the way.

After repairs, she was sent out on patrols again. But within the month, on May 2, 1917, she suffered an engine-bed fracture at sea, and once more had to be towed in, this time by a minesweeper. After at first planning to tow her once more to Quebec City or Sorel, it was decided to pay her off, as her engines could neither be repaired by their original builders, Yarrows, nor by the Bath Iron Works in Maine, where she had been maintained by her prewar owner. So, on May 10, 1917, she was removed from active naval service, and by July 30 it was resolved to scrap her as being unrepairable. Her turbines were removed and sent for instructional purposes to the west coast dockyard which later became HMCS *Naden*. The hull was eventually sold in June 1918 to Charles Brister & Sons of Halifax, who stripped it of any metal value. But the hulk could still be seen on the shore of the Northwest Arm behind Halifax in the mid-1930's. In 1937 permission was granted for HMCS *Naden* to sell the turbines for $200 for scrap disposal. So *Tuna* served her purpose, and the government got $1,000 for the remains of the ship they had bought from Jack Ross for one dollar.

HMCS *Grilse* lasted out her days in the Navy. By October 1915, she was patrolling off Cape Breton, looking for U-boats that the United States Navy predicted would soon be foraging off the east coast. A typical duty can be described in a little detail to show the sort of job these inshore patrol vessels were required to undertake. In those days there was no detection equipment like sonar or radar, or direction finding electronics, only, as sailors say, "the Mark 1 Eyeball!"

With the American prediction, the false alarms started, adding to the spy scares which were rife among the civilian population already. Since the most up-to-date German submarines had only sufficient range to cross the Atlantic, they would obviously need refuelling bases on arrival. And since such bases would surely require agents ashore to arrange for the supply of fuel oil, it was natural for the two types of reports to be connected, either at their source or when they reached the authorities. Thus when a submarine was reported off the Little Bras d'Or, near Cape Dauphine, Cape Breton, and a mysterious foreigner was reported living nearby, the coincidence called for investigation.

On October 13 Lieutenant Ross was sent by the captain of patrols at Sydney to Little Bras d'Or Bridge in *Grilse*, to interview William Carey, a miner who had reported the submarine. The trail was cold, since the sighting turned out to have been made on September 5, a month and a half before. The report had not even been forwarded to Halifax until September 24! The best Jack Ross could do was discuss the matter with Carey's landlord, who was also the local customs officer, for Carey was then at work down the mine. The two men were positive it had been a submarine. Ross also asked after the suspicious stranger boarding at Big Bras d'Or, within sight of Cape Dauphine. He was said to be working at farming and fishing for his landlord, and it was rumoured he had been trying to arrange to buy a fishing vessel at Ingonish, down the coast a bit. Ross returned to Sydney in *Grilse*, to report progress, and was then sent to Ingonish to investigate this suspicious stranger. It should be realized that anyone not at least second-generation born in Cape Breton would have had some suspicion attached to him as a "stranger" on that highly clannish island.

When Ross sailed again on October 15, the naval motor launch *Two Brothers* also sailed under his command, to assist in the operation. Midshipman R.F. Lawson, RCN, was in charge of this small vessel, which was painted black for the occasion, while he and his crew were dressed as fishermen. He was to pretend to fish off Cape Dauphine, keeping a lookout for the submarine, and for any suspcious activities ashore. On reaching Ingonish, Ross was informed by the customs officer that no fishing vessel had been bought or even a sale requested that year, and as it was by then blowing hard, *Grilse* anchored nearby. The *Two Brothers* could not clear the headland outside Sydney due to the gale from the open Atlantic, so returned home. Thus the whole exercise was abortive. But it was deadly serious and all too typical of those duties assigned to the local forces at that time.

During the winter of 1915-1916 *Grilse* was loaned to the British Commander-in-Chief America and West Indies Squadron, who was based on Bermuda. *Grilse* was sent down to Jamaica for anti-U-boat patrol duties there. Although she left Halifax with some 13,110 gallons of fuel oil, she burned about 3,000 gallons a day at normal operating speeds. So due to heavy weather and not necessarily running at her most economical speed, with about 150 miles to go to Bermuda, she was all but out of fuel. The only thing to do was to stop engines, rig a sea anchor, and call ahead for help. Twenty-four hours later the RN cruiser *Cumberland* was close alongside and passed a towline. *Grilse* arrived at Ireland Island, Bermuda, at the end of *Cumberland*'s leash on December 18. After several months of sybaritic existence in the West Indies, her return voyage, although not plagued by bad weather, also resulted in *Grilse* being out of fuel and under tow, this time entirely due to a miscalculation of consumption, which brought down the admiral's wrath on the commanding officer's head. She was again in Halifax by May 1, 1916, where she was taken in hand for a refit. Before it was completed, Sir Robert Borden had requested Ross's release from the Navy to take up the post of chairman of the Pensions Commission, which was then being established. He was relieved by Lieutenant Walter Wingate, RNCVR, and Jack Ross finished his war in Ottawa. But due to his continuing deep interest in the Navy, he maintained a close liaison with the new Royal Canadian Naval Volunteer Reserve when it was formed in 1923, and was made one of its early honorary commanders, a rank which very few were accorded, and which considerably delighted him, albeit one he richly deserved. He had contributed more than most to the small successes the Royal Canadian Navy had achieved, and was known in many circles until his death as Commander Ross, and deservedly so. A remarkable Canadian.

For the summer, *Grilse* again operated on patrols off Sydney, in the Gulf of St. Lawrence. However, in September, Admiral Kingsmill, on an inspection tour of the port, decided she was too extravagant of fuel for this work, and he ordered her to Halifax. He gave instructions that she was only to be used on special patrols when important ships were to enter or leave harbour, and that her cruising speed was not to exceed 13 knots. In

December 1916 she again sailed for the Caribbean to work for the British for another winter. This time she did not reach her destination at all. The story of that attempt is one of the most harrowing tales of a storm at sea.

Grilse left Halifax dockyard at 2:25 p.m. on Monday, December 11. Early on the night of the 13th, the radio office at naval headquarters in Ottawa decyphered the following telegram:

> From: Captain Superintendent,
> Halifax
>
> At 0800 12 Dec. *Grilse* reported position, moderate southeast wind. At 1900 reported southerly gale; returning; shall I proceed Shelburne? To this I replied proceed Shelburne. 2328 Cape Sable reported *Grilse* calling S.O.S. in position (225 miles SE of Nova Scotia). 2340 from Cape Sable: *Grilse* says now sinking. Barrington called at intervals. Nothing heard. Messages were sent by wireless to ships on outer patrol, also en clair to all ships from Barrington. Telephone to shipping master Liverpool calling for all available help.

(Barrington Passage was the naval radio station just outside Halifax.)

But at 11:15 p.m. on the 14th a telegram was received in Ottawa from the Captain Superintendent, Halifax:

> A rumour afloat that Halifax Morning Chronicle received message from Shelburne that *Grilse* slowly limping into harbour. Have you any information?

It seems that once again the newspapers were the only source of information that was current, for this telegram crossed one from Ottawa to Halifax:

> Telegram reached here from telegraph operator, Shelburne: *Grilse* at Shelburne. Press informs me *Grilse* is there. Have no official report. Have wired.

By 9:37 a.m. on Friday December 15, Halifax was able to wire Ottawa:

> Following from Wingate (*Grilse*'s C.O.) begins: *Grilse* at Shelburne 2230. Six men lost overboard: Wilkinson, Artificer Engineer; Clements, Wireless Opr; Trimbee, Chief Petty Officer; Ashwin, Leading Seaman; Harris, A.B; MacAuliiffe, Signalman. Chandler badly injured, leg broken. Sub -lieutenant Fry seriously injured about head. Ship making water forward. Mess deck flooded.

A court of inquiry developed the whole story within a few weeks. I am indebted to the Directorate of History at DND for permission to quote at some length from this harrowing tale of the dangers of "the steep Atlantic stream" that had little to do with the supposed enemy.

Grilse had sailed with sufficient fuel this time to reach Bermuda, by shipping an extra 2,000 gallons in barrels lashed securely along the sides of the cabins and the engineroom skylight, and in the "torpedo racer," the knee-high rail on which the torpedo tube revolved. When she sailed, the weather forecast was favourable, and she had a fair passage overnight.

But during the forenoon of the 12th, the wind got up and came in heavy gusts from any direction between southeast and southwest, whipping up a heavy confused sea, in which *Grilse* would roll and pitch tremendously. At 10:20 it was so high that *Grilse* could make no headway, and, to save fuel, the captain decided to lie to a sea anchor he had made for just such an occasion. Forty minutes later a sudden shift in the wind brought the sea anchor hawser (the best four-inch manila rope in the ship) hard across the sharp bow, which chafed through it before anything could be done. By 11:00 another sea anchor was rigged but it was not satisfactory in holding her bows to the sea, so *Grilse* got under way again an hour later. By this time she had received a forecast from Boston which predicted moderating weather, and besides, the wind had dropped to Force 2, light breezes only, although the swell was still running high.

During the afternoon, however, wind and sea rose again, and at 2:00 p.m. *Grilse* turned to run for shelter at Shelburne. Later the captain gave orders to jettison the oil barrels. Five or six had been emptied into the ship's tanks, but the remainder were still full and the engineer officer protested that the oil was necessary to be sure of a safe passage to Bermuda. The captain overruled him and a party of hands set to work. They punctured all the barrels, so that they would partly drain and be light enough to handle, then started throwing them overboard. This was designed to lighten the top-weight, which would tend to make the ship roll even more than normal. At 5:10, when the work was finished, Leading Seaman Frederick Chandler was found in the torpedo racer with his leg broken. He was also dazed and could give no clear account of how it had happened. A short while after that, the First Lieutenant discovered that two men were missing, Leading Seaman Gilbert Ashwin and Able Seaman Albert Harris. They had been working with Chandler, but he had not seen them go. The ship was rolling violently at the time and the deck was slippery with oil from the broached barrels. The seas breaking inboard and the violent and rapid motion of the ship did minor damage to various parts of her gear, notably to her radio equipment. At 6:30 a green sea carried away the aerial trunk, protecting the antenna lead where it passed through the deck, and broke the deck insulator. Up to that time the ship had been in regular contact with the shore stations, but now she could not transmit or receive. The wireless operators, Simon McLean and Ernest Clements went on deck and, lashing themselves to the mainmast, rigged a jury lead through the hatch, since water pouring through the broken insulator earthed any lead they rigged that way.

Soon after this the captain sent down instructions to the radio room to make a distress message and at 8:00 p.m. the senior operator began sending an S.O.S. message: "In distress Lat 4340 N, Long 6450 W, require immediate assistance. He heard no reply. After adjustments to his gear he continued transmitting. Still he received no reply, but at 8:30 he did hear the radio station on Sable Island send something about *Grilse* in distress, with position, saying we required assistance." The antenna lead was then found to be earthing on the mast, so the operators again went on deck, put on lifelines and tried to get their gear working again. The senior operator returned to the office to try to send a signal but his assistant remained on deck. He took off his lifeline and was probably preparing to follow down the hatchway when a roll or heavy sea surprised him. He was not seen again.

The boats, one hoisted at her davits and the other secured on chocks over the engineroom skylight, were by this time causing some anxiety. They were damaged and partly filled with water. This weight so high above the waterline tended to reduce the stability of the ship, just as the extra oil had done, causing worsening rolling, so the captain ordered them cut away. Chief Petty Officer Walter Trimbee and Able Seaman Allan Brazier undertook the work, but by the time they received these instructions they had been modified — they were merely to free the boats of water and lash the boat over the skylight more securely. Brazier took the plug out of the sea-boat hanging at the davits, and punched some holes in her steel bottom to let the water out faster.

As this was done, the other boat broke loose from her lashings and took charge, sliding and crashing across the skylight as the ship wallowed and rolled, and seas washed aboard. The two men looked around hastily for lines to secure her, and Brazier's eye fell on the davits of the port sea-boat which had been left behind at Halifax. He cut off some of the hauling part of one line. Trimbee secured one end to a ring in the boat while Brazier was catching a turn with the other on the nearby davit. Two other men were hanging onto the gunwale of the boat to try to hold it still. At the same time, Clements, the wireless operator, was by the "booby hatch" near the mainmast; two men, Able Seaman Malcolm Macauley and Leading Signalman Harry MacAuliffe were by the wardroom door under the bridge, taking shelter, and Mr. Robert Wilkinson, the artificer engineer, was making his way along the deck from the engine room hatch toward the booby hatch.

The captain, keeping his weather eye on the horizon on the port quarter, as well as the work progressing on deck, sighted a mountainous sea bearing down on the ship. He shouted an order for all hands to hold fast for their lives, but nowhere is it mentioned that the order was heard above the gale, and by now it was almost totally dark. *Grilse* was in the best possible attitude to ride the sea but even so she broached to, or was knocked parallel to the troughs and crests of the waves. The sea beat her down and threw her over to starboard on her beam ends. The pendulum in the engine room showed a roll of 89°. The bridge wing supports buckled, the after funnel was crushed, the engine room skylight was stove in and the mainmast went overboard.

Macauley and MacAuliffe, under the bridge, went over the side together. Macauley's right arm fouled the lanyard of an oil bag (being towed astern to try to dampen the breaking seas) so that he remained alongside and managed to haul himself back inboard (the scars left by the rope were visible on his wrist when he gave evidence at the inquiry). But MacAuliffe simply vanished.

By the engine room skylight, Brazier was swept toward the rail, but it caught his trouser leg, stopping his slide just long enough to let him grasp it, and he did not go over the side. As he recovered himself, he saw Chief Petty Officer Trimbee lying face downward in the water, apparently unconscious, with the back of his life jacket split open. He was soon carried away by the sea. No one saw Mr. Wilkinson or Earnest Clements go, but when the senior wireless operator came on deck, which he did immediately the ship rolled more or less upright again, the mast was lying where he had last seen Clements.

Slowly the ship rolled back, but the sea which had broken aboard had smashed the skylight over the engine room and filled the compartment to a depth of four feet over the bed plates and gave the ship a list of 20° to starboard. For some hours she had been leaking forward through strained seams and holes of sheared rivets, and now the mainmast strengthening plate was lost too. (The carpenter who examined the ship at Shelburne gave it as his opinion at the inquiry that the gun-mounting forward and its support were too rigid, and caused the weakening around the plate edges.) The bilge pump in the engine room and a hand pump and a bucket brigade gained on the water forward, but so slowly that no-one could be spared for the engine room itself. The engines could run almost under water, and did so until the following afternoon when the shaft bearings started to overheat for lack of lubrication. But the dynamos were put out of action at once, ending any chance of making further signals by radio.

Sub-Lieutenant Cyril Fry, with a working party, improvised a cover for the skylight with timber, blankets and carpets to prevent another green sea from swamping the ship completely. In the process, he was thrown by a heavy roll and was badly cut about the face and head. He had to be taken below, to join Chandler out of action.

Meanwhile the gale continued, but with no more giant seas. The men pumped and bailed throughout the night and the next day, December 13. At 4:00 p.m. the engines had to be stopped and the pumps and all but four buckets were put to work freeing the engine room of water. She was so much down by the head that as soon as she lost steerage way, the wind caught her stern and swung it away, aggravating the roll. But the wind shifted about this time so that *Grilse* was laying with her head to the west-northwest. At 6:00 a.m. the next day, the artificers were able to start work on the engines and at 10:00 a.m. *Grilse* got under way again. The wind, which had been blowing at Force 7 or 8 gales for over thirty-six hours, now began to moderate and by noon it had dropped to Force 5 and there was a ship within hailing distance. She was not the first vessel sighted, but all others had been most suspicious of the long, low silhouette of *Grilse*, which, with seas breaking over her, must have resembled a U-boat. They had not dared to come near her, and had ignored her distress signals, no doubt suspecting they were a nasty German ruse! The SS *Petrolite* of New York, however, at noon on the 14th and in moderating weather, came close enough for *Grilse* to pass a message to her by speaking trumpet from bridge to bridge. She promised to report the torpedo boat's plight, but for some unknown reason no signal from her was ever received at Halifax.

During the forenoon there was evidently breathing space to survey the damage, for the ship's log contains the entry:

> Lost overboard:
> 1 Patent Sounding Machine
> 1 After Steering Compass
> 1 Torpedo with warhead. No pistol fitted. No gyroscope. #2803
> 2 Patent Steel Lifeboats
> 1 Life Raft
> All wash deck gear, buckets, etc., tackles & heaving lines stowed in deck lockers.

The torpedo was evidently the reload which was stowed on chocks on the starboard side of the engine room skylight, lashed down to the deck. There would be no space to stow it below in such a ship and no way of bringing it on deck when it was required, to replace one stored in the tube for firing if that one were expended on a target.

So *Grilse* limped, bows almost awash, into Shelburne harbour at the south tip of Nova Scotia. The court of inquiry stated:

> The Court is of the opinion that the ship was properly navigated. That the primary cause of the loss of life and damage to the ship was the extreme violence of the weather encountered.
>
> Reviewing the circumstances, and having considered the evidence, we are of the opinion that no blame is attributable to the Commanding Officer, officers, or ship's company of the *Grilse*.
>
> A regrettable feature is the communication of the wrong position with the S.O.S. signal at 7 p.m., on the 12th instant. This could hardly have occurred had Lieutenant Wingate checked it, and the subsequent search for *Grilse* would not have been conducted over the wrong area.
>
> We would recommend that a steel hatch or skylight replace the damaged one over the engine room of *Grilse*.

Grilse was recommissioned on May 10, 1917, under Commander John T. Shenton, RCN, with new officers and a new ship's company. The rest of her wartime career was uneventful. Her name appears in the regular reports of movements of the patrol vessels at work in Canadian waters, but nothing special is recorded. She was probably laid up with reduced complement in winter time, for the plans for the winter of 1918-1919 simply remark that she was not available for the season, even for work in the Halifax approaches, and certainly she would be expensive and unhandy for a harbour craft. The Canadian Navy List shows that from January 17 to February 12, 1918, she was left under command of Mr. Thomas Cotton, late ,RCNVR, who before and after that period served as her First Lieutenant. She was paid off from the naval service soon after the armistice, on December 10, 1918, but it was not until over a year later, on April 26, 1920, that the commander in charge at Halifax reported that she was nearly stripped of her fighting equipment and would soon be available for sale. She was then offered for sale shortly after, together with the elderly cruiser *Niobe* and *Canada*, a smaller, ex-Dominion Marine ship, all at $25,000 apiece. Only one tender for *Grilse* was received, for $1,025 from John Simon, of Pictou, N.S., which the captain of the dockyard considered "too absurd for consideration." Thus she remained in naval hands for some years longer, during 1921 and 1922 technically as a tender to the youth training establishment at Halifax, HMCS *Guelph*. She was not manned most of the time, being visited daily by a petty officer to inspect the ship and turn over the engines by hand. In the cold weather of November 1921, a pipe burst in the galley one night, and when it thawed out in the morning, water flooded the forward compartments of the ship. This was pumped out, the pipe sealed off to keep her watertight, and two watchmen hired to keep the small steam boilers lighted for internal heat.

The youth training establishment fell victim to the budget cuts of 1922, as did the Naval College, the new cruiser *Aurora*, and the two submarines, CH 14 and CH 15. *Grilse* was again put up for sale, and this time there were two bidder, one for $3,000 and one for $25,000. The latter was of course accepted, and on May 10, 1922, the deal was closed. This, and other sales, left the Navy with but two destroyers and five trawlers, but did allow funds for the establishment in early 1923 of the Royal Canadian Naval Volunteer Reserve, the famous RCNVR, which was to flourish moderately during the years of peace.

Grilse's purchaser was Solomon R. Guggenheim of New York, the mining magnate. He had her towed to the United States and fitted out as his yacht again, and renamed *Trillora*, the name of his estate on Long Island Sound. She remained in his possession until 1938, being seen frequently at major yachting events in the area, and lying at his dock, or on the way to lower Manhattan. But in a hurricane on September 21, 1938, she foundered alongside the jetty to which she was secured in the harbour at Roslyn, Long Island Sound. The loss of *Trillora* was not necessarily a disaster for Solomon Guggenheim. She was rather elderly and old-fashioned and he had only used her occasionally. In fact, he had been trying to sell the vessel for quite some time, with no buyers. When he was told that she had sunk at the jetty, according to his biographer, he was delighted. She was, of course, insured!

The wreck was eventally ordered removed by the U.S. Coast Guard, and Mr. Guggenheim turned her over to a salvage firm at no cost. She was not finally removed from the Yacht Register until October 1941.

Stadacona had been commissioned for patrol service out of Sydney, Nova Scotia on August 13, 1915, an elegant, clipper-bowed, two-masted vessel, as unlike *Tuna* and *Grilse* as a destroyer and a submarine. She and *Hochelaga,* were much more in the traditional "yacht" design than the two racy, low-slung, fast and aggressive predecessors had been. *Stadacona* was employed on general duty patrolling and visiting the outports in the lower St. Lawrence, the Gulf, along the Nova Scotia coast, and out as far as the western shores of Newfoundland. Whenever valuable ships were coming out, or expected inbound, these vessels were despatched to keep an eye open for surfaced submarines, even though they were equipped only with a small deck gun and machine guns. One report by the Commodore Superintendent admitted that "these 4 inch guns were obsolete, but ammunition was available, and anyway they were the only guns available for arming patrol vessels."

With the onset of heavy winter weather, *Stadacona* was put into refit at Halifax, and recommissioned in March 1916, again working out of Sydney. For a while in mid-1916 she was provided with V.I.P. "mess traps" (crested fancy china and silver) and bedding, and used to transport important naval and government people around the coast. The special equipment had to be landed when she reverted to patrolling again in the fall! During the summer of 1917 she took Commodore Sir Charles Coke, RNR, and Captain Pasco to Newfoundland, and gradually reverted to her prewar yacht status as a senior officer's despatch vessel, a handsome one at that. She did perform at least one valuable service, in salvaging the schooner *Triton* in September 1917. The owners of that vessel, when the Navy declined to claim the usual salvage amount, which could have run as high as half the value of the ship and her cargo, asked if they could make a donation to the crew of *Stadacona,* which, surprisingly, was allowed, the amount of $300 being divided among the ship's company. The reverse of this munificence was a later claim by H.J. Stabb & Company of St. John's, "for damage to one of their wharves on October 5th, 1917". There is no record if the Navy ever paid it!

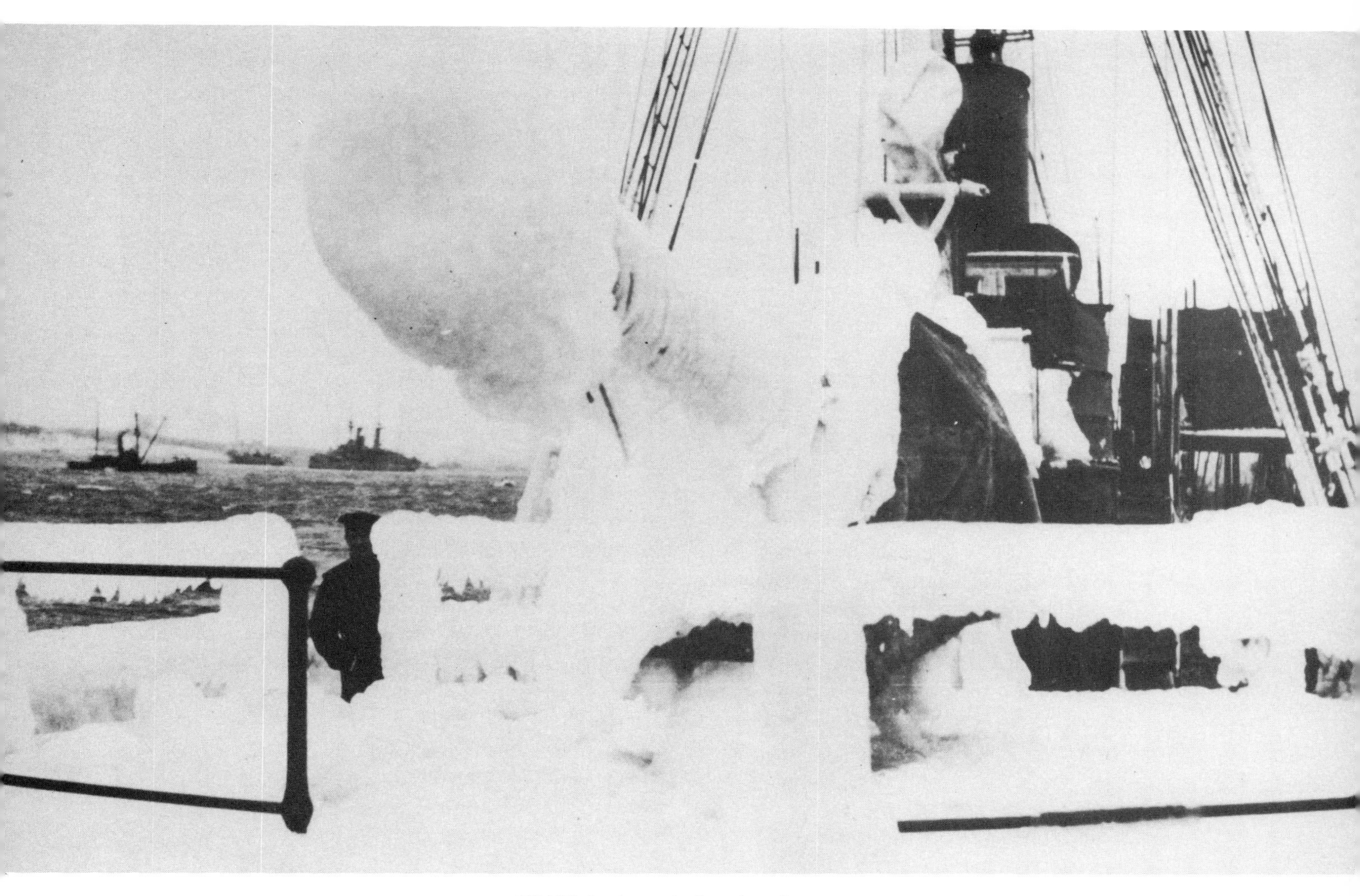

HMCS *Stadacona*'s foc's'le, after a winter patrol in 1916. At Halifax.

HMCS *Stadacona*, leaving Esquimalt in 1919. Lieutenant A.F. Thomas, RNCVR in command.

At one point there was a flurry of paper back and forth between Ottawa and Halifax about *Stadacona*'s actual length, which was causing confusion and apparently concern, due to her long clipper bow and bowsprit protruding forward, and her overhanging stern. Finally, after a month's exchange of messages and queries, it was resolved that she was 168′ along the waterline, 198′ from the rudder post to the top of the stem (where the bow emerged into the bowsprit fairing), and 211′ overall. She carried the Minister of Marine on several voyages, and was at Halifax on December 6, 1917, when the merchant ship *Mont Blanc* exploded with devastating results in the Narrows at the inner end of the harbour, injuring six of *Stadacona*'s crew. The crew by this stage were all RNCVR men and officers, and an interesting note is on file from Admiral Kingsmill to the Halifax commodore: "I have also, ready to come with this draft, 46 ratings RNCVR, trained as efficient, which means that they still have to be taught a good deal".

The officers and ratings of the patrol craft were borne for record purposes in the cruiser *Niobe*, which maintained offices ashore or on board, with paymasters and records officers and clerks. Hence the notation on most service documents: "Borne in *Niobe* for *Stadacona*" and so forth. Toward the end of the war, when acting as a senior officer's ship, she had pay officers and clerks on board, so she in turn had the crews of some of the smaller patrol vessels on her books, although they would rarely have seen her.

After the war's end, it was decided to send some ships to the west coast, where, by that stage, and with no threat, there were no modern warships stationed. *Stadacona* and four new trawler minesweepers were sent around in January 1919, via Port Royal, Jamaica, and the Panama. Off the Oregon coast she lost her rudder in a gale, and had to hurriedly put into port, and hence did not reach Esquimalt until August, five months after departing from Halifax. On the coast, in addition to her new fisheries patrol duties with the other naval and coast guard ships, she was slated to be "at the disposal of the Lieutenant Governor." But soon the Minister of Marine and Fisheries was advising that in the postwar economies, it would be impossible to obtain the necessary appropriations to keep *Stadacona*, as well as the minesweepers, in naval commission. So, in all too typical government fashion, she was to be "transferred to the Fisheries Protection Service or laid up" — no saving at all, since he was also the Minister of the Naval Service! However, for the time being she was retained in service, used as a despatch yacht for the rest of the year, at one time taking the Director of the Naval Service from Vancouver to Victoria to meet Admiral of the Fleet Lord Jellicoe during his work tour of the Commonwealth, and another time taking the members of the Air Board along the B.C. coast in December 1919. Royal Naval College cadets were also taken to sea in her for practical seamanship, and when she was at last paid off from the navy, on March 31, 1920, and hoisted the blue ensign of fisheries protection of the coast guard on April 1, it was on the condition that "RNCC training was not to be affected."

During the summer of 1920 she not only carried fisheries branch personnel about the coast, but the Governor General of Canada, the Duke of Devonshire, as well, for some fishing at Campbell River in September. In Ottawa, meanwhile, the deputy minister was cautioning that the fisheries appropriations were running out, and that *Stadacona*, as well as four other ships, would have to be paid off. While she was actually retained by the department for occasional use through to 1922, and laid up in 1923, on March 11, 1924, she was sold, ostensibly to the Central America Shipping Company of Vancouver, who sold her again almost at once to the Ocean Salvage Company. The actual owner was Joseph W. Hobbs, who had taken advantage of the passage of prohibition by the United States in January 1920, and brought over from Scotland two shiploads of liquor, which he arranged to reach his thirsty customers south of the border without the inconvenience of customs. Hobbs bought *Stadacona* (and two other ex-naval vessels, HMCS *Naden* and *Exmouth II*), at Esquimalt, and reconverted her into a yacht, before despatching her to

Scotland for a cargo of his personal solution to the rising and increasingly lucrative American demand. She was then sent to the southern California coast and to the west coast of Mexico, where small, fast motor launches sped the cases ashore after dark, *Stadacona* in effect acting as their "mother ship". The Canadian Navy was cognizant of this nefarious trade, but since Canada itself was not directly involved, felt they could not intervene. However, they did resent the ex-naval ship being associated quite so directly with this enterprise. So on December 23, 1924, the senior naval officer at Esquimalt wrote to the Naval Secretary asking that *Stadacona*'s owner be told to change the ship's name "since she is a rum runner" (no distinction being made as to the actual contents of the bottles involved, which all contained perfectly good and legitimate Scotch!) In February 1925, Hobbs was officially told to change the name. That stalwart, searching for a name not yet in use, yet one that might be difficult for the U.S. coast guard radio stations, noticed on a B.C. map the name of Kuyakuz Mountain, surely never before used. *Stadacona* was then refitting in a British shipyard, and the British workmen were instructed to paint the new name on her bows and across the stern. But Mr. Hobbs made an error in his estimation of the shipyard hand's understanding, for on the ship was painted "*Kuyakuzmt*", a mouthful that confused and baffled even her master and crew, who wondered what Hobbs was about, and made no sense at all when wirelessed to the watchful U.S. coast guard.

When the cream had been skimmed from the illicit liquor business, and prohibition was undoubtedly on its last legs, the ship was reconverted again, this time as a legitimate yacht for Joe Hobb's use, as the *Lady Stimson*. Hobbs made and lost several fortunes, and is reported to have spent $5,000 to repair and rehabilitate the yacht. Even so, he sold her in 1929, and she became the *Moonlight Maid*, owned by W.P. Dewees, a wealthy theatre owner of Vancouver. She was once more fitted out luxuriously for cruising by her new owner, who retained her until November 1941, when, with a new war on, he sold her to Captain Paul Armour of the Armour Salvage and Towing Company of Seattle and Prince Rupert, B.C. He stripped out her fine fittings and converted her into a tow boat for towing barges up and down Puget Sound and the coast, still with her original 1200 horsepower engine. In 1942 she was once again to change hands, this time purchased by the U.S. government, and used to tow supplies to their army bases in Alaska and the Aleutians, after the Japanese had been chased out. She survived the Second World War, to finally be sold to the Foss Launch and Tug Company of Seattle for scrap. They stripped out all equipment of any value, and then on January 31, 1948, set fire to her oil-soaked wooden fittings, leaving only the stout steel of her hull for scrap.

In the midst of his career as a scotch whiskey importer, Joseph Hobbs surfaced in another role in Vancouver. On April 15th, 1925, Acting Lieutenant J.W. Hobbs, RCNVR was appointed the Vancouver Half Company's first Commanding Officer when the Naval Reserves were established there. Hobbs had served in the RNVR in England during the First War, so when the RCNVR was approved for formation in 1923, he received the appointment as the designated C.O., due to his obvious background and continuing association with shipping. But the naval authorities at Esquimalt did not approve his philanthropic pursuits involving circumventing the bonded warehouse system, so his initial appointment was brief, and on their recommendation his appointment was not approved by Ottawa. However another C.O. could not be found locally to take on the fledgling naval reserve unit, and it was not until a year later that the internal wrangling between the sponsoring bodies in Vancouver (who were not unduly concerned about Mr. Hobbs' civilian pursuits!) and the navy were resolved, and Hobbs confirmed as C.O., and allowed to raise the first naval half company on that coast.

After prohibition was repealed, Joe Hobbs moved to Scotland, where he owned and operated the Great Glen Cattle Ranch, and, not too surprisingly, a distillery. The

Stadacona's final demise.

Hochelaga, at Pictou during the 1930's, as a ferry to Prince Edward Island.

Canadian Navy and the U.S. Coast Guard may have found Hobbs a bit hard to swallow, but his townspeople at Fort William in western Scotland made him a Freeman, and tendered this testomonial:

"Joseph William Hobbs, Commander of the Venerable Order of St. John, Liveryman of the Worshipful Company of Shipwrights, Freeman of the City of London, in recognition of his pioneering achievements in industry, agriculture, and stock-breeding, unprecedented in the history of the local economy ..."

No mention of rum running!

Hochelaga also had a long and useful life. Like *Stadacona*, she was assigned to patrols off Halifax and in the Gulf, out of Sydney, throughout 1916, 1917 and 1918. She was remembered by Admiral of the Fleet Lord Fisher's daughter-in-law, a daughter of Randal Morgan, the original American owner, for in January 1916, while at Halifax, a parcel of knitted wool helmets arrived from Kilverstone Hall, England, for the crew of the ex-*Waturus*, "In memory of many pleasant months spent on *Waturus* in American waters". In January 1917 she was the only patrol vessel active at Halifax, the rest being up on the slips for repairs. At one point *Hochelaga*'s navigator was suspended from duty, as his real (as different from his calculated position proved to be one hundred miles apart! One of the problems of the too-rapid growth of the RNCVR, one suspects. In December that year, she, too, had several men injured in the Halifax explosion. Then, as the war drew to a close and the convoy system defeated the U-boats, occurred *Hochelaga*'s only brush with the enemy, which left her commanding officer under arrest for a court martial and very nearly charged with an offence which could have him executed.

On August 25, 1918, about 1:45 p.m. *Hochelaga*, returning from a convoy escort to Cape Race, Newfoundland, in company with the new patrol vessel *Cartier* and the two patrol trawlers TR 32 and TR 22, was steaming southeast across a calm sea, not far from Miquelon Island. The ships were in line abreast, about three miles apart, with *Hochelaga* second from the left, *Cartier* on her right, and the two trawlers on the outer wings. At this moment two schooners were sighted from *Hochelaga*, well ahead of her on her port bow. Her commanding officer, Lieutenant Robert D. Legate, RNCVR, altered course toward them, with her neighbouring ship TR 32 following her motions, with a view to intercepting the schooners and warning them that submarines were in the area.

At 1:55, the schooner towards which *Hochelaga* was steering, disappeared, and almost at once a submarine was seen on the surface close to the now wrecked schooner, which was seen to be on her beam ends. At this point *Hochelaga*'s course was altered away from the scene by about 60° to the south, toward *Cartier*, some distance to starboard. Only then was "Action Stations" sounded, and a signal made from *Hochelaga* that a submarine was in sight, and another to TR 32 ... "Follow me." There seems to have been some lack of signalling skills, for at this point *Cartier* made a signal to *Hochelaga*: "What does your signal mean and what have you seen?" *Hochelaga* relied: "Submarine in sight, bearing East," upon which *Cartier*, much more valiantly, altered around promptly toward the scene and rang on full speed.

At this *Hochelaga* asked *Cartier*: "Do you see reinforcements astern? Don't you think it better to wait for them?" to which *Cartier* tersely and pointedly replied "Negative." *Hochelaga* then formed up on *Cartier*'s port quarter as they approached the engagement between the surviving schooner and the submarine. It could then be seen that the U-boat had disappeared, having noted the warships' approach, leaving the schooner still on her side, with debris and several dories floating nearby. *Cartier* began rescue operations at 2:30, with the others circling around, in theory to keep the U-boat at bay.

Things did not improve for the unfortunate Lieutenant Legate, for on return he was placed under arrest on board *Cartier*, the senior ship, as reported by the senior officer patrols, Sydney, "Pending a disrespect Court Martial." *Cartier* was then ordered to Halifax, and Legate placed under close arrest in the cruiser *Niobe* pending court martial, an unusual step, as officers were usually held under open arrest at the most, confined only to a building or ship.

After some indecision, the final charge was the very serious one: "When in sight of a ship of the enemy which it was his duty to engage, did not use his utmost exertion to bring his ship into action." He only barely avoided the charge of cowardice, through it being very difficult to prove that motive. The lesser disrespect charge was dropped, in the prosecution of the more serious one. The court martial was held in early October, and on the 4th the five members reported:

> The Court considers that the *Hochelaga* should have been steered at full speed toward the enemy vessel or her last observed position and all means of offence available made use of in an effort to inflict damage or destroy the enemy. This was not done and the Court therefore finds the charge against the Accused proved.

The sentence was passed on October 5, "To be dismissed from His Majesty's Service," and was approved by naval service headquarters a week later. Altogether it was a sour note on which to end an honourable naval career.

A new commanding officer was appointed, and *Hochelaga* continued patrolling until the war's end. Like *Hochelaga*, it was soon realized that there would not be enough naval funds to retain the two yachts as well as the two new destroyers that were being negotiated, and the newish cruiser *Aurora* that Commodore Hose, that tireless fighter for the survival of the Navy had bargained away from the RN. The story was later told by Admiral Hose himself that when he went to England to obtain a cruiser to replace the ancient *Rainbow* and not much newer *Niobe*, he was told that all the Royal Navy could spare would be a coal-burning ship. Hose, not at all satisfied with such an out-dated cast-off, advised the Admiralty that Canada would much prefer an oil-fired, newer ship. When they remained adamant, he countered with the veiled threat that in such case, no oil fuel stocks would be maintained at Halifax, only coal. Since Halifax was counted on by the RN as one of their main world-wide fuel depots, and their newer ships would undoubtedly be oil-fired, the Admiralty relented and *Aurora*, built in 1913, was obtained.

In July 1919 *Hochelaga* was recommissioned for service during the visit of the Prince of Wales to Canada, and for a cruise by the Governor General down the St. Lawrence River and up the Saguenay with Admiral Kingsmill in attendance. In October, 1919 *Hochelaga* was used for inspection trips of radio stations and lighthouses along the shores of the Gulf of St. Lawrence and as far as Newfoundland. Even after the war, life was no bed of roses during these trips, as evidenced by the telegram of October 29, shown on next page; gales still blew in the Gulf, war or no war. She was even used as an icebreaker in the harbours west of Halifax, and to help fishermen get clear of ice in the Strait of Canso. Panelling and tapestries were again added for a cruise by the Lieutenant-Governor of Nova Scotia, but then she was put up for sale, being paid off from her new operators, the Coast Guard, on October 30th, 1920. Due to an inflated idea of her value, she was not sold until February 23, 1923, when purchased for commercial use by John Simon of Halifax for $11,000. Later that year she was put into service under ownership of the Hochelaga Shipping and Towing Company of Upper Water Street, Halifax, to operate between Pictou, Nova Scotia, and Charlottetown, Prince Edward Island, as a passenger and freight ferry. She was a singularly handsome ship, with her long clipper bow, tall raked funnel and masts, and sweeping deck line. She ran like clockwork, and the cry often went up among the cottagers along the shore of Pictou Harbour, "There's the *Hoch*!" as she swept in just at the day's close from her daily run to the island. We children watching her then little knew that she had already had an illustrious career as a naval vessel.

With the advent of the Second World War, and the reduction in tourist and package freight trade, *Hochelaga* was put up for sale. In 1940 she was considered for war use again,

OFFICIAL COPY

GREAT NORTH WESTERN TELEGRAM

Z.A. LASH, PRESIDENT — HEAD OFFICE, TORONTO, ONT.

LET US NOT DEMOBILIZE PATRIOTISM

A 1 38 MOE 46 DH AND 47 COLLECT RADIO — H M S HOCHELAGA 29 — OCT 29 1919

NAVAL

OTTAWA

HOVE TO TUESDAY NIGHT STRONG SOUTHERLY GALE AND HIGH SEA STOP MIDNIGHT WIND SHIFTED TO WEST NORTHWEST INCREASED TO HEAVY GALE AND HIGH SEA STOP HOVE TO OFF CAPENORTH BEARING WEST NORTHWEST ABOUT TEN MILES STOP WIND NOW NORTHWEST GALE VERY HIGH SEA

HOCHELAGA.

BUY VICTORY BONDS

but still being coal-fired, and over forty years old, was rejected as impractical. Thomas C. Wilwerth of New York City, an ex-telegraph operator, had obtained a contract from the South Puerto Rico Sugar Company to ship several thousand tons of sugar from Puerto Rico to U.S. ports. Searching for a ship to handle this project, no easy task with the U.S. entry into the war and their taking up most available vessels for patrol and transport work, he happened on *Hochelaga*, and bought her at Halifax in November 1942. Wilwerth sailed her from New York on Christmas Eve, and on arrival had the ship dry-docked at Sullivan Shipyards, where he intended to have her converted to oil-burning and prepared for bagged sugar cargoes.

At this stage the purchase and transportation of the ship had already cost some $72,000. Then she was unceremoniously chased out of Sullivan's due to U.S. Navy requirements for their facilities for repairs, and after trying to refit the ship alongside at his own piers in Upper New York, he had her docked once more, this time at Todd Shipyards. Then it developed that several hull plates needed replacing, and the U.S. Coast Guard licensing authority advised that she would have to be manned by a crew of about twenty-four, instead of her Canadian complement of twelve or thirteen, thus necessitating more accommodation. To obtain funds for this added expense, a partnership was formed, which was not a success, and when bills eventually reached $136,000, the creditors had her seized by the U.S. Marshal on July 3, 1943, just as she was due to sail for Florida. She was then bought by a subsidiary of the United Fruit Company, who had taken over Wilwerth's sugar contract, and towards the end of the war sold again to either Greek or Jewish buyers. At this point *Hochelaga*'s history becomes rather vague. She surfaces but once more on the world's stage, as an "illegal" immigrant ship, trying to transport Jewish refugees into Palestine to break the British blockade in the last days of that unhappy Palestine Mandate.

The thousands of survivors of the death camps and garrets arriving at ports all over Europe found everything from quite decent newer ships to the most hazardous of wrecks, some of which could not even be persuaded to run long enough to leave their loading harbours. Which of these categories our old friend *Hochelaga* belonged to is not known. For although she was shown on shipping registers as the property of Em. Fostinis of Marseilles, flying the Honduran flag, and operated by a Panamanian subsidiary, Cia. Mar. Las Palmas, this might simply be a front for the Aliyah Beth, the illegal immigrant bureau, or could be a local shady merchant trying to make a fortune on one or two trips to Palestine. She was shown in some records as *Hakhayal Ha'irvi* or *Jewish Soldier*, although in other registers she was still *Hochelaga*.

Through connections with the Cuban Consul in Antwerp, Fella Perlman obtained visas for the transportation of five hundred refugees from Belgium, the alleged destination being Cuba. In mid-July 1946, ex-*Hochelaga* slipped into port and took aboard the five hundred, "right under the nose of the Royal Navy", with no suspicions aroused, no questions asked, as Belgium was relieved to get rid of this drain on her strained economy. But on July 31, 1946, she was intercepted by seamen of HMS *Saumarez*, Captain W.H. Selby, at the entrance of the Palestinian port of Haifa. The vessel stopped when challenged, and on boarding, the British sailors found that the refugees' food supplies were mostly provided by UNRRA, the United Nations relief organization that was providing food for the refugee camps and travellers, which also flowed into the ships, illegal in British terms or not. The ship was taken over by a boarding party, secured alongside in Haifa harbour. There were no incidents, as occurred in *Exodus* later, and the crew were arrested. The unfortunate refugees were herded into temporary camps by the police and officials of the Jewish Agency, not for the first time in their lives. They were then mostly transported to camps on the island of Cyprus, to await the solution of an unsolvable problem between Britain, the Arabs and the Jews.

At this time *Hochelaga* disappears from history, although she remained listed in Lloyds to 1953. She was probably scrapped shortly after her arrival, for no one could complain about what the Jewish Agency did with her once she was seized, and her value was almost nil. It would not have been unusual for the British to use her for a trip or two to carry the refugees to Cyprus.

And thus the five first armed yachts ended their careers, one of them having survived long enough to outlive most of her Second War counterparts, whose story we must now take up.

CHAPTER 4

AFTERMATH OF WAR, AND FINANCIAL HARD TIMES

With the end of the First World War, retrenchment was the order of the day. Not that Canada's Navy had been any great size, for at most she had operated two elderly cruisers, two submarines, a depot ship or two, five armed motor yachts, and quite a respectable fleet of trawlers, drifters, large and small patrol launches and other miscellaneous service vessels. But none of them were of much use for the protection of Canada's shores. And the demands on the Royal Navy during the war had shown that the days were past for relying on Britain to provide the exclusive seaward defence of her huge dominion across the Atlantic. While there had often been a cruiser or two at Halifax, and even the odd battleship from time to time, the demand on destroyers and other escort vessels had been too great to ensure any form of standing Royal Navy patrols, (although they did provide many of the ships used), or even anti-submarine hunting groups off Canada's east coast. And of course none at all on the west coast, where in that conflict, there was considered to be no risk.

So if it was an evil now passed, the war had at least opened most knowledgeable Canadians' eyes to the potential for a coastal defence force of its own, if required. The Royal Canadian Navy, and its auxiliary arm the Royal Navy Canadian Volunteer Reserve, had proved its competence in battle and in storm. This force had reached the respectable total of almost 6,000 men (no women were recruited directly into the Canadian Navy in that war), and another 2,350 Canadians had served with the Royal Navy, the Royal Naval Division in the trenches of France, the Royal Naval Air Service, and other sea arms of the mother country. For a change, there was now scattered across the country a band of civilians who maintained at least an awareness of a navy's role, a familiarity with its capabilities, and, in a great many of these cases, a respect and even a love for "the Service."

With the end of that war to end wars, demobilization was the order of the day. Already we have seen in tracing the postwar histories of the four surviving armed yachts, that even their modest upkeep became too great a strain on the naval purse. In May 1918 the British Admiralty had put forward the proposal that all naval defence of the Empire, Canada included, should lie in British hands for reasons of efficiency, and that local naval boards should only control dockyards, schools, repairs, recruiting and other essentially land functions. The Admiralty would, on their part, be responsible for questions of strategy and the entire utilization of the Navy as a fighting force. This proposal was put to the prime ministers of the several dominions. After study and consideration, Canada's Sir Robert Borden decided that the proposal could not be accepted. The concept obviously did not recognize the status of the Dominion, and would offend the newly awakened sense of nationhood, fostered by the recent war, when, for the first time, Canadians had fought as "Canadian" units up to divisional size in the army, and, off Canada's shores, as the Royal Canadian Navy. It was a bit too early for independent commands for a Canadian Air Force, but then, the air force was a new concept everywhere. While agreeing that the Admiralty's proposal was probably the best from a standpoint of efficiency, Borden thought it politically impractical, a view echoed by other prime ministers. The Royal Navy's case was not helped by their problems of distant support in the late war. So the concept was dropped, and this meant that while the Royal Navy had proven the need for a concentration of force to meet any future threats, Canada was going to have to provide something for its own defence locally, or have none at all. The problem came in for detailed examination during 1919, and arrangements were made for an inspection visit and a report by Admiral of the Fleet Lord Jellicoe, who was specially commissioned by the Imperial government to examine the defence requirements of the major dominions. He arrived in Ottawa from Victoria on November 27, 1919, and on December 22 attended a meeting of the cabinet, where he presented his carefully considered proposals concerning a new naval policy for Canada.

In general, these recommended a local defence force adequate for Canadian needs, on two coasts, and consisting of the following ships, to be acquired over a period of ten years, in four steps:

> 1. First Phase: 4 local defence destroyers, 8 submarines, 8 anti-submarine patrol craft, 4 trawler minesweepers.
> 2. Second Phase (to be completed within seven years): Add the following ships: 3 light cruisers, 1 destroyer leader, more submarines and a parent ship.
> 3. Phases Three and Four: Add the following: 2 battle cruisers, 4 more light cruisers, 12 large destroyers and a parent ship, 2 aircraft carriers, 4 fleet minesweepers, 8 more submarines.

Meanwhile, in April 1918, Borden had asked the British Admiralty confidentially whether Canada could arrange to take over some Royal Navy units, as with the war's end in sight, Britain would possess many more warships than she would presumably need in time of peace. The reply was that the British government would be willing to transfer to Canada a number of warships of various types, and if the Dominion would undertake to keep them in repair, man and pay for their operation, the ships would be given free of charge. A decision was delayed on the details of this plan, in view of Lord Jellicoe's pending visit, and was not finally made until March 24, 1920, when a modest request was forwarded for one cruiser and two destroyers. The Admiralty promptly replied that the Bristol Class cruiser *Glasgow* and the two relatively new destroyers *Patriot* and *Patrician* had been selected. The minister of Marine and Fisheries then announced that they were to replace the obsolete and useless training ships *Rainbow* and *Niobe*. However, looking their gift horse in the mouth, the Canadian government pointed out that *Glasgow*, although having a gallant war record (she had participated in the battles off Coronel and the Falkland Islands in December 1914), had been built in 1910, and was coal-burning. Captain Hose went to the Admiralty to request a newer, oil-fired vessel, and undertook, unbeknownst to his Ottawa superiors, the modest blackmail for *Aurora*.

With the balmy days of peace, these three vessels turned out to be about all that ever appeared of Lord Jellicoe's grandiose plans, except for the transfer of two new H Class submarines CH 14 and CH 15, which Borden had accepted in June 1919.

By 1922 no one in Canada outside the naval service was interested in building up a naval force, and the total strength had dropped to 336 officers and men. *Aurora* and the two submarines had been sold. The two destroyers and four small trawler minesweepers were all that were retained. Even these were always undermanned, relying heavily on the newly formed Royal Canadian Naval Volunteer Reserve to fill out their complements with basic seamen, after its formation in 1923, as well as the professional merchant seamen and fishermen of the Royal Canadian Naval Reserve a few years after, when they could be spared. The Navy struggled along with no men, no money, and almost no ships. When *Patriot* and *Patrician* outlived their useful life spans in 1928, they were replaced with two more ex-RN ships, *Champlain* and *Vancouver*, the first ships to receive Canadian names on their transfer to Canada. One of the trawlers had also been lost on the west coast.

As the years rolled on, the fact that Article 1 of the Treaty of Versailles required that Germany surrender all submarines, and build none in the future, was taken as a sort of guarantee that another "Battle of the Atlantic" was highly unlikely. The London and Washington naval conferences of the 1920's and early 1930's lulled the general public into a false sense of security about their sea defences. False because the powerful and peaceful nations such as Britain gave up their strength, America at least agreed to restrict hers, while the smaller nations refused to agree to the outlawing of submarines. It had always been felt that such vessels were the weapon of the weaker nations, and here the point was proven, for the weaker nations would not sign the agreements unless provision was made for submarines to be retained, albeit under the operational requirements of international law, whatever that was.

Whatever the causes — and the onset of the Depression was one — Canada's Navy was involved in a very real and desperate struggle to survive at all. By the early 1930's she had added two new destroyers, *Saguenay* and *Skeena*, built for the first time to her order, in England. They were rather disparagingly referred to as "the Rolls Royce of destroyers," because of provision for steam heating in the messdecks and in the wardroom, and because of extra strengthening in the forward part in case of encountering ice in the Gulf or the North. The Navy retained the two older destroyers, and the three First World War trawlers. And that was all. There were some motor launches with names, for there had to be a "ship" in which the commander-in-chief's flag could be flown, at least in theory. (It was not until the onslaught of the next war, with all its practicalities, that this requirement was dispensed with.) When Hitler marched into the Sudetenland, and abrogating the peace treaty in 1937, the Canadian government could still find no money to build up its forces except in the most modest of fashion. To look at 1938, just before the Munich crisis, the naval expenditures rose from a level of $2,171,000 to $4,763,000, which was enough to support a total naval personnel strength of 1,965 officers and men in the RCN, and the following fleet:

4 destroyers, *Skeena*, *Saguenay*, and the two replacements for *Champlain* and *Vancouver*, *Fraser* and *St. Laurent*, also bought from the RN.
3 old trawlers, two of them in the dockyard under care and maintenance only.
4 new "Basset" Class minesweepers, building.
1 sail training schooner, *Venture*.

The seagoing ships were divided pretty evenly between the two coasts, and of course, there were no ships in the Arctic, or even interest in that area from a naval point of view. Admiral Hose had retired, and Rear Admiral Percy W. Nelles had assumed command of what navy there was. In naval circles in Ottawa, and with the senior officer staffs at the coasts, there was a rising concern that if war was shortly to come — as most naval officers were now sure was inevitable — many more ships would have to be produced from some source. Dr. Hugh Keenleyside describes the scene exactly when, in an article about the acquisition of the Second World War armed yachts, he says, "Of course the Naval authorities had for years been making conventional complaints about the lack of ships and crews." But, in their own quiet way, the staff had looked about them on the coasts, and made an assessment of which vessels could be requisitioned for use in an emergency, and were already taking some steps to lay in some stores of small guns, minesweeping wire and winches, and such vital war equipment. The vessels they saw were, apart from those already in naval service, several belonging to the RCMP Marine Division, some of which were still coal-burning vessels of the Department of Fisheries, and those serving the coast guard and hydrographic survey departments. But, even in their lists, there was some confusion between what was desirable and what was attainable. Lieutenant Commander F.G. Hart, in a report to the Director of Naval Stores, listing the equipment that would be required to man an auxiliary flotilla on each coast in the event of an emergency, allows for nineteen anti-submarine craft on the east coast and twenty-one on the west, but added a note at the bottom: "At present there are only 5 vessels on the East Coast and none on the West Coast possibly suited for fitting as A/S craft."

When war was clearly approaching, Prime Minister Mackenzie King, on September 1, 1939, asked the British to indicate what kind of military cooperation between the two countries would be acceptable. On September 6th, having had a communication from England, Sir Gerald Campell, the High Commissioner for the United Kingdom in Ottawa, stated the nature of the cooperation the Admiralty would seek from the Canadian Navy:

— 6 destroyers, to be placed under Admiralty operational orders;
— Fit out ships with Asdics for anti-submarine hunting;
— 3 anti-submarine vessels at St. John's, Newfoundland (that island still being a British crown colony);
— Small craft for minesweeping and anti-submarine to assist in West Indies local defence;
— Fit out 3 Armed Merchant Cruisers;
— Defensively Equipped Merchant Ships (DEMS) arming, and manning these ships with gunlayers;
— Surplus RCNVRs to Canadian requirements to be made available on loan to the Royal Navy;
— Recruit civilian officers and technicians for direct entry into the RNVR.

It should be noted that almost all of these suggested arrangements were indeed met, entirely at Canada's option and choice, as her immediate contribution to the Empire's naval defence and war effort.

However, the first requirement for the Canadian destroyers to be placed under Admiralty operational orders, while agreed to by Admiral Nelles as the only practical way to use them in the upcoming war, was refused by the Canadian cabinet as politically unacceptable. In fact, this fundamental problem was resolved by the order-in-council of September 14 which said these destroyers were "to cooperate to the fullest extent with the forces of the Royal Navy." This happy solution meant, in fact, that Nelles's concept of a single naval battle control was met, and yet Canada maintained a right to control its own forces, a vital point later in the war.

When war as at last upon us, the government of the day acted swiftly. Plans were put in hand for doubling the manpower of the Navy, although no proposals were made for recruiting any women into naval service. The two west coast destroyers were told to leave at once for Halifax, and a rapid agreement was reached to acquire another destroyer from the RN (to become HMCS *Assiniboine*). The first transatlantic convoy sailed promptly on September 16. For this time, unlike in 1914, the Allies knew that the Germans, although making considerable play with their new, large and powerful battleships and battle cruisers, were fully ready to start the submarine war again, with fifty-six submarines in commission, forty-six of which were ready for action, and twenty-two of which could operate across the Atlantic right away.

And this time there were "few doubting Thomases" as to the potential range and hunting grounds of these U-boats. They would assuredly appear off Canada's Atlantic coast. The question was "when". Fortunately, Germany's Admiral Erich Raeder was not prepared for war when Hitler precipitated it, as he had hoped for two hundred operational Uboats by war's outbreak. In this the Allies were fortunate, for they had only a few destroyers available — those not tied up with their designated battle fleet protection duties, and a few older anti-submarine sloops and trawlers that were fitted with Asdic, the underwater detection device. There were no small ships fitted with radar, or even with H/F D/F radio direction finders, later used to detect U-boat radio transmissions. There were few depth charges, no aircraft dedicated to hunting submarines, nor any suitable bombs if they had found one. If Germany was not yet ready for a major submarine war, the Allies, and especially Canada, were certainly even less prepared for an anti-submarine one!

The Canadian naval staff realized at once that the new ships ordered in the early months of the war could never be ready for the coming winter, and most of them not before late 1940 at the earliest. Several armed merchant cruisers were fitted out with guns, three of them small Canadian liners, *Prince David*, *Prince Henry* and *Prince Robert*, requisitioned from the Canadian National Railways, and fitted with 1895 pattern 6″ guns stored in Montreal for the purpose. Several British merchant liners were similarly armed in Montreal, Quebec and Halifax, but these were of no use to hunt the anticipated submarines. Those few ships that were acquired from the RCMP and Fisheries were soon fully engaged in minesweeping the harbour approaches, on patrols, and as guard and inspection vessels off the ports of the east coast, at Halifax, Sydney, Saint John, and so on. Obviously some more suitable ships would have to be acquired to be fitted out as anti-submarine hunters. The loss in the first few days of the war of the large liner *Athenia* was sufficient to prove to the navy that the U-boat war was to start where the depredations of 1917-1918 had left off. There would be no slow build-up of the submarine war, and the aircraft carrier *Courageous* was sunk by a U-boat on September 17, to underline the danger.

The Canadian naval staff were in agreement that the primary area of concentration would be in the North Atlantic, that heavy ship defence could only be provided by the Royal Navy, and that Canada's most useful contribution would be to make her destroyers available to the RN on an integrated command basis. This was a remarkably altruistic attitude, giving up command control of Canada's only warships, one that was later to be re-opened both navally and politically, as the RCN gained in size, experience and self-confidence. But defence of Canada was of much lower priority than defence of the United Kingdom.

In addition, the Navy appreciated that local defence, of Nova Scotia's and New Brunswick's harbours, and of the St. Lawrence exits, would have to be assumed by the RCN, in addition to the provision of armed merchant cruisers, and naval control of shipping personnel.

While these local defences would not require sophisticated warships, they would require considerable numbers of credible and seaworthy vessels. This had exercised several naval minds over the last four years, and hence gave rise to Commander Roy's visits and correspondence, and Captain Murray's appreciation of the situation. It was of too low a priority to enable ships to be acquired in the post-depression years, and yet was potentially politically sensitive.

A quick look at the Canadian shipping registry showed that there were few vessels in this country that could be acquired that would not disrupt the fishing industry or other necessary pursuits, which it was desired to continue if possible, food being as necessary as defence.

Large private motor yachts would be the answer ideally, for they would not be of much use to their owners in wartime, and their requisitioning would not disrupt any vital enterprises. But where to find them? In fact, only one Canadian yacht seemed practical, Charles H. Sheppard's steel-hulled vessel *Ambler*, which he used in Georgian Bay. There were many, many others, of course, who gave their large motor yachts, even sailing vessels, for naval training purposes, such as Stuart Playfair's *Pathfinder*, used in Lake Ontario and Georgian Bay throughout the war as a sea training ship, as was Eddie Watts's *Haidee* and many others. The rest were rather more difficult to find.

CHAPTER 5

BUY YOURSELF ANOTHER YACHT

With the very real need to obtain some suitable anti-submarine ships quickly, to hold the fort until the newly ordered corvettes and minesweepers could arrive, the navy early began casting its nets wider, and not too surprisingly, looked enviously to the south. There, under the much-vaunted affluent society, was quite a respectable number of large steel motor yachts, some of them very large indeed. The names of J.J. Astor, J.P. Morgan, W.K. Vanderbilt, and the movie stars of Hollywood only need be mentioned to bring to mind opulent, fast yachts. And with German U-boats prowling the coasts, it was unlikely that these owners would be risking their yachts at sea as in the balmy days of world peace. True, the United States was neutral, and still quite decidely so, and Canada was now a belligerent nation. But really there was no other source.

In discussions between the navy and other departments of the government in Ottawa, the Canadian Shipping Board, represented by Dr. Hugh Keenleyside, and the Canada-U.S. Joint Board of Defence, resolved that action must be taken to see if some large American yachts could be bought. Consequently, in mid-December 1939 Commander J.W.R. Roy (later to lose his life in the sinking of HMCS *Margaree*) went to the United States in civilian clothes to have a quiet look at what yachts might be available. He proceeded to New York, where he spent two days, ostensibly as a rich Canadian yachtsman looking for a large yacht for himself, visiting yacht brokers and inspecting yachts. He then went to Boston to continue his rounds of vessels, and looking at photographs and listings in brokers offices. He was reasonably optimistic:

> "Generally all the yachts seen were in excellent condition and will most probably prove so under a proper steamship inspection. It is probable, however, that few if any of these ships will do the speeds claimed for them, in fact few will do better than 12 knots and a great many will not do that.
>
> It is not considered that this type of vessel will require extensive alterations for adapting to Naval purposes. They all have quite adequate deck space aft for depth charge chutes and throwers if required. The biggest alteration would be to provide space forward for a gun. In most cases it will be necessary to take away the dining saloon, almost invariably on the foc's'le, and deck over and strengthen the foc's'le deck for the gun mounting. Most of these ships will take a 4″ gun. Asdics, Type 123, can be fitted in at least all the larger ships. Accommodation is plentiful but expensive furnishings and a considerable amount of woodwork will require removal.

Commander Roy then appended a list of vessels offered for sale, or considered to be available or suitable, although he had not seen them all, the listing being provided by the ship-brokers he had visited. Cautiously, he recommended:

> "Taking price into account, it is recommended that consideration be given to acquiring four of the vessels for A/S duties on the east coast and Gulf next summer. The prices quoted are only approximate, though in some cases a lower offer of cash might be accepted. Should it become known that the Canadian government was in the market for yachts the prices would rise immediately. It is considered that having ascertained the condition of the vessels by survey, the purchase should be made through a reliable broker.

At that point, he made an interesting comment in his letter to the Deputy Chief of the Naval Service:

> In addition to the vessels mentioned on the attached list, there is another steam yacht worthy of mention — The *Winchester*, built in 1916, which I saw. She is of extremely light construction but if her boilers are in good condition and she can be bought cheap, say $25,000, she might be worth spending money on. She can probably still do in excess of 25 knots.

Although there is no indication that Commander Roy was aware of it, this *Winchester* was a larger and faster sister-ship of Peter W. Rouss's *Winchester* that had become HMCS *Grilse* during the First World War. This one was Rouss's last venture into high-speed commuting yachts, and was owned in 1939 by General Cornelius Vanderbilt. So the matter of yacht purchasing to fill Canada's need for patrol vessels had come a full circle. And of the seventeen ships Roy listed, Canada was to buy eight, plus the *Winchester*, and another whose name was added as a pencilled note at the bottom of his list, *Aztec*, in Boston, at 230 feet the largest of the yachts bought for war service. But he was probably correct in his caution that the government should not let the word get out about wanting to obtain the yachts, for the eventual delivered prices were almost one-third higher than his estimates. By the time the purchases were being arranged, although the affair was kept as secret as possible, it soon became known that Canadians were buying large yachts en masse, and for cash too!

Dr. Hugh B. Keenleyside of External Affairs, the director of the yacht purchasing program in 1940.

The largest yacht, Arthur Burrage's *Aztec*. Also the oldest, built in 1902, and she had served in the USN in the First War as SP 590. Elegant rather than lovely.

Aztec in the slips at Boston for inspection and repairs, after purchase by T.H.P. Molson.

There were three reasons that there were so many large and expensive motor yachts on the American market. First, there was a war on; memories were still fresh of the violent U-boat campaigns of 1917, when the Germans — the same Germans who were once again prowling the oceans in their U-boats — opted for a "sink at sight" campaign, with little attention paid as to belligerent or neutral flags flown from their targets. This had occurred only twenty-two years before, and the yacht owners were not too confident that the boastful new German Kriegsmarine would respect their flag on the high seas. Second, the Depression was only just over, and in some cases the yachts had changed hands several times as the fortunes of their owners had waxed and waned, with consequent lack of meticulous care. Some owners were just beginning to recoup their finances by the greatest of energy and industry, with little time for large motor yachts, some of which were from twenty-five to thirty-seven years old, and no longer speedy.

But one of the prime causes that some of these yachts were on the market was a relatively new requirement introduced in the late 1930s by the U.S. Coast Guard (who arranged the licensing of all ships), that a certain minimum crew had to be carried, no matter how short the voyage might be. So even if an owner was only day-running down the coast, stopping and shutting down at night in a yacht haven, he was now obliged to carry sufficient deck and engine-room hands to stay at sea on a watch rotation basis. Thus, some of the ships that could have operated with three or four deckhands and the same number or less in the engine room, now were required by law to carry maybe nine deckhands and the same below, which made the whole enterprise doubly expensive. The owners were prepared to indulge themselves in the operation of comfortably large motor yachts, but felt aggrieved when required to solve the unemployment problem of seamen as well. Thus many of the yachts were put up for sale.

With several ships apparently available for purchase, and discussions going on actively with naval and External Affairs personnel, the flow of correspondence rose quite quickly on the matter of yacht acquisition and future use ...

Commander Roy to the Deputy Chief of Naval Staff:

> With reference to my report on American owned yachts, it is disappointing that the speeds of vessels available will not allow them to carry out duties as escorts for fast liners. They have, however, sufficient speed for convoying the majority of cargo vessels.
>
> As there is no chance of new construction being available by the opening of navigation in 1940, it is strongly recommended that at least four vessels be purchased, fitted with a gun, Type 123 Asdics and depth charges in order that we can give some measure of A/S protection to shipping in the Gulf.

A good idea of the desperate plight of the Canadian Navy in trying to provide even the most meagre of protection for the merchant ships now under the close control of Captain Oland's Naval Control of Merchant shipping organization is contained in Commander Roy's next paragraph:

> Consideration should also be given to giving A/S protection by fitting numbers of smaller vessels with depth charges and a light gun.
>
> (Note no Asdics for detecting submerged U-boats!) These could be stationed in divisions of 3 or 4 at strategic points such as Gaspé, Magdalene Islands, etc. There are any number of fast motorboats, 80-100′ in length, available for sale at reasonable prices and though they would be of no value in bad weather, the weather is fine in the Gulf for a large percentage of time in the summer.

To which the Deputy Chief of the Naval Staff, Captain Leonard W. Murray, later to command all the escort forces operating out of Newfoundland on the Atlantic convoys, noted sourly on January 4th, 1940 to his Chief of the Naval Staff: "The Gulf of St. Lawrence is a very unfriendly part of the ocean and I cannot agree that boats of 80-100 feet will be able to escort fast ships very often, even in the finest part of the summer, July-August."

But he went on to urge that three additional large yachts be purchased that Commander Roy had seen and recommended. He might also have given a bit more thought to using slower motor launches in the view of later knowledge acquired by the Navy in ocean escort work, when they found to their considerable surprise that many merchant ships to be escorted could do no more than 8 or 10 knots at their best speed, about 11 miles an hour.

With plans obviously going forward to buy what were in effect 'war vessels' in a neutral country, a committee was formed in Ottawa to examine how this was to be accomplished. It was headed by Norman Rogers, then Minister of National Defence, and included C.D. Howe, Minister of Transport, who were charged with acquiring "certain vessels." They in turn issued instructions to Dr. Keenleyside of External Affairs and Mr. Lesslie R. Thomson of the Department of Transport to look into the details and evolve a plan.

To lend the necessary urgency to the matter, Admiral Nelles, the CNS, wrote on January 4 to the Deputy Minister (Navy):

> As tenders for the construction of our A/S - M/S vessels do not become due until 11 January (i.e. contracts would not even be settled to have them built until that date), it would appear most improbable that deliveries of ships in quantities commensurate with our needs will become available before October next.

Lesslie R. Thomson, the Department of Transport executive who organized all the details and people.

Dependent on the completely unknown action of the enemy, it is essential that steps be taken as soon as practical to render the minimum naval protection to shipping in the Gulf and River St. Lawrence as and when these waters are re-opened to navigation in 1940.

As far as can be ascertained there are practically no vessels in Canada of a type suitable for conversion into A/S vessels. With this in mind, Commander J.W.R. Roy, as a civilian, visited (the U.S.) to form an opinion of the suitability of the yachts available on the sales lists at those ports. To achieve the minimum naval protection in the St. Lawrence it is considered we should acquire approximately a dozen vessels.

On the Pacific Coast it is considered that a minimum of four A/S vessels should be maintained. The *Sans Peur* (by then loaned to the RCN from the RN, to whom she had been turned over by the Duke of Sutherland) and *Macdonald* (from the RCMP Marine Division) are now being equipped.

Admiral Nelles then spelled out the requirements for these yachts:

The principal attributes of a vessel suitable for conversion into a submarine hunting craft are:

(a) being able to keep the sea;
(b) having hull plating heavy enough to carry A/S equipment;
(c) deck strong enough to permit the mounting of at least one 4″ gun;
(d) capable of being equipped with depth charges;
(e) a minimum speed of 12 knots.

Admiral Nelles then listed fourteen suitable yachts seen or considered in the United States, of which seven were to end up in Canadian hands. And as a somewhat surprising indication that at least the Navy had its equipment plans developed reasonably far into the future, even if the other government departments were by no means ready for war, he concluded his letter to his deputy minister:

It is anticipated that the A/S equipment for these vessels will be available from the United Kingdom about mid-March.

As and when our A/S - M/S building programmes commence producing ships the above named craft will be made available for service further afield, e.g. in Newfoundland waters and in the West Indies; in other words they will be required to perform useful service for the duration of the war so long as they continue to be seaworthy.

It is requested that the War Supply Board be asked to devise ways of acquiring these vessels.

Considering that this letter was written in early January 1940, it is a remarkably far-sighted document by a very astute naval officer, with very little experience to guide him. He foresaw the use these vessels could be put to clearly, their shortcomings, and their potential extended value; he had equipment ready for the ships if and when they arrived. He detailed the basic requirements when selecting yachts, not asking for any qualities that were not essential to their task.

The committee decided to officially open negotiations with the United States. A telegram was sent from the Secretary of State for External Affairs to the Canadian Minister in Washington, explaining in some detail what was required:

No. 17. CODE. SECRET.

With reference to our telegram of the 16th ... and Mr. Kleenleyside's conversation on the telephone this morning ... concerning the desire of the Canadian Government to acquire certain privately owned yachts for naval patrol purposes, please approach the

State Department and ask for a definite ruling in relation to these two cases.
(a) The Canadian Government wishes to purchase a privately owned yacht registered in the United States between 125 and 200 feet long, to be brought to Canada in its present condition and subsequently to be outfitted for naval patrol purposes;
(b) A private individual in Canada wishes to purchase a privately owned yacht registered in the United States and bring it to Canada in its present condition. It is the intention of the Canadian purchaser ultimately to resell the yacht in question to the Canadian Government, and the Government will then outfit the vessel to be used for naval patrol purposes.

The Canadian Government is anxious to know whether there will be any objection on the part of the United States Government to either of the procedures envisaged above. It is the impression of our representatives, who recently discussed related matters with the United States Maritime Commission, that such procedures would not be contrary either to the letter or the intent of United States laws or regulations. It is the view of this Government that the terms of Title 18, Section 23, to which reference has been made by United States officials do not apply to transactions such as those mentioned above. As the Canadian War Supply Board is anxious to move in this matter in the near future, I shall be grateful if you will endeavour to obtain a favourable reply from the State Department as soon as may be feasable.

Nine days later a secret message was returned by the Canadian Minister in Washington to the anxiously waiting committee, indicating that this official request was perhaps a rather serious error in strategy in the plans to acquire American yachts: "State Department has given careful consideration to this question and have come to the conclusion that Title 18, Section 23 of United States Code definitely prohibits transactions referred to in your telegram."

The minister followed up this telegram with a more detailed interpretation of the laws involved, which is worth quoting in some detail, as it not only spells out the problems to be faced by the Canadians in acquiring these yachts, but the hazards faced by both the individuals sent down to get them and even the American owners who might be persuaded to sell them, knowing their eventual use.

Construction, Fitting out and Arming of Vessels in the United States, against Friendly Powers
1. The United States Criminal Code provides:

"Whoever, within the territory or jurisdiction of the United States, fits out and arms ... or procures to be fitted out and armed, or knowingly is concerned in the furnishing, fitting out, or arming of any vessel of any foreign prince, or state, ... to cruise, or commit hostilities against the subjects, citizens, or property of any foreign prince or state, with whom the United States are at peace, (i.e. Germany), shall be fined not more than $10,000 and imprisoned not more than three years. And every such vessel, her tackle, apparel and furniture, together with all materials, arms, ammunition, and stores which may have been procured for the building and equipment thereof, shall be forfeited; one half to the use of the informer and the other half to the use of the United States." (R.S. Sec. 5283; Mar. 4, 1909, c. 321, Sec. 11, 35 Stat. 1090).

2. The foregoing section has been interpreted to mean that it is an indictable offence *either* to fit out or to arm a vessel.

3. it is not necessary that the vessel should be armed or in a condition to commit hostilities on leaving the United States, *in order to convict* a party concerned in the

enterprise, who (would be) indicted for being concerned in fitting out a vessel with intent that she should be employed in the service of a foreign state ...

4. It has been suggested that if a ship were duly purchased by a private party, who, in order to be enabled to transfer such vessel to a belligerent, when beyond the jurisdiction of the United States, should obtain a clearance for some foreign port. The United States Government has stated emphatically that such a circuitous transaction, including a violation of the law, *is as much forbidden as a direct one.*

5. A vessel constructed in a United States port for a hostile attack on a friendly sovereign will be arrested, under United States law, even though she is not yet complete, and the intention is to send her to a foreign port for completion.

6. It would seem that the proposals of the Canadian Government, to purchase in the United States certain privately owned yachts, to be brought to Canada and there be outfitted for use as naval patrol vessels, would constitute a clear violation of the terms of the United States Criminal Code.

This exchange of telegrams properly let the cat out of the bag. Not only was it forbidden to buy the yachts even in a roundabout manner, and then arm them in Canada, but the U.S. government was now semi-officially cognizant of the fact that the Canadian Navy was interested in such a project. There was now no official way to acquire the yachts, and the Canadian government could hardly jeopardize the freedom of any of its citizens, let alone American yacht owners or brokers by openly sending down delegates to buy up the yachts needed.

When J.K.L. Ross had bought his two yachts in 1914 and in 1915, the two Governments had not been involved until the matter was completed, although the naval staff in Ottawa knew what was afoot. When AEmilius Jarvis was asked to buy *Waturus* and *Columbia*, it was apparently presumed that this civilian purchase of the yachts was allowed, as no official questions seem to have been asked. In 1940 matters, unfortunately, had reached a rather higher plane.

With the Navy basing its plans for local convoy protection and anti-submarine patrols off Nova Scotia on the acquisition of at least eight east coast and two west coast yachts, their pressure on Ottawa diplomatic circles to take some action was mounting. As there was almost no standing patrol force at either coast, and the war was already five months old, with submarines sinking major passenger ships, the Navy was in desperate straits, and the yachts had suddenly become essential. So in Ottawa a modified plan was put forward by Dr. Keenleyside to Dr. O.D. Skelton, the Under Secretary of State for External Affairs. The proposal was that the committee should select a few influential Canadian yachtsmen and requisition their present yachts, if this had not already been done, and then encourage them to purchase substitutes from private owners in the United States. When these replacements reached Canada, they in turn would be requisitioned, and the Navy might return the first smaller requisitions as "not being as suitable as at first thought."

It was now also necessary to avoid any real explanation to the Canadians selected to buy the yachts, so that they could truthfully say that they had not been informed that their new playthings would be taken over by the Navy. And of course it was necessary to avoid *any* explanation of the exercise to the American owners, as they otherwise might be charged with conspiring to violate United States laws.

Dr. Skelton agreed the plan was possible, but insisted that highly informal and secret discussions should be held with trusted State Department officials in the United States, and Dr. Keenleyside went to Washington on February 1. Despite the "official" reply above, the contacts in Washington were not too surprised at the visit. In fact, Dr. Keenleyside says they were fully cooperative, although unable to tell any other departments of the proposal.

Shortly after, due to some press comments already appearing under the hand of some of the more watchful and astute reporters, the State Department became nervous, and asked Canada to give an undertaking that none of the vessels would be used for belligerent purposes for six months. Canada stalled giving a direct reply until all the ships selected had been transferred, making the question somewhat academic, although as it turned out none of them were used for actual "belligerent" purposes within the six months.

In the meantime, on the supposition that all would be well, plans were proceeding in Canada to select yachtsmen, make funds available, and organize the arrival of some dozen yachts for conversion. Allthough formal approval for the plan and the necessary funds were not in hand until February, the operation was already under way, adding a touch of unaccustomed spice to the lives of the otherwise very proper civil servants involved in several departments. The Navy at this stage was being kept out of it altogether, for the presence of uniformed officers around the yachts would have made it all too obvious that some illegal skullduggery was afoot. This exclusion rather annoyed some of those in the naval hierarchy, who felt that they should be involved in the acquisition of what were, after all, ships for their use, the cost coming out of their budget. Even after the war was over, the Navy was still aggrieved at being left out. In April, 1946, an Amercian claimed commission for putting the Government onto several yachts, which was not concurred in. The question was asked of the Navy if they had any comment on the claim, eliciting the reply,

> The Naval Service had no say whatsoever in the ships which were made available for Naval use at the start of the war. Hence their general unsuitability. It is my opinion that this Department is in no way implicated with Mr. White.
>
> Rear Admiral,
> CNAS

It soon became known in U.S. ship brokerage circles that Canadians were out to purchase several large motor yachts. It must have considerably annoyed the committee, and caused no little worry, when an all too specific letter arrived in Ottawa:

> January 27, 1940
> From: W.R. Givens, St. Petersburg, Florida.
> To: W.L.M. King, Prime Minister.
>
> We understand it is the intention that the War Supply Board will purchase 15 - 18 yachts, and that Henry Hill (his step-son) and Andrew B. Side & Co., with CDR Roy searched out yachts for Admiral Nelles, to be purchased at attractive prices ...

In fact, Givens was only worried that Hill and the Sides Company would get no commissions, and that the War Supply Board would buy from the owners direct. It would appear from this early correspondence that Commander Roy had not been universally discreet.

In fact, in March 1940, the nominal broker with whom most of the actual purchasers dealt, Cox and Stevens of New York, agreed to give over 33⅓% of their commissions to Hill and Sides on seven of the yachts, "in the interest of amity."

But secrecy was still considered to be essential, maybe more so in view of this leak of information. The Department of Transport was delegated to handle the whole affair, and put in charge was a Montreal engineer by the name of Lesslie R. Thomson, who had come to Ottawa as a wartime assistant in C.D. Howe's department, and later in Munitions and Supply. Thomson was an ideal choice; not only did he know his way around the Ottawa inner circles, but he was an amateur sailor of some skill and repute, and had many contacts in yacht clubs throughout Canada. He could move and deal easily with the well-to-do sailors , knew enough of ship requirements to be able to discuss problems and solutions technically, yet was an astute businessman in his own right.

Having therefore tentatively selected the yachts, and set the government requirements in motion, the next step was to select the yachtsmen to go south. This was done personally by Thomson, who, after confirming the whole procedure with Admiral Nelles, with Captain Murray and Commander Roy, between February 14 and March 3 came to agreements with thirteen prominent yachtsmen in various parts of Canada.

The following gentlemen were approached, all of whom agreed, sometimes with some reservations, and whose names should be recorded as valiant helpers in the Canadian naval war effort, certainly unacknowledged until now!

At Halifax, belonging to the Royal Nova Scotia Yacht Squadron, Donald R. Turnbull, a Scot, and manager of the Acadia Sugar Refining Company was contacted, and his sailing yacht *Wanderer IX* was requisitioned.

Also of that squadron and contacted was, Ralph P. Bell, a shipping operator, president of several offshore shipping companies and fish-packing and supply houses, and the past secretary of the Halifax Relief Commission from 1917 to 1919. Later in the war he was to be appointed Aircraft Controller from July 1942 to December 1944, responsible for all Canadian wartime aircraft construction.

Another RNSYS member was Colonel Sidney C. Oland, managing director of the famous Oland brewing interests, an ex-artilleryman and 66th Battery Commander in the First War, aide-de-camp to 3 governor's general, and whose sons and brothers made considerable names for themselves during the war and after.

Two others at this yacht club who were contacted were B. Pearson McCurdy, a Halifax newspaperman, whose small sailboat *Joann* was requisitioned, which considerably puzzled him; and Colonel Frederick H.M. Jones, MC, an active militiaman, small yacht owner, and the general manager of the Eastern Trust Company.

In Montreal three yachtsmen were contacted: Tom H.P. Molson of the Molson Brewing interests, who was in turn secretary, vice-president and chairman of that family firm. He had owned, at various times, a sloop, a schooner and two power yachts, and became commodore of the Royal St. Lawrence Club. His brother, Senator Hartland Molson, gives a good picture of him: "He was good company, with a sense of humour and was well educated and travelled. He was a lot like the rest of us: keen on sports, but not exactly a world's champion."

The second Montrealer was George H. Duggan, Past Chairman of Dominion Bridge Company and Dominion Engineering Works, an honourary LLD and DSc of three universities, and in the large racing yacht world. He won international cup races as long before as 1896 and 1901, and was a designer of large racing yachts, a founder of the Royal St. Lawrence Yacht Club, and at this time, seventy-eight years of age. Also, Philip S. Ross, a well-to-do insurance and printing business executive, also of the Royal St. Lawrence Club, became the third Montrealer approached.

In Toronto, the Royal Canadian Yacht Club formed the base for those contacted: first, Stuart B. Playfair and A. Montye MacRae, both in the investment business with their own firms, and keen yachtsmen. Stuart Playfair, although a well-known power and sail yachtsman, was like Colonels Oland and Jones, also a soldier, having served in the South African War for over two years in the Queen's Own Rifles and as a Lieutenant in the 48th Highlanders during the First War. His large requisitioned steam yacht, *Pathfinder* was to be retained by the Navy in the Great Lakes as a training ship for new recruits throughout the war. At the end of the war, when he and his son-in-law, Garfield Lorriman, went to pick her up in Hamilton, she had been so knocked about in naval service for five hard

D.R. Turnbull, of the Royal Nova Scotia Yacht Squadron, Halifax, bought *Caribou* in New York.

Henry Ripley's *Elfreda*, that was bought by D.R. Turnbull of Halifax, and became HMCS *Caribou*.

B. Pearson McCurdy of Halifax picked up Vanderbilt's *Winchester*.

Thomas H.P. Molson of Montreal, who brought up the elderly yacht *Aztec* from Boston.

LT.-COL. H.F.M. Jones of Halifax, who bought the yacht *Avalon* for the Navy.

Wild Duck, when owned by Margaret and Charles Levy of Virginia. Bought by George H. Duggan of Montreal, she became HMCS *Husky*, had a varied career after the war, and is still afloat today in New Orleans.

George H. Duggan of Montreal, an accomplished yachtsman and engineer, who bought *Wild Duck*.

Stuart B. Playfair, Toronto stock broker, who bought *Arcadia*, and loaned his own *Pathfinder* to the Navy.

years that she was not considered by them to be worth recovering, and Mr. Playfair could only sell her "where is, as is." The yachts were just not built for such continuous and hard use.

Also in Toronto, Tom K. Wade was contacted, later to be a stalwart of the RCYC as commodore, an executive in the Salada Tea Company and, like Ralph Bell, he too served in Ottawa as a "dollar a year man" under C.D. Howe for the duration of the war.

Out on the west coast, contact was made with Clarence Wallace, president of Burrard Dry Dock Company, and with Dr. Keenleyside's brother, E.W. Irvine Keenleyside. Mr. Wallace was later to become the lieutenant-governor of British Columbia. Irvine Keenleyside was to eventually bring three yachts north, for Mr. Wallace did not in fact go south himself, but had Mr. Keenleyside act as his agent in the transaction.

Since the whole operation had to be kept strictly secret, some idea of how the contacts were handled is gained from the story of Colonel Jones in Halifax. He was a bit surprised when his sail yacht *Wanderwave* was requisitioned "for naval service" in February 1940. He then received a visitor from Ottawa (Lesslie Thomson), who suggested that the government would not object if he were to go south and buy himself another yacht to replace his.

"But I don't want another yacht," he told his visitor. "There's a war on, and I'm not going to have time to sail it anyway."

"Look sir," said the caller, in effect, "The government would like you to buy another yacht. We'll give you the name of one we suggest might be satisfactory, and the broker to contact."

At this the light dawned, so Colonel Jones asked: "How much is this yacht likely to cost?"

"About $150,000."

"And just where do I get that kind of money?"

"Ask your bank manager for a loan for it."

"WHAT? My bank manager isn't going to loan me that kind of money to buy a yacht at this time!"

"It's all right, Colonel Jones. Just ask your bank manager, and I think you'll find it's quite in order."

Once again the light dawned, and sure enough on application to his manager, Colonel Jones found he had an open letter of credit to, if he wished, buy a new yacht! The same story occurred in each of the cities, as Lesslie Thomson made his contacts, and arranged for the yachtsmen to go south, or send representatives.

Most of the men went themselves. Those that did go were entitled to charge their reasonable expenses to their account, but were held fully accountable for those expenses. Again and again, the purchasers were advised to tell no one of the negotiations, so they were reticent to even discuss the matter with other yachtsmen friends, some of whom, unknowingly, were on the same mission. Stuart Playfair was cautioned, in an excess of secrecy, not even to tell his wife. But after several U.S. phone calls and a visit to New York, he told Thomson that "his wife was becoming suspicious that there was something funny going on and he might have a girl friend he was hiding!" Upon which it was allowed he could tell his wife the story, but she was to be sworn to secrecy!

On the west coast, when Clarence Wallace's 140-foot diesel yacht *Breezin' Thru*, arrived he had to use her for a couple of weeks, in common with several of the other purchasers, to maintain the illusion that he had bought her for himself, and because not all yachts could be taken in hand for conversion at once. Wallace's sudden affluence and his folly in buying a very large yacht in the middle of a war puzzled his yachting associates. He did nothing to enlighten them, cruising very comfortably among the Gulf islands for a week or so — a modest reward for his trouble in arranging the purchase.

The actual purchases varied considerably. In some cases these men went south for a particular vessel, bought it through a brokerage firm, and returned with the yacht's original crew to man her as far as Halifax or Victoria. In other instances, the yacht examined was found to be unsatisfactory, and the Canadian then looked around for a better buy. This was the case with Clarence Wallace's *Breezin' Thru*. The yacht he was originally requested to consider was not, in his agent's opinion, worth taking up at all. She was the *Machigone* of Long Beach, California, and had suffered from age, being over thirty years old. He suggested Leila Post Montgomery's *Breezin' Thru* instead. After some delay, Ottawa agreed, and arranged to acquire his selection.

But not all yachts in poor shape were rejected, and this was where the careful selection of knowledgeable yachtsmen paid dividends. The yacht that Tom Molson bought was found to be partly flooded, sunk in Boston harbour, for her engine room had flooded in a hurricane before the war. In fact, *Aztec* had been laid up from 1932 to 1939, after her owner had died. Molson bought her essentially for scrap value, for he paid no more for her than any other ship, yet she was the largest of the armed yachts, at 260 feet and over 800 tons. She was also the oldest, being built in 1902, originally to the order of Henry Clay Pierce of Mexican oil fame, but he had decided not to take delivery of her while still building. She was completed for Albert C. Burrage, a lawyer and copper mining executive, who, with his wife, were *Aztec*'s owners for thirty-eight years, until bought by Tom Molson. He dealt with the Burrage Estate lawyers, and made the best deal he could, without revealing the vessel's ultimate destination.

He then had her towed to an East Boston dry dock for repairs and a proper marine survey inspection. Preparing her for her trip to Canada was no small job, requiring a new

Commodore Tom K. Wade of the Royal Canadian Yacht Club, who brought up the yacht *Ramona*.

E.W. Irvine Keenleyside, who bought one yacht in his own name, two others for other West Coast yachtsmen.

Clarence Wallace, Vancouver shipyard owner, whose name was used to buy *Breezin' Thru*.

Breezin' Thru, ex-*Sabalo*, in May, 1940, when in use by Clarence Wallace of Vancouver, to the surprise of his friends.

Sabalo, just after building in 1916, with U.S. Navy's notes regarding her purchase as SP 225. She became HMCS *Cougar* in the Second War.

propeller shaft, a dory to replace the smashed lifeboats, new Edison batteries, a rebuilt generator, and so on. There was also fuel to take on, the survey to be paid for, and then repairs once again when it was found that a garbage chute passing through a fuel tank had corroded and allowed the diesel oil to spew out into Boston harbour through the garbage outlet!

No crew was available in this case, of course, and this was quite a worry for Tom Molson. He eventually arranged with Foundation Maritime, the Halifax towing company, to provide a crew for the sea trials and the passage home, as they were already under a Naval contract as crew for the Halifax anti-submarine net guard vessel. He arranged on his own for the cook and a steward to come from the Molson family yacht at Montreal, the *Curlew*, which the Navy had, of course, requisitioned. As well, he invited two yachting friends to join him as, he says, "An After Guard of officer complement for the trials and the trip." The Canadian government had nothing to do with all these manning arrangements, but did help in another facet of this particular purchase. When the time came to transfer *Aztec* from American to Canadian ownership, the U.S. Coast Guard had become suspicious of all these Canadians buying big yachts, having been told nothing by the U.S. State Department. They refused to allow the transfer. Molson, very disturbed, contacted Ottawa, who suggested he personally contact President Roosevelt directly, and say something like "Accustomed as I am to yachting in the Gulf of St. Lawrence, I request that the Neutrality Act by bypassed, since the Navy has requisitioned *Curlew*." This call was made, had immediate effect, and he received permission to have the ownership transferred. No doubt a telephone call from the executive office to the coast guard, without explanation, was word enough for the wise.

After the repairs and hull survey were complete, trials run, defects in the gyro compass and radio direction finding set made good by a very helpful local coast guard staff, they sailed from Boston, more or less hugging the shoreline due to concern about marauding U-boats, and the scratch crew's navigational accuracy in a strange ship. *Aztec* arrived in Yarmouth, Nova Scotia, about 3:00 in the afternoon. There was a strong wind blowing on arrival, and in handling the unfamiliar vessel they hit the jetty quite a crash, breaking three pilings. Tom Molson later received a bill for $150 for repairs from the port authority. After contacting the customs, he went to the Bank of Montreal in the town, fortunately finding that the manager, Mr. Cairns, was an old friend from Montreal. So he had no trouble raising the necessary but completely unanticipated $10,000 for customs duty and sales tax on his new purchase. The Canadian customs had also been told nothing of the official intentions for the yachts.

By 7:00 p.m. all was cleared, and they resolved to run for Halifax during the night, to avoid being seen by any watching U-boats. Despite the Shelburne and Lunenburg fishing fleets being out, they ran through the night with all lights out, except for one on the port boat boom which they could not find a switch to extinguish. Eventually it was broken by a blow from a boat hook, and they arrived safely at Halifax the next day, passing up the harbour into the Northwest Arm and an anchorage. Shortly afterwards they were ordered to Dartmouth, and secured alongside another new acquisition, the large turbine yacht *Winchester*, where Molson turned over "his" yacht to what he referred to as a rather piratical RCN crew in civilian clothes (to continue the ships' disguise as a civilian vessel). The Foundation Maritime crew returned to their company, and Molson, his two friends, the cook and the steward returned to Montreal. Within a few days *Aztec* was in turn officially requisitioned by the Navy "for war service," as HMCS *Beaver*, and *Curlew* was returned to Tom Molson. Oddly enough, after the United States became embroiled in the war in December 1941, they obtained *Curlew* as a patrol yacht, and she saw duty on the American west coast in their navy. Although only 117 feet long and, in 1940, considered too small for Canadian purposes, she was well found, having been built at White's in England in 1927, and was quite satisfactory for the USN in the fairer waters of the southern U.S. west coast.

It had taken from February to May 24 to complete the deal for *Aztec*, at a total acquisition and delivered cost of some $73,600, and yet this made her one of the cheapest purchases. Molson said, "It was a lot of trouble for me, but looking back on it, it was in a way fun."

Despite the Canadian government's best efforts to prevent any publicity about the purchase of the yachts getting out, by mid-March the word was in the public press in the United States, to the considerable distress of the Canadian purchasers, even though the press was usually most supportive of the concept of the yachts being used to fight the Germans. Stuart Playfair, in Miami, noted in the *Marine Progress Weekly News Report* of March 18 the report of transfer from American owners of no less than five yachts, to Canadians Colonel Jones, David Turnbull, Tom Wade, Philip Ross and Signey Oland. As this was not enough to cause concern, the cat was completely let out of the bag by an article in the Miami Daily News of March 17, headlined "GHOSTS OF GREAT STALK PLEASURE YACHTS AS CANADA SEEKS FAST SLEEK U.S. SHIPS FOR WARTIME COASTAL PATROLS." Following photographs of the luxurious fitting of the Miami-based yachts, there were several paragraphs to ensure there was no mistaking the purpose of the Canadians, even if they themselves continued to say nothing, becoming very concerned at the distinct possibility of long prison sentences or heavy fines.

> Luxuriant trappings may be scrapped if several yachts familiar to Miami's harbour are transferred by their owners from American registry to Canadian. These comfortable fixtures would be transformed into war gadgets by fighting men defending Canada's coast. Already the war is calling these trim pleasure craft to grim duty in dealing death. There are reports, for instance, the *Lyndonia*, aboard which the late Cyrus H.K. Curtis entertained two presidents and dozens of cabinet members, will be sold to Canada. If the *Lyndonia* is sold it means the luxurious chairs in which the great of this nation once lounged will be replaced by racks of iron holding deadly depth charges to be used in submarine attacks. It means that fore and aft will be mounted rapid-firing naval guns and that in the mahogany staterooms will be placed hammocks in which sailors will sleep fitfully, ready for a call to action ...

Arcadia, owned by Mrs. H.R. Hardwick of Boston. To become HMCS *Elk* in the RCN.

The yacht *Dolphin* "... to be used very largely for entertaining purposes ..." became *Ramona*, and then HMCS *Lynx*, but only lasted until 1942 in naval use.

The ill-fated *Nourmahal*, owned by Vincent Astor, which then became *Conseco*, and then HMCS *Otter*. Lost by fire off Halifax in March, 1941.

A close-up of *Cleopatra*, that became HMCS *Moose*, and the only one to be reconverted to a pleasure yacht after the war, for Joseph Simard.

Despite all the hyperbole, the *Lyndonia* was not taken into Canadian service, but the paper named seven of the yachts that were actually right then in the process of changing hands to Canadian ownership. All this publicity was a cause for much anxiety.

In retrospect, it is a bit surprising that the U.S. government was not forced into taking some official notice and delaying action. Maybe the German-American Bund did not subscribe to the Miami papers. A few sales were disallowed, such as the yacht *Ranley* to Sidney Oland, but this was due more to the mercantile arrangements whereby any American could override an offer by a foreign buyer of a U.S. flag ship, in order to protect their merchant marine from falling into the hands of foreign buyers. There were two or three other cases of this in the purchase offers of the Canadians. The law made no distinction between genuine cargo-carrying merchantmen and these large motor yachts.

Meanwhile back in Canada, the government was valiantly protecting the secrecy of the negotiations, despite what might appear in the American press. Even Canadian papers joined in. The Toronto *Globe* on March 15, 1940, noted that Stuart Playfair's yacht *Pathfinder* had been requisitioned for war purposes, which was accurate enough, and then added that on the same date, naval authorities requisitioned the *Anitra*, a 52-foot sailing yacht owned by Mr. A. Montye Macrae. John W. Magill, a marine broker of Chicago, wrote to Mr. Playfair on March 29 that he noted that Playfair had bought a U.S. yacht of 188 feet, He continued:

> I wrote to Mr. J.O. Cossette, Naval Secretary in Ottawa, about the sale of some yachts and he informed me on the 18th instant that the Naval Service was not contemplating the purchase of yachts from the U.S. I have a list of 8 yachts suitable for war work on the Lakes if you are interested.

Maybe Mr. Magill was contemplating a renewal of the War of 1812 on the Great Lakes, and a renewal of the Provincial Marine! At any rate, he had been fed an unequivocable answer by a public servant who had received his orders.

In some cases, the Canadians met and even dealt with the American owners. Stuart Playfair paid Mrs. Margaret Hardwick $125 for china, glassware and linen left on board. Her *Arcadia* was sold "as is," and the description by Playfair of her fittings has a plaintive note:

> My den has a lovely chesterfield and several chairs, besides writing desks and a table that would look well in the best of homes. The staterooms are furnished very luxuriously and tastefuly with dressing tables, etc., that are most attractive but hardly of use for sailors. I am wondering what will happen to these beautiful things which are not suitable for service. Are they to be stored in some shed until after the war and then probably not wanted and sold off by auction or dumped overboard and just disappear? Also re the two launches. The starboard owner's launch is a 26′ mahogany boat with a Ford V8 engine, and the port crew's launch is a 24′ boat similarly equipped. Both are dandy little pleasure boats suitable for going ashore, but are certainly not the type of boat that will be required for service on the high seas. If your Department has no use for some of these things I have mentioned and consider it is advisable to dispose of them now, I would like to have a chance of buying them in.

In view of the fact that Playfair was almost entirely correct, and those yachts that arrived in Canadian hands fully furnished had their fine fittings stripped out, which then just "disappeared", it was a rather less than fair approach to these businessmen, many of them not necessarily very wealthy, who gave months of their time and even quite a bit from their own pockets to bail of the penny-pinching government, not to let them buy some fittings. In interviews with six of these gentlemen, the only one who had anything but a large photograph of his purchase (provided by the government) was Pearson McCurdy of Halifax, who had wisely kept a small but handsome brass wheelhouse clock from his ship *Winchester*.

Just to add one final ungenerous touch to this not very edifying part of the story, we may quote a final paragraph in a letter from a Department of Transport spokesman, again to Stuart Playfair, after all the transactions were completed:

> You will recall that it was the original intention to add on 5% to the cost as a nominal commission to yourself, and you will also recall that you most generously agreed to return this commission to the Crown upon the conclusion of the work. The Government, of course, is still willing to proceed with this interchange of cheques. Moreover, the whole situation has so changed since the original arrangement was made that many of us here doubt the necessity of camouflaging the final transaction by the

appearance of a payment of such a transaction. Therefore, unless you have some strong reason for differing from this suggestion, I would suggest that we omit all question of this 5% commission.

Even the trips up to the Canadian ports were not without their problems. To quote Mr. Playfair once again:

Cape Lookout, N.Y.,
Monday, April 22/40

Dear Mr. Thomson:

In my letter from Charleston of April 17, I reported progress and expected to get away next day, but the weather reports continued very unfavourable, and although I asked my Captain to tackle it, first coaxing him to go out and try it, next practically commanding him, and almost threatening to fire him if he wouldn't, but I might as well have been talking to a post for he simply wouldn't take his ship around Hatteras in weather such as reported on the way.

It was exceedingly disappointing, but we stayed in Charleston until 11 a.m. Saturday, April 20, and left with weather reports only fair. A strong south-westerly blow which we hoped would round to west so as to be off-shore continued and increased during the night, and became a gale and knocked us around good and proper. At six a.m. Sunday the Capt. said the weather report was lousy, and he drew in behind Cape Lookout and dropped our hook. And then did she blow! We couldn't even get a message ashore, so we dropped a second anchor and remained all day.

Am putting this in a bottle and a fishing boat has signalled they will pick it up and mail it. Will advise you when we get to New York. As you know, we cannot use our wireless until we get permission.

This last restriction was imposed by the U.S. Government because the yachts were now owned by Canadians who were not licensed to transmit wireless messages while in American waters. So they travelled without wireless. This was not quite so unusual in the early 1940's as it would be now. Even a few of the older merchant ships were still without reliable wireless.

Again a ludicrous note is added later in the summer by a rather officious letter from the Canadian Registrar of Shipping, complaining to Playfair that in registering the motor vessel *Arcadia* in Canada, he had not declared sufficient assets, and that this was not acceptable. This was a requirement to ensure purchasers could meet all the licensing and personnel safety and maintenance requirements as a ship operator. Stuart Playfair was requested to insert on an attached form "attachable assets to the required value, such as real estate. The amount of the assets required to be declared will be $1,800.00." To this nonsense, generated out of the secrecy of the transaction preventing the customs and excise people from being in on the game, Playfair answered testily but justifiably:

I have your letter of June 21st informing me that my declaration of assets is not satisfactory, but as I do not own any real estate directly in my own name, I cannot improve on it. I am, however, enclosing a form duly signed by Mrs. Playfair which will cover your requirements.

As the *Arcadia* has been taken over from me by the Government for war purposes, I cannot see what difference it makes whether I have any assets or not.

On the other hand, customs and excise's problems can be understood by quoting two confidential memoranda, written by Lesslie Thomson as late as April 5 and 12, marked "PERSONAL AND CONFIDENTIAL, AND TO BE DESTROYED" telling how the yachtsmen were to transfer their purchases to Canadian registry, still concealing that the Navy or government were in any way involved!

2. The next step to be taken is that of the entry of the yachts into Canada, i.e. clearing Canadian Customs duties and the payment of Canadian sales tax.

3. Would you be good enough, therefore, to write at your earliest convenience a letter to Hugh Scully, Esq., the Commissioner of Customs, Ottawa, and mark it for his personal attention.

4. I would suggest that your letter to Mr. Scully cover these points:
(a) That your own yacht was requisitioned some little time ago by the Canadian Government;

(b) That you went to the United States and bought from Mr. ... of ... another yacht (give its name) to replace her.

And so, on the letter went, giving in detail the protocol for the new owners in bringing their new purchases north.

The second memorandum aimed at indicating to outsiders that the requisitioning and subsequent purchases were all at the instigation of the individual purchasers.

1. In order that the Government files may be complete and could demonstrate to any future enquirer the sequence of the steps that have been taken, it seems to be highly desirable and indeed almost essential that some further correspondence should be on record between each of the individual yachtsmen and the Government. It seems also highly desirable that some consideration should be passed between the Government and each individual yachtsman, in the nature of a "token payment", to indicate that the requisitioning was a valid undertaking of the Canadian government. Will you, therefore, be kind enough to co-operate along the below mentioned lines.

2. First of all will you write a letter to the Government in reply to the previously mentioned telegram. Your reply should be dated within a day or two of the day upon which you received the telegram and it should be addressed to the person or the Department signing the telegram. You should say something along these lines:

(a) You acknowledge receipt of the telegram and admit that the yacht is no longer under your control;

(b) you ask, as a matter of interest, for particulars of the service in which the Government proposes to use your yacht; and

(c) you ask whether the yacht is to be bought or chartered, and upon what basis will the remuneration to you be determined.

3. In order that there may be some variety between the letters which the Government will receive, I wish you would be kind enough to insert in the letter several other points which may occur to you other than those which I have suggested. Ask other questions; make suggestions, if you like, as to where, in your judgment, the yacht would be most serviceable for the period of the war; and the like.

Then followed two paragraphs describing in detail what answers will be given to these letters, ending,

5. iv) as a method of binding the arrangement a *small* payment will be made to you, say $1.00 on account, when the matter will have been passed by the Department of Finance. (This may take some little while, and it may be in April before the cheque can be finally despatched). ...

7. If these steps are taken, any future enquiry would reveal the apparent intention of the Government at the time.

8. After you have complied with the request in this Memorandum No. 2, will you kindly destroy it.

Despite all this laboured official subterfuge, and rather heavy-handed instructions to the businessmen involved, it is interesting to see how carefully the officials were organizing their tracks, on the chance that American isolationists might come sniffing around, not only to embarrass the Canadian government, but to use information that might be disclosed to beat the sympathetic Roosevelt into providing less help to beleaguered Britain and its Dominion.

As late as February 1946, Lesslie Thomson, in connection with an American's claim for commissions, wrote to the then Deputy Minister of National Defence (Navy), saying ingenuously:

"Finally, I may say that I can assure you from personal knowledge, that the Department of Munitions and Supply did not purchase this yacht on behalf of the Department of National Defence ..."

He just did not happen to mention that it was done by another Department. There are lessons to be learned here in interpreting official Government answers to questions!

The story of the purchases ran similarly for each of the yachtsmen, and while some kept extensive records, despite the exhortations of Mr. Thomson to destroy all government correspondence on the secret instructions, Tom K. Wade of Toronto retained nothing, and remained very secretive about the whole matter, even with members of his family.

In the case of Ralph Bell's purchase of *Cleopatra*, that was to become HMCS *Moose*, Mr. Bell dealt only with the yacht brokers in New York. In purchasing *Halonia* from R.A. Van Clief, of the jewellery firm of Van Clief & Arpels, Mr. McRae, although purchasing her through the broker Sparkman and Stevens, made contact with Mr. Van Clief, and received the papers for the ship directly from the owner before sailing, with his son Donald, for Yarmouth, encountering the same gale as Stuart Playfair, off Hatteras. He was very closely attached to the yachts he owned on his own behalf, and felt strongly enough about them as 'ships with souls' to the extent that when he died, at his request, his family took his large sailing yacht *Patricia* out into Lake Ontario and sank her, so she would not fall into other hands of which he might not have approved.

Sidney Oland lost the first yacht he bid on to an American buyer, who was allowed to override his bid with an equal one. He then located the 140-foot motor yacht *Mascotte* at Houston, Texas. She was in very fine shape, with beautiful panelling, some of which was painted over in an exotic red laquer paint found normally on Chinese furniture. As there was considerable and worrysome delay in completing the purchase arrangements from the estate of Henry Plant, which was her technical owner, Colonel Oland arranged to sail her to New York under the American flag. Effectively on charter, she would be closer to home when the approval to transfer the ship to Canadian ownership came through in case there was a problem about permission at the last moment. It also avoided the necessity of putting into another American port for fuel, if there was a last-minute hitch. The ship had been used by two brothers on alternate weekends, primarily as a "party ship," and she was loaded with a rather excess quantity of Scotch and other potables. The owners wanted to remove these cases, but Colonel Oland, nervous about the secrecy conditions, refused on the grounds that trucks alongside removing stores would draw attention to the pending sale, which he wanted to avoid. And anyway, the vessel had been bought "As is, with stores as existing." On arrival in Halifax, the Olands managed to smuggle ashore some individual bottles in their suitcases, but again were apprehensive about drawing attention to the negotiations even at that late date, by being seen to be bringing a significant volume of "stores" ashore. And once again, these supplies just disappeared into naval or dockyard hands.

Halonia on arrival at Yarmouth, N.S. in April, 1940.

Capt. Fox and Mr. A.M. McCrae, Master and owner of *Halonia* for a few weeks.

Col. Sidney Oland of Halifax brewing fame, who bought *Mascotte*.

Mascotte, in the mid 1930s, owned by E.S. Burke Jr. of Cleveland. Became HMCS *Reindeer*.

Ralph P. Bell, Nova Scotia businessman, who bought the *Cleopatra*, and into whose care all Halifax yachts were placed for a time, on paper.

On the way up from New York the new owner received a bad scare, when a submarine surfaced astern of them, presumed to be one of the U-boats referred to and anticipated by the Canadian authorities. They were vastly relieved when after what seemed an eternity the American Stars and Stripes was hoisted behind the conning tower! When the ship arrived off Halifax, Victor de B. Oland, a brother of Donald, and Sydney's son, was stationed with the artillery at Fort Ogilvy at the harbour mouth. He asked for leave to visit the ship, but so ingrained was the secrecy plan by this time that when asked by his C.O. why he wanted leave, Victor refused to tell him, on the grounds that it was a military secret not open to the artillery. This did not engender good relationships with his C.O!

Mr. Pearson McCurdy of Halifax was asked to buy *Winchester (the third)*, then owned by General Cornelius Vanderbilt, the New York banker and railroad tycoon. While there was quite a delay in arranging the transfer, there was no real problem. However, so keyed up were the Canadians by the secrecy instructions from Ottawa, and this hazardous and unfamiliar role to a newspaperman like McCurdy, that he became convinced that his bags had been rifled in his New York hotel room while he was at dinner. Fortunately for his peace of mind, his letter of credit was at his New York bank, and not in the bags! After the purchase had been completed, Mrs. Vanderbilt came down to the ship to recover some of her paintings from the saloon. But Mr. McCurdy's captain would not allow her on board due to the very stringent instructions given to him by his new owner. Of course McCurdy contacted her at once, and arranged for her to come down again, but only when he was there to accompany her. McCurdy signed on most of the original crew for the trip to Canada, being particularly glad of the chief engineer, a German now naturalized as an American. Unlike the simpler diesel-engined yachts, *Winchester* operated on forced draft for the engine room, which was sealed when running, with about 5 pounds per square inch pressure, and the ship would do over 30 knots at full speed, with two turbines on direct drive. At Yarmouth, because they had entered a war zone, the crew were offered the choice of continuing to Halifax, or being returned to New York by air. Three-quarters signed on for the last lap, including the engineer, who later applied to join the RCNR, but was refused because of being an American, and McCurdy feels, because of his Germanic name. As an experiment, off Chester, N.S. they laid a smoke screen, to the consternation of the coastal defence forces, and then off Halifax picked up a pilot and the examination officer. For the benefit of these gentlemen in this strange "torpedo-boat," they made a few runs along the coast, and then the ship was turned over to the harbour pilot. He ordered "Half ahead," and within seconds the vessel was doing 15 knots. He then ordered "half astern," and the ship quickly came to a stop. "Say, Captain," said the pilot, "Won't this ship go slowly?" After a few test runs he got the hang of it, and they proceeded to anchor in the Arm, the pilot requiring 52 engine movements to bring her to her mooring!

The yacht *Avalon* was one of the newest and handsomest purchased, being built in 1931 by Pusey & Jones of Wilmington, Delaware, to the order of Ogden L. Mills, the Secretary of the U.S. Treasury. F.H.M. Jones went first to Boston to review yachts being offered there by the brokers. But the ones produced for consideration by Colonel Jones and another friend from the Royal Nova Scotia Yacht Squadron, Hugh Bell, were too often in poor condition, some almost write-offs, as the brokers seemed to be unloading what they had. When Bell called a close friend in the business in Boston, he confirmed that there was quite a move afoot "to make a killing," They then passed on to New York, and had a meeting with Dan Cox of Gardiner and Cox, and with Philip Rhodes, both yacht brokers, who also turned up some unsatisfactory vessels. Then Cox produced *Avalon*, for sale by a Mr. Smith of the Greyhound Bus Company. She was lying in Gulfport, Mississippi, and shortly a purchase price was arranged and matters set afoot to arrange the transfer to Canadian ownership. It took a month for the passage from Gulfport, via Miami, and up the U.S. coast, to Shelburne, Nova Scotia. Of the original owner's crew, only the captain, the senior engineer, and two crewmen remained with the ship, so Colonel Jones hired the

Avalon, a handsome yacht owned by Fred Smith of Dixie-Greyhound Bus Lines, lying at Gulfport, Mississippi. Became HMCS *Vison*.

balance locally in Gulfport, and paid them off in Shelburne, and like others, taking on a Canadian crew there to complete the passage to Halifax. The yacht had a considerable outfit of beautiful and genuine English furniture when purchased, but none of it was in evidence when the author served in her in early 1944.

On the west coast, Irvine Keenleyside was involved with the acquisition of three yachts. He was in the investment business, and took the time first to go to Long Beach to pick up *Machigone*, an old but reasonably sound vessel, which had been built as a steel sailing yacht in 1909. She had later been equipped with a steam engine, then with German submarine-type Foos diesels. After arrival at Esquimalt, unfamiliarity with these unusual power plants resulted in their being burnt out, and *Machigone* never served as a powered armed yacht.

Then, on behalf of Clarence Wallace, Irvine Keenleyside went south again to buy *Breezin' Thru* from Leila Post Montgomery, of the Post Cereal family and a sister of Marjory Post Hutton Davies. As mentioned before, Mr. Wallace was allowed to retain his ship for a few weeks. He was out with Irvine Keenleyside on one of these jaunts, and came down from the bridge one day to announce grumpily "I've been kicked off my own bridge!" Not all paid captains took a subservient approach to the technical owners of "their" ships. While on the mission to the south for Mr. Wallace, Keenleyside saw the yacht *Blue Water*, and assessed her as being ideal for the Navy's requirements. Although old, having been built in 1915, she was available cheaply, and in good running order, having been well maintained. He cabled Ottawa for permission to buy her in the name of his partner, E.A. Riddell, who, at this stage, knew nothing of the deal at all. After some delay, this was approved, Mr. Riddell's 45-foot yacht was requisitioned, and he suddenly found himself owner of the 172-foot diesel yacht *Blue Water*. She turned out to be one of the best buys the Navy got.

The two vessels obtained from Canadian sources were the only ex-yachts that did not need a change of name to conceal their origins, but are still classed as "Animal Class Yachts" in the records. These were *Ambler*, owned by Charles H. Sheppard of Aurora,

Machigonne, a yacht from Long Beach, California, that became HMCS *Grizzly*, but never ran.

Ambler's crowded engineroom, with two large diesel motors.

Blue Water, owned by Marian Huntingdon of San Francisco, that served the USN in the First War, and the RCN as HMCS *Wolf* in the Second.

Ontario, and the palatial *Sans Peur*, owned by the Duke of Sutherland, a Scottish native, who turned over his ship on Canada's west coast.

C. H. Sheppard was a retired Ontario lumberman, who had worked for his father's company, and used *Ambler* around Georgian Bay as a pleasure yacht. He made an outright gift of the ship to the government, although to regularise matter she is shown on the records as chartered by him for one dollar, and she technically remained his property until sold by the Navy on his behalf at the end of the war. She had originally been built for the American millionaire Merrill B. Mills, was then owned by Louis K. Liggett of drug store fame, before being bought in 1935 by Mr. Sheppard.

Until 1935, Charles Sheppard had owned rather modest-sized cruising motor launches, which he operated from a summer home at Waubaushene, particularly for fall deer-hunting on the northeast part of the Georgian Bay shoreline. When Stuart Playfair bought the 110-foot *Pathfinder*, Sheppard was rather put out, and determined to do him one better. *Ambler* was for sale in the United States, as Louis Liggett's drug business had run him short of funds in the course of the Depression, so she was bought and turned over to Sheppard at Midland, Ontario.

As it turned out, she was far too large for local cruising, and was very difficult to handle at low speeds in the small harbour of Waubaushene and the other backwaters in which he had been accustomed to wandering. There was usually a paid skipper (although sometimes Charles Sheppard took the helm himself), an engine room chief, and five or six mill hands from his father's Georgian Bay Lumber Company. The furnishings that came with the ship from Liggett were magnificent, down to engraved table silver and china with the ship's name on them, and even decks of cards with the ship's photograph on the backs. By the time of the war's outbreak, Sheppard was using *Ambler* very little, and when she had been turned over to the Navy, he bought a much more practical and smaller boat.

Charles Sheppard had opened correspondence in the fall of 1939 with the government regarding acquisition of his vessel, but before any details could be resolved, she was frozen into her harbour at Waubaushene for the winter. When finally accepted by the Navy, in May 1940, a crew was sent up to Midland, to which port she had been sailed. Acting Lieutenant R.S. Kelley, RCNR, was directed to take command. According to his instruction, "the Blue Ensign is to be worn from the day of comissioning until 0800 on the day of arrival at Montreal, after which the White Ensign will be worn."

This rather unusual procedure arose because of an agreement with the United States. In 1819, following the naval engagements on the Great Lakes in the War of 1812, and the ruinously expensive shipbuilding races, wherein the two protagonists built bigger and bigger ships, a treaty was signed, the Rush Bagot Agreement. Therein it was stipulated that no more than a very small number of armed vessels were allowed on the Lakes at any one timer. This treaty was still in effect in 1940, and remains so today. Thus warships built on the Lakes at first had to proceed at least to Montreal before being armed, and not under the Navy's White Ensign, but rather the government ships' Blue Ensign. Later an agreement had to be signed for the duration of the war when this system became too cumbersome in the face of massive shipbuilding programs. So *Ambler* departed from Midland on May 8, arriving in Montreal on the 14th, for conversion to a warship at Quebec City, and for patrol duties in the St. Lawrence area.

On Canada's west coast, the Duke of Sutherland's large new private yacht *Sans Peur* turned up by chance. The Duke of Sutherland was a British businessman, with interests in the timberlands of British Columbia, through Sutherland Canadian Lands Company. He had served in motor launches during the First World War in the North Sea and the Adriatic, as a commander, RNR, so he was no stranger to large motor vessels in his own right. When the war broke out, His Grace was on Canada's west coast, combining business with pleasure; a visit to his operations there, and a world cruise with friends. *Sans*

Sans Peur, one of two non-U.S. yachts the Canadian Navy obtained. This one owned by the Duke of Sutherland, and turned over in 1939 at Esquimalt, British Columbia.

Peur arrived at Vancouver on September 12, 1939. With the outbreak of the war with Germany, the duke at once left by train across Canada for his wartime duties in Britain, and turned his yacht over to the British Admiralty in London, although she was left at the Canadian naval base at Esquimalt on Vancouver Island. The Admiralty formally requisitioned her in October 1939, and they then informed Canadian naval headquarters to say that she had been requisitioned for war service as of October 7, that for the time being at least she could be made available to the RCN, and suggested that "she would be suitable for A/S duties," and that they (the Admiralty) would take her up if the Canadian Navy did not want her. Headquarters replied that they could certainly use her (at that stage there were no warships on that coast whatsoever except a couple of small steel minesweeping trawlers). She was commissioned as an HMC ship, on charter to the RCN by the British Ministry of War Transport. She had been technically hired by that ministry from the Duke of Sutherland for 569 pounds 10 shillings per month; then on August 8, 1941, she was purchased outright for 45,000 pounds, or about $225,000 in those days. All this time she was "on loan" to the Canadians for patrol use, and no monies changed hands, except that Canada paid for her manning, repairs, fitting out and upkeep. Then, in April 1943, since fairly obviously *Sand Peur* was not going to be required by the Royal Navy, approval was sought to sell her to Canada. An order-in-council passed on March 16, 1943, approved this, for $305,191, for monthly hire and purchase price, to be refunded to the Admiralty.

Sans Peur herself was a most unusual vessel, with an uncommon background. She had been built in England in 1933. Dr. Ernest G. Stanley, an English surgeon practising in Paris and a nephew of Rudyard Kipling, had decided to make the useful gesture of ordering a new and large yacht as his personal contribution towards easing the 1930's shipbuilding depression for at least one firm. His choice fell on John I. Thornycroft (now

Vosper-Thorneycroft, to whom I am indebted for this history), and Stanley accepted their design for the 821-ton *Trenora*. This outstanding vessel was one of the first to break away from the traditional arrangement of a low-strength main deck and an upper superstructure carried on stanchions above this deck. This new design involved making the upper level boat deck the strength deck, which involved considerable argument with Lloyd's Register assessors for insurance purposes. It was finally necessary to go directly to the then chief surveyor so that dispensation from the existing rules could be granted. Thorneycroft's skill of design paid off well, for she is still afloat, even after five hard war years.

With twin large Polar Atlas diesel engines, she had a world cruising speed of 12½ knots for 7,000 miles, and a top speed of almost 16 knots, suitable for wide-ranging cruises. *Trenora* proved an able sea boat and the firm received an enthusiastic report of her behaviour in a severe gale in the Bay of Biscay. The well-known marine artist Norman Wilkinson had suggested to the owner that a black funnel would suit the yacht better than the usual buff colour. This may have been correct from an artistic point of view, but it led to a story reaching Dr. Stanley that she must have "terribly dirty diesel engines," and the funnel was soon painted in the traditional buff. Later in the 1930's the duke bought her, renamed her *Sans Peur*, the Clan Sutherland motto, and in 1939 was cruising off the coast of California when she grounded on a sandbank. The only damage incurred was to a lady guest, who had been holding a lion cub at the time of impact and was badly scratched by the alarmed cub. In the history provided by Vospers, no explanation of how a lion cub came to be present at sea off the coast of California is provided. It must just be taken as an eccentricity of the British nobility!

Before going on to their war services, a brief review should be given of the past history of the American yachts. Out of the fourteen, five had already seen war service in the United States Navy in the First World War, in very similar guises to those they were to adopt for another war.

Aztec, later to become HMCS *Beaver*, had been leased to the American Navy in June 1917, and was the flag ship for the commander of the 1st Naval District. Apart from use for his inspection tours, *Aztec* convoyed submarines from Boston to New London and back, and troopships from Boston to Halifax. On December 29, 1918 she embarked Assistant Secretary of the Navy Franklin D. Roosevelt for a naval review honouring the return of the USN battleships from European water. It is worth noting from naval records that her crew was shown to consist of ten officers and eighty-six men, quite a crowd for a ship that would have been designed as a yacht with maybe four or five officers and not more than twenty-five seamen, stewards and stokers. She continued on District duties until decommissioned in March 1919, and was returned to Mr. Burrage. Despite the fact that the original loan was arranged as a "free lease," on October 25, 1920, a payment of $239,202 was ordered made to Mr. Burrage for the use of his craft for two years, and her reconversion.

Machigone, later to become HMCS *Grizzly*, was built in 1909 for William L. Douglas, a shoe manufacturer, and later mayor of Boston and a governor of Massachusetts. She was taken up by the USN on May 15th, 1917, and christened merely SP 507 in Naval parlance, on a purchase price of $55,000. She was armed with three 3-pounder guns, two machine guns, and a "Y" gun depth charge projector, also being employed on patrol duties on their East coast.

The yacht *Sabalo* was almost brand new when the USN acquired her from her original owner and builder, W. Earl Dodge of New York City, a local financier. Built in 1916, she was taken over for $25,230 on May 11th, 1917, as SP 225, armed with two 3-pounders and machine guns, and also for "section patrols" throughout her USN service. She was returned to Mr. Dodge in March, 1919, and passed through several hands before being owned by Mrs. Montgomery from whom the Canadians bought her.

During World War One *Blue Water* was known as USS *Wenonah*. Here she is all rigged out for service in her fashionable camouflage and with guns mounted on fore and after decks.

With *Winchester*, only being built in 1916, Peter Rouss was not particularly happy at the thought of the Government taking up his new, very fast and swanky vessel. USN records only state enigmatically "Owner is averse (sic) to turning vessel over to Govt. Will be taken over May 29, 1917. Serial 33619 DELIVERED." So much for Rouss's reluctance. His feelings must have been salved to some extent by the $300,000 purchase price paid. *Winchester* was fitted with one 3"/50 calibre, and one 6-pounder gun, machine guns, and a "Y" gun for depth charges. She was commissioned in September, 1917, and assigned for duty with the Bureau of Construction and Repair. After her war service, she was re-sold on March 9th, 1921 to Peter Rouss again, for $65,000, through yacht brokers Cox and Stevens, and remained in his hands until his death in 1926. She was then owned briefly by Vincent Astor, sold to Russel A. Alger, and in 1930 to General Cornelius Vanderbilt, from whose estate Pearson McCurdy bought her in 1940.

Although many of the Vanderbilts had marital problems leading to divorce or separation, Cornelius Junior did not, although he did feud with his father and never spoke to him in later years. He even became estranged from his wife, the grande dame of New York society of the 1920's and '30's, and spent his latter days living aboard his two last yachts, *North Star* and *Winchester*. One summer day in the late 1930's, he arrived at their country home, Beaulieu, at Newport, Rhode Island, to find that because of some heart trouble Cornelius had, his wife had installed an elevator to save him the climb to the second floor. He was so insensed that he stalked from the house to remain almost exclusively aboard *Winchester*, until his health and mental faculties faded, refusing to even allow his son aboard. He later sailed to Miami.

The last of the Canadian yachts to have seen USN service was *Wenonah*, which became HMCS *Wolf*, on the West coast. She proved so satisfactory to the Navy that she remained in their hands for 12 years. Taken up as a Naval patrol ship on June 8th, 1917, and assigned their number SP 165, she remained in Naval service until April 12th, 1919, when she was transferred to the Department of Commerce's Coast and Geodetic Survey. But after only 3½ years, *Wenonah* was transferred back to the Navy's 13th Naval District on the West coast, classified from a "patrol vessel" to the more descriptive "converted yacht". It is quite possible that the Commandant of that Naval District, when he saw the very handsom 172-foot ex-yacht, soon set wheels in motion to keep her for his tours of that extensive district, rather than use a more utilitarian warship. After remaining in naval use from November, 1922 until June, 1928, *Wenonah* was stricken from the Navy list, and sold on May 15th, 1929 to H.W. Goodall of Santa Barbara for a mere $7,000. He renamed her *Stranger*, and later sold the ship during the Depression to Mrs. Marian Huntington of San Francisco, from whom she was bought by the RCN.

Thus the sixteen ex-yachts came into Canadian naval hands. Some smoothly and normally, like *Ambler* and *Sans Peur*, turned over by patriotic citizens. Others through a series of secret visits, subterfuge, hidden deals and mysterious bank transfers that would sound appropriate only to Grade B movies, but which at the time were treated as deadly serious. Even to this day, more than one of the yachtsmen purchasers are reluctant to talk of how the deals were made. As one said, "No one has yet told me that I am relieved from my promise to keep the whole matter top secret." Even many of the files in the Department of National Defence and Public Archives are still marked and treated as "Restricted."

At Halifax, the ten American yachts were collected in the Northwest Arm, or across the harbour at Dartmouth and the purchasers from inland returned to their civilian or Militia pursuits.

The yachts at Halifax were turned over to the care of Ralph Bell, as the local "agent" by the owners from out of town, although once again this was only for bookkeeping records. All this was dutifully recorded on the Merchant Shipping Register, and Mr. Bell soon was shown as being responsible for quite a respectable fleet. Then, after a few days, the Navy itself took over the ships, one after another, as soon as caretaking naval crews could be provided. While the final details of the purchase dragged on until September, 1940, the matter was essentially closed with their deliveries to Halifax and Victoria. In the fall, each of the yachtsmen involved received an invitation to a testimonial dinner in Ottawa from C.D. Howe, where those who attended received a letter of thanks from the prime minister, and a large mounted photograph of "their" yacht. Since attendance in Ottawa was at the yachtsmen's expense, not all went, and the letter and photograph were all they got, plus some trips to the United States, and, for most, a sea trip.

As an aside, it is interesting to note that a year and a half later the United States Navy was no more prepared for an anti-submarine war and for convoy and ship escorting than Canada. Their historian, Samuel Eliot Morison says it was the Navy's own fault when they were not prepared for the 1942 U-boat blitz along their coast. The Navy had not asked Congress for small patrol vessels, and even President Roosevelt, an ex-Secretary of the Navy, said "The Navy couldn't see any vessel under a thousand tons."

The Canadian and Royal Navies were not immune to this destroyer and larger attitude, and fleet operations governed practically all naval policy decisions, not anti-submarine and convoy protection.

Five yachts in the Northwest Arm at Halifax, in May 1940. Front to rear: *Arcadia/Elk*, *Wild Duck/Husky*, *Winchester/Renard*.

CHAPTER 6

CONVERSION AND OFF TO WAR

Now that the Navy could be said to have the sixteen yachts, the next thing was to convert them for war service, and arm them. The conversion turned out to be an expensive arrangement in some cases, for there were dining saloons to be removed, even new boilers to be provided; decks needed strengthening to take the thrust of a modest gun being fired, with its complicated forces extending in all directions. Similarly, the after decks had to be reinforced to take the rails for depth charges, each of which resembled metal garbage cans and weighed over 300 pounds. The ones to be dropped from the chutes at the stern took only a simple stowage rack to hold two or three, with a rocker arm to control their release. But the ones to be projected into the air, outwards from the sides of the vessel, required a heavy depth charge thrower, mounted on a base plate and exerting a considerable deck thrust forward when fired. With the charges rolled from the stern and one fired from each side by a thrower to a range of 35 yards, a diamond pattern was formed by the explosions underwater, increasing the chance of trapping a submarine therein.

One problem that arose was, in the advice from the United Kingdom, that while they could supply four hundred depth charges in an initial order, they could provide no primers or detonators or pistols: the items required to be fitted inside depth charges to make them explode at the U-boats' depth. These had to be provided from Canadian sources, and it took some time to get civilian firms geared up to produce them.

Apart from these items (and not all yachts were found suitable for all equipment), stowage had to be arranged for rifles and revolvers under lock and key, and mounting for .303 and the heavier .5 calibre machine guns, either on each side of the wheelhouse on the bridge, or aft of the funnel and mast. *Vison* (ex-*Avalon*) for instance, was fitted with 5" twin Browning water-cooled machine guns on each wing of the bridge, hand-controlled on a pedestal mounting.

In addition to this armament fitting, considerable changes were required in the accommodation, as weapons crews were required in addition to seamen and enough sleeping spaces for more than one watch of seaman and engine room stokers. For the exercise of naval discipline and authority, it was necessary to have a wardroom for three or four officers, a separate mess for the petty officers (a senior coxswain, or Cox'n; two or three petty officers of the watch, and an engine room chief or two), and then hammock space or pipe rail berths for most of the crew. Because they had been luxury yachts, the wardroom arrangements were little trouble to provide. In fact, the problem was often how to divide up the extra, and sometimes sumptuous, cabins between the P.O.s and the crew, for in most cases there were far more cabins than were needed and the crew space was too small for the wartime complements. The petty officers could be accommodated two or four to a cabin, and in the larger yachts they could even have a separate small mess to themselves for eating and relaxation. As well, space was now needed for extra radio gear, armament stowage for shells and ammunition, Asdic power and operating rooms for the submarine detection technical bits and pieces, and some secure stowage for each man, albeit small. In the smaller vessels, the best that could be arranged was what became known as the "hot mick system," whereby there were enough hammock spaces provided for two out of the three watches of seamen and stokers, on the presumption that one watch of each would always be on duty. In harbour, when only one or two men were required to be up and about, this system created uncomfortable crowding, resulting in the extra off-duty watch having to sleep on tables, benches and even on the deck. Each man had his own hammock, but not always a place to sling it, and too often he perforce laid it down, with its meagre mattress and blanket, on a hard bench for the night. This was all very fine in decent weather, or after only a short trip out. But too often the weather at sea had been abominable. The decks leaked, the green new entry seamen had been sick constantly, coffee had spilled, life jackets had split, spilling kapok around, and the mess deck was a shambles. The crew in the hammocks could get above it all, but those on the settees or cupboards were in danger of rolling off into the mess during their sleep, such as it might be. Even for the crews who slung their hammocks, there was not always room for all of them, and thus, men coming off watch just climbed into the hammocks of the men who had relieved them, thus the term "hot mick system." In the larger yachts such as *Renard*, *Sans Peur*, *Beaver* and *Elk*, this was not much of a problem, as their length allowed far more mess deck space for the same number of crew than had to be packed into the little 130-foot *Moose*.

The initial estimate of the conversion costs of the yachts to naval service was based on two misunderstandings by the naval staff themselves. *Sans Peur* was the first yacht taken up that was adapted for an armed A/S vessel, with guns and Asdic. The cost of outfitting her was seen to be about $22,000, and it was presumed that the other yachts, most of which were smaller, would cost somewhat less than this to equip. Also, in initial discussions among the naval staff, and with Lambert and German, the Montreal firm of naval architects who were engaged to oversee the design and fitting out of the yachts, the original conception was simply to install A/S listening gear, depth charge racks, a small gun and simple stowage in each vessel. It was hoped that existing accommodation could be utilized without any great modifications. These vessels were expected to provide some protection to meet the immediate danger, and were viewed as a stopgap until the corvettes and minesweepers, then being contracted for, could arrive in service. The yachts would be used only for simple, local duties, requiring minimal crews and equipment. Thus contracts for the conversion were awarded on a cost plus basis, for if tenders had to be called, an unacceptable delay would have occurred, entailing surveys of each ship by the bidders, detailed plans and an allowance for unexpected findings of problems during the conversions. The ships were required at once, and although costs far exceeded the initial estimates, the final costs were probably as low or even lower than they would have been under a tender system.

Basing conversion costs on *Sans Peur*'s conversion was wishful thinking, for she was a relatively new, strong, well-fitted ocean vessel, broad of beam, and even with some extra deck strengthening already built in. Some of the other yachts were thirty years older, less well-built originally, and by no means designed for the rough work they were to face. However, at the operating level, especially on the west coast, the Navy itself was at first very scathing of the yachts that were arriving, some senior officers stating that there was no way they could be made into fighting ships and armed. This attitude was partly due to the secrecy of their purchase, where the eventual owner, the Navy, was not allowed any voice in the selection and acceptance of the ships, despite Commander Roy's visit and selection, of which the other service officers of course knew nothing. They also obviously didn't know that on that coast two of the four yachts had already served in the US Navy in the First World War, and were already strengthened to take a gun forward. Providing they proved sound vessels, their use was, in effect, already proven.

Then, too, by the time the yachts were in the shipyards' hands, the situation at sea was changing. There would now obviously be a continuing need for these ships, not just a one-year tide-over and then relegation to unimportant duties.

The corvettes and other escorts were taking longer to fit out than anticipated, due to the unfamiliarity of the yards with warship construction, which differed considerably from building merchantmen and fishing trawlers. The shipyards also had to deal with the new technologies associated with Asdics, radios, guns and other war materiél. There were often conflicting and changing priorities assigned to the various construction jobs. Sometimes the completion of a corvette would be the top priority, then this would be changed by naval headquarters while a large armed merchant cruiser was fitted out and armed, often with minimum drawings. In the case of one Montreal yard, the new designs of deck cabins and funnel locations were simply marked on the decks in chalk, and the cutters and welders worked to that. Into this complicated fabric, the sixteen yachts were woven, to take their place in the builders' schemes. And it was a bit hard to convince these yards that these little luxury motor vessels were as vital war ships as the more obvious ones.

With the experience of war indicating that it would be longer and harder than at first hoped, it was then seen, at least by Mr. H.W. Milne, of Lambert and German's, that it would be sound policy to make these vessels as efficient as possible for anti-submarine defence for a longer period of time. This raised the necessity for better accommodation and division of living space, for providing necessary safety measures in the stowage of explosives, more subdivisions in the event of damage or collision. It also entailed a closer scrutiny of machinery, the replacement of some elderly minor motors and other equipment, and the provision of adequate spare parts to ensure the ships would not break down at a critical moment.

"The result of the above," said Milne in a report to the Navy at the time, "is that, generally speaking, the Department will have a number of vessels capable of giving efficient service for the duration of the war, long before new vessels now under construction can be delivered; vessels that will give practically the same protective service at less operating cost and a fraction of the capital expenditure, and we have no hesitation in endorsing the policy of the Department in the purchase and modification of these yachts." A prophetic statement that was, in the main, true, with only the odd yacht proving less than useful.

In order to finance the fitting out, a preliminary financial estimate was raised through the Treasury Board of $20,000 on each yacht. As the work on them was starting and the naval architects soon saw that this was far too little, Lambert and German were soon suggesting that an average cost of about $40,500 should be expected, more in some cases, less in others. This gave rise to the ridiculous government approach that since further financial estimates must be raised, and the practice being that the new ones should replace the old $20,000 ones, the Department of Munitions and Supply tried to avoid book work by paying *nothing* out of the earlier estimates so that their cancellation would be simplified. As late as September 1940, Captain L.W. Murray, the Deputy Chief of Staff, was urging the civil deputy minister of the Navy to allow the new estimates to be raised for *some* amounts, so that at least progress payments could be made to the yards, who so far had paid all their costs from their own funds.

Some fairly complicated construction details had to be arranged, such as re-calculation of the yachts' stability due to fitting guns and depth charges on the upper deck, and the Asdic operating gear in a new small "hut" built in most cases above the bridge for visibility for the operator. Although now-a-days the Asdic (now called by the American name Sonar) is placed well down within the ships' superstructure and the operators concentrate only on the video displays before them, in 1940, the rudimentary Asdic sets made considerable use of the operator's ability to see for himself where the submarine might be. Lambert and German estimated that fitting out might take approximately 35,000 man hours per ship (at a wage rate average of 50 cents an hour), with allowances for extra work required when the ships were dry docked. As the ships came to hand, and by September with more than half of them back in the water and in service, Lambert and German reported the following conditions that required additional work beyond that demanded by the Navy for warship conversion:

> *Beaver:* due to her age and size, she required more modifications to render her fit for service. A long bowsprit extending from her clipper bow had to be removed. The heavier gun with which she was to be fitted (an ancient 4″ hand-operated breech loader) required considerable stiffening of her foc's'le deck. Stability considerations called for the removal of a mast, shortening the funnel, and lowering the lifeboats closer to the deck.
>
> *Caribou:* The forward part of this ship was in very bad condition, for when she was scaled (whereby the loose paint and rust is chipped away from the plates) the scaling hammer punched the hull in a number of places. Eight shell plates together with frames and floors were partially or completely renewed. Lining up of engines indicated that structural castings were out of line, which was probably the reason why this vessel was never satisfactory to her former owners on account of the continuous expense of renewing propeller shafts, the excessive vibration and frequent breakdowns. Machinery repairs on this vessel have proved excessive. The electric wiring in the engineroom was renewed.
>
> *Elk:* Heating system completely inadequate for North Atlantic service. New heating system and boiler fitted. Necessary to renew two shell plates which were badly corroded.
>
> *Husky:* Normal conditions throughout. (Fortunately the same was said of *Vison*, and of *Sans Peur*, which offset to some extent the large expenditures on some of the others.)
>
> *Lynx:* Considerable additional expense was involved on account of corroded parts. Heavy machinery renewals were also found necessary.
>
> *Moose:* This was a heavy job, considering the size of the vessel. It was necessary to fit bilge keels on account of lack of stability. Extra expense in modifying the stern of the ship to accommodate depth charge racks. Funnel increased in height.
>
> *Otter:* Two shell plates removed, and internal fresh water tanks which were corroded completely and leaking badly. Expenses due to heavy machinery renewals, approximately $5,000 worth of spare parts being found necessary. One generator was found defective and a new diesel generator was purchased and installed. All electric motors were found to be more or less defective, and required removal to the shop and overhaul.
>
> *Reindeer:* Reasonably normal condition, but several shell plates were corroded to an extent which called for renewal.
>
> *Raccoon:* (Report not yet available, as ship just being dry-docked).

Renard: Considerable extra work has been found necessary after opening up this ship. Repairs of boiler amounting to approximately $5,000. Shape of stern necessitates additional expense to permit depth charge chutes being fitted. The decision to fit a second 12 pounder (gun) aft and to install torpedo tubes, and the fact that examination of the hull revealed many holes in the structure, all of which are to be repaired by patching, will necessitate additional expenditures. The entire top of the oil tank requires removal. It was also found that this ship required a complete new forward deckhouse. New uptakes, inner funnels and seacocks required.

This recitation of problems by Lambert and German illustrates in some detail the difficulty the government always gets into when estimating repair or refit costs of their ships, such as the later infamous *Bonaventure* case. A repair officer, or in this case maybe an inexperienced yachtsman, walks around the ship, even poking into tanks and compartments, and estimates, probably accurately, the costs of repairing the problem areas he sees. But the contractor, in accepting or offering a bid, must wisely add a phrase to the effect that the bid is subject to adjustment when the ship is opened up or hauled into dry dock, or layers of old paint are chipped away. Pearson McCurdy, and the inspecting naval dockyard staff, could hardly be expected to know that *Renard* would need new funnel liners.

Two examples of the adjusted estimated costs will suffice to show what the Department of Defence faced in the way of cost adjustments:

Vessel	Original estimate	Inflated time & workmen's compensation	Newly found extras	Totals	
				Estimated	Actual
Elk	$40,000	$3,000	$6,000	$49,000	$49,000
Renard	40,000	3,000	20,000	63,000	129,444

While these sums may seem vast, even in these inflated days, especially for "used" ships, and only ex-yachts at that, they were far below the cost of new built ships that would otherwise be needed to do their work, and since most of them lasted through the war, the investment was still well worth it. There was no option, anyway, if escort vessels were to be available in 1940 at all.

The only unmitigated disaster was the case of the elderly *Grizzly*, ex-*Machigonne*. Over thirty years old, she had served successively in the U.S. Navy as a coal-fired auxiliary-engined schooner, and as a diesel yacht for four owners between the wars. There is considerable argument between the participants involved in her purchase as to whether her German-made engines really broke down on the way up to Victoria from Long Beach and she had to be towed in (rather a suspect argument, for her original German engineer came up that far with her), or whether she arrived safely and the naval engineers, in a fit of pique over not being consulted about her purchase in the first place, refused to spend a day or so at sea with the yacht's original engineer and ruined the elderly power plants during the first day of trials due to lubricating oil problems. Be that as it may, and memories seem to favour the latter event, she never operated under her own power again, and was thus relegated to use as an anchored harbour or channel guard vessel on the west coast. Some bookkeeping savings were thus realized in not fitting her to drop depth charges or with Asdic or a heavy gun. However, she is always classed, like *Ambler*, as one of the Animal Class Yachts.

Despite all these vicissitudes in expense, the departmental estimates were astoundingly accurate when compared to the final actual costs:

Estimated purchase and delivery costs: $1,800,000 (for thirteen ships, at an average of $138,500 each).

Mascotte, ex-*Josephine*, bought by Colonel Sidney Oland, and which became HMCS *Reindeer*.

Branch Office
148 STATE STREET
BOSTON, MASS.
CAPitol 2966

SPARKMAN & STEPHENS
INCORPORATED

NAVAL ARCHITECTS — YACHT BROKERS
MARINE INSURANCE

11 EAST 44TH ST.
NEW YORK CITY
VAnderbilt 3-7244
Cables: Sparstep

For Sale by an Estate — Diesel yacht MASCOTTE *ex* JOSEPHINE. 140′ o.a., 132′ w.l., 24′ 2″ beam, 8′ 6″ draft, 337 gross tons. Built by Newport News Shipbuilding Corporation. Dining salon, galley, pantry, living room and library on main deck. Sleeping accommodations for ten in owner's quarters with four double and one single staterooms and five baths. Powered with two Winton Diesels of 400 h.p. each. Electric refrigeration; Diesel generators. Other auxiliaries include Radio Direction Finder, Gyro Pilot, Radio Telephone and Gyro Compass. Built in excess of Lloyd's and has a cruising radius of approximately 5000 miles. Available for inspection in New York City. *For further information, price and location consult* SPARKMAN & STEPHENS, INC., 11 East 44th Street, New York City, or 148 State Street, Boston, Mass., *or your own broker*.

Actual purchase and delivery cost: $1,791,354 (for fourteen ships, at an average of $128,000 each).

The eventual grand total cost, including conversion, and ready for service, was about $2,955,500, including *Ambler* at a purchase price of only one dollar, and *Sans Peur* at $328,841. So the project could be considered to be quite a success, despite HMCS *Grizzly*.

In the United Kingdom, much the same program was under way, only the need for secrecy was not present, as there were enough large British yachts that became available, or were brought out from Europe when France and the Low Countries fell to the Germans. They were nations accustomed to ocean travel in private yachts.

The best known of the yachts converted into armed patrol ships for the RN was probably T.O.M. Sopwith's large *Philante*, later to be used as an anti-submarine training ship at Liverpool, where many Canadian 'V.R.s brushed up on their submarine techniques.

As in the RN, and certainly in the RCN, trade protection had a very low priority in the USN, where this protection initially was provided for by a motley collection of old gunboats, World War 1 destroyers in reserve, and the Coast Guard. It was not until the European war was well under way, and the U-boats were already taking a considerable toll even from the convoys run from Canada to the U.K., that the Americans realised their shortage in this critical field.

The USN acquired 10 yachts before December, 1941. Those over 1,000 tons, and there were eventually to be more than a dozen, were classed as gunboats, those of 500 to 1,000 tons were classed as patrol yachts, and those below 500 tons were called coastal armed yachts. With the selection of vessels for the USN ranging from the destroyer-sized ships down to the little 95 footers, their average length was only slightly longer than the RCN's, 179 feet versus 168 feet. But as far back as 1939, CDR Roy had been correct when he pointed out how vital it would be to keep the purchases secret for as long as possible to prevent price gouging, when it became evident governments were desperate for yachts. The Americans in late 1940 and during 1941, paid an average of $284,300 for their ships.

There was still some consideration to be given to the often sumptuous fittings that came with the yachts, yet would have to be removed for their war service. In May 1940, Lesslie Thomson had reported to Norman Rogers, Minister of National Defence, and to his own boss, C.D. Howe, the Minister of Transport, on the matter of the yachts' fittings:

> 7. Fittings are worth $5,000 to $30,000; pianos, oriental rugs, china, silver, etc. It is recommended that such fittings be conserved to the utmost degree, in order that the ultimate resale value of the yachts be enhanced. Many potential purchasers would be influenced as much by the internal fittings as by the exterior vessel herself.
>
> 8. Recommended storage ... None of the present luxury equipment should be permitted to go into ordinary Naval service. In short it would be truer economy to furnish these yachts with strong, simple furniture and fittings rather than to attempt to appear to save money by utilizing some of the existing luxury equipment under active service conditions.

It could certainly be argued that the wardrooms at least would have been glad to retain some of the finer china and table silver rather than the Navy's utilitarian silver plate and coarse china mugs. Fortunately for some of the future commanding officers, their cabins in some ships retained pieces of furniture from the former owners. The odd armchair and settee was to be found, perhaps a fine mahogany table, and at least one west coast yacht had rather handsome brass beds. Bathroom fittings aft in almost all yachts were of a style and make that the Navy would never have accepted had the vessels been new built, but were left in the "owner's suite" for convenience and haste. In the crew areas due to crowding and the need for "heads" for an expanded complement, the replacing fittings were strictly utilitarian.

In many of the yachts the wood panelling was removed in rearranging cabins and mess decks, and in a few ships, for fire safety purposes. In others, notably on the west coast again, the fine wood-grain panelling remained to the end of the yacht's service. This was certainly true in the case of *Sans Peur*. And there were some surprises for the new crews, left over from idiosyncrasies of their prewar owners. In *Grizzly*, when checking the electric circuitry and various buttons, one was found carefully moulded into the panelling beside the bed of the commander. When pressed it caused a panel in the bulkhead to slide aside, revealing the bed in the next cabin close beside, presumably, in the old days, occupied by one of the guests.

Although the list of repairs indicated that often the electric wiring was replaced, in many yachts it was not, and this was to cause problems throughout their naval service, and possibly the loss of one yacht. Too frequently, when faced with service at sea in very rough weather, with seas coming aboard, the salt water got behind the elegant panelling, where it soaked into the old cloth-covered wiring, causing short circuits and fires. Certainly in *Vison*, this occurred on several occasions in the wireless office, at main deck level, even as late as mid-1944, and the wireless operator was frequently required to cope with minor fires and electric shocks from the wet wiring as part of his duties.

Each of the yachts was strengthened in the dockyards to take a small (by naval standards) gun forward, and in two cases — *Renard* and *Sans Peur* — another gun aft. The only exceptions were in *Ambler*, where the raised coaming around her tiny foc's'le was found to be needed for seaworthiness, yet did not permit the use of such a gun, and in *Grizzly* where her immobility made such a weapon unnecessary. *Beaver* was fitted with her elderly 4″ gun, controlled entirely by hand levers. The others at least had what were called "quick firing" or Q.F. guns, where the breech closed automatically with strong springs when a shell was inserted by the gun's crew. The guns that were supplied consisted of seven 4″ Q.F., retained fortuitously in naval stores when the old destroyers *Patriot*, *Patrician*, *Champlain* and *Vancouver* had been scrapped between the wars; six 3″, referred to as 12-pounders from the weight of their shells; and one much smaller 6-pounder. Additionally *Sans Peur* was soon provided with a 40mm anti-aircraft cannon, called a "pom-pom" from the sound it made when firing. Since at this time she was still based on the west coast, neutral waters in 1940 and 1941, it can be presumed this was for training, and not to drive off potential German aircraft. It speaks well for the foresight of some naval or civil service officer that the guns should have been stored, and useable, against an unforeseen future need. For if they had not been available in Canada, there would have been a major problem in trying to obtain any from hard-pressed Britain.

Depth charges for dropping on the anticipated submarines, although a remarkably simple weapon, were by no means in plentiful supply. Although the racks for them to be released over the stern of the yachts could be constructed by any machine shop, and due to the small size of the yachts few throwers would be required, and those obtainable from Britain, the depth charges themselves were only becoming available as the local manufacturers acquired expertise and built up their supply lines. Essentially the depth charge was a sealed steel drum, about the size of a household garbage can, with a hollow central tube about 5″ in diameter running from end to end. The rest of the inner space was taken up by 300 pounds of the explosive, at first Amatol, and later the more powerful Torpex. Into one end of the hollow central tube was fitted a "primer," consisting of a soupcan-sized container of rather less stable explosive, with a handle and a rubber sealing ring at one end and a small finger-sized hole at the other. Into the opposite end of the same tube went the "pistol," a water-pressure actuated firing device, with a depth-setting key and the various depths marked on the outer face, and a very sensitive detonator

Winchester, 3rd of that name to be built for Peter Rouss of New York. A very fast turbine yacht. Became HMCS *Renard* in the Second War.

Winchester as Patrol Vessel SP 156 of the US Navy during the First War. In 1918.

Winchester between the wars, now owned by General Cornelius Vanderbilt, in the 1930s.

HMCS *Renard*, ex-*Winchester*, off Halifax, in her wartime camouflage.

protruding from the inner end, which slid into the finger-like depression in the primer when it was slid home and sealed by a turn of the handle. Not very complicated, but their manufacture took some careful organization, although thousands were needed as soon as the war started.

An idea of the original shortages is given by the story out of Sydney, Cape Breton, where there was a major shipping port for convoys. The naval officer in charge there when war broke out, Commander J.B. Prentice, asked for a supply of depth charges for his little fleet of motor launches and ex-RCMP vessels on guard duty. He was told there were none available. Being the hub of the island's mining community, and since the depth charges were not really very complicated, he resolved that they could make their own, using mine explosives which were not affected by water. An ordinary farm milk can was stuffed with 100 pounds of Forcite, a small hole was drilled in the can's lid, and the lid taped firmly in place. A detonator attached to a length of ordinary mining fuse was inserted through the hole and sealed, the whole to be fired by the simple expedient of lighting a match to the fuse! On the first "sea trial" in the old coal-burning steamer *French*, the fuse was lit, and the can simply kicked over the side. To the horror of the watching naval personnel, it was suddenly realized that the air-tight can was not going to sink. It sat bobbing on the surface, fuse burning quickly, as the *French* all too slowly chugged away at barely 10 knots! The quarterdeck was cleared just in time, as the makeshift charge exploded on the surface with a tremendous roar, showering the ship with water and small pieces of milk can. In future the home-made depth charges were pierced at the bottom and weighted with rocks so that at least they would sink before detonating.

As time went on, depth charges were provided in numbers enough for the yachts to acquire their normal complement: rarely more than twelve, even in the larger yachts. Even this represented just under two tons; quite a weight at the upper deck level, which had to be taken into account during stability tests, with extra ballast, and without making the ships too low in the water overall.

The Asdic sets themselves arrived from England just in time to meet the fitting out timetables for the yachts. In the 1920's and 1930's the whole concept of Asdic was a closely guarded secret, and the sets' operation and success came as a complete surprise to the U-boat command. The name was derived from the Allied Submarine Detection Investigation Committee of 1917, set up in desperation when no detection equipment seemed able to cope with the unrestricted German U-boat war. All sorts of bizarre experiments were tried at the time, and the Canadians carried out some of the earliest experiments in HMCS *Cartier* with hydrophone listening and echo-ranging during 1917. As the sets developed from the simple listening hydrophones to the active echo-ranging sets, whereby the set sent out a sharp burst of sound to be echoed off any submarine within range, so the sets became more of a secret weapon of the day, and the Allied committee was dissolved in the mid-1930's. By 1935, half of the RN destroyers were equipped with Asdic sets, and the Navy thought it the final and easy answer to the U-boat menace, more efficient than it proved to be in actual combat. The main problem lay in the fact that its "beam" of sound covered a relatively shallow angle, rather in the shape of a narrow flashlight beam, in the direction in which it was aimed, ahead or around the ship. It lost contact with the submarines being tracked, especially deep-running ones, some 200 or 300 yards ahead of the attacking ship. This rather extensive "dead space" allowed the submarine to duck sideways before the slow-sinking depth charges could reach a lethal range, about 35 yards. This problem was not solved until the advent of ahead-thrown "Hedgehog" bombs of 1943 and the heavier "Squid" ahead-thrown depth charge of 1944, which could be fired while the Asdic set was still in contact, and sank faster, ahead of the attacking ships.

By 1939, four of the six Canadian destroyers had Asdic fitted (two of them being on the west coast), and four more trawler-type smaller sets had been ordered but not yet fitted in the "Basset Class" minesweepers. *Skeena* and *Saguenay* soon had their sets fitted, and other larger requisitioned ships of 1939 and early 1940 were equipped with Asdic as the sets arrived from Britain. In fact, there were few serious delays in equipping ships that became available, and again it is a tribute to foresight in the Admiralty's supplies section, that there was not an insurmountable delay in meeting the demand.

Trained operators and officers was another matter entirely, and here the RCN was woefully unprepared for expansion. The four destroyers were intially suplied with but two seamen submarine detectors (S.D.s), sometimes required to man their sets for days on end at sea. There were a few more seamen on training courses in the United Kingdom, as there were no courses of any kind available in Canada. There were only two trained anti-submarine officers in the whole Canadian Navy, qualified in 1927, but they had not been seriously connected with the A/S field since that time. In February 1940, a training school was set up at Halifax, with an Attack Teacher, a Canadian development, as part of the equipment. Two ships, HMCS *French* and *Acadia*, coal-burning ex-RCMP patrol vessels, were assigned for sea training, together with an elderly RN 'L' Class submarine. At Halifax, lack of trained maintenance staff familiar with the new equipment meant that repairs were often attempted by the new, enthusiastic and keen S.D.s, who often caused a worsening of the defects. It was not until electrical maintenance staff could be recruited from civilian sources that this problem was solved, during 1940, resulting in many ships being out of service for A/S purposes, although they continued their patrols all the same, on the theory that the U-boats would not be aware of their shortcomings. Even spares ordered from Britain were lost when the ship *Manchester Guardian* was sunk in a collision off the Halifax harbour entrance, and it was only by shipping A/S spares from a small stock at Esquimalt dockyard that the ships on the east coast were kept in operation at all.

The problem of shortages of trained operator S.D.s and Anti-Submarine Control Officers (ASCOs) was not to be resolved until late in 1941. In the meantime, the ships and the training school just ran very short handed.

When war broke out, Lieutenant Commander Arthur R. Pressey was in England to review the Canadian plans for harbour defences with the more experienced Royal Navy counterparts, and while there, took the opportunity to visit the A/S training establishment, HMS *Vernon* in Portsmouth, to up-date his 1927 knowledge. On return to Canada, he was appointed director, anti-submarine, and made an acting commander, responsible for all anti-submarine measures for the Canadian Navy, whether they be port defensive mines, nets, booms, or the equipment being fitted in the ships, and the training needed therefor. Soon his efforts at recruiting civilians qualified in electrical maintenance bore fruit, and the sets ceased to fail as frequently at sea due to more systematic inspections and servicing by knowledgeable experts. The A/S school, originally set up in Esquimalt, was transferred to Halifax, closer to the source of trainees and their ships, supervised by Lieutenant J.W. White, on loan from the RN, together with a submarine detector instructor, Chief Petty Officer Cheeseman, R.N.

Thus it was at a critical time that the yachts came on the scene, and it was only by the most strenuous and ingenious efforts that their Type 123 sets could be made available, and operators trained to run them. These sets comprised a 3-foot diameter disc "transducer", housed in a watertight "dome" fastened to and protruding below the hull of the yacht, about under the bridge. There were also various electric motors to train it around and power supplies to create the sound, in a compartment immediately above the dome. And above the bridge was a glassed-in hut to house the operator. The initial operating equipment consisted of a ship's magnetic compass binnacle, some fitted with a small ship's wheel on the operator's side, others with a car steering wheel on the top. The operator wore a set of headphones, over which he could hear the transmitting "ping" of his set. He was listening for the much fainter potential returning echo from a submarine — or a shoal of fish, a rock, or any other echo-returning object in the sea. By turning the wheel through 5° arcs, the Asdic beam could sweep around, rather like an underwater sound flashlight, the direction of the beam at any instant being indicated by a small red arrow on the outer edge of the compass inside the binnacle. At first the length of time taken for the echo to return indicated the distance away of the object. This was soon supplemented, in the Type 123A sets, with a paper trace recorder to show the range on a scale based on time. As well, there was the change of the unstable magnetic compass to the more steady electrical gyro compass.

While some of the yachts were to be modernized, many kept their original sets throughout their naval lives, with only the change to gyro compasses, as the yachts became the training ships for operators destined for the ships in the Atlantic battle. The duties of S.D.s were soon carried out almost entirely by Reserves, despite the remarks of one early report that "To date difficulty has been encountered in obtaining suitable Reserve ratings. RCNR ratings lacked the necessary intelligence and 'V.R.s lacked the sea time. A group of sixty 'V.R. ratings earmarked for A/S have been sent to sea specially to enable them to obtain sea experience prior to taking their course."

Training required time, for there were at the start not enough instructors for potential students, and certainly almost no instructors with sea A/S experience, apart from the two loaned from the RN. And the A/S school could only handle a dozen or so seamen trainees at a time. It should also be realized that the new and often inexperienced ships' commanding officers also needed some instruction in the use of this new "box of tricks" and how to take advantage of its information, and the ASCOs needed yet another type of supervisory course in the details of controlling the operators' searching and in digesting the information for their captains' use. It can be appreciated what a monumental problem was faced absolutely from scratch, in having ships not only equipped with the sets, but provided with seamen and officers at least moderately competent to operate them. It is not too surprising then that the U-boats had a fairly easy time at first, for at least their crews were well trained in their trade, although even they did not appreciate how effective the Asdic could be in trained hands.

After their theoretical courses ashore, the operators and the officers in the ships, be they destroyers or armed yachts, expected too much from their sets, under varying conditions of sound transmission, and often in wildly rolling vessels, and were often fooled by wily U-boat commanders. Also, the U-boats soon found that the best way to attack a convoy at night, or even at dusk and dawn, was on the surface, which was not appreciated in the early days by the protecting escorts, the submarine only diving if detected and attacked. They would run in on a convoy, usually from one of the leading corners, trimmed down with decks awash, with the captain alone in the conning tower. If undetected, torpedoes would be fired from about 1,000 yards, and the boat alter away, or, if right ahead of the ships, dive to pass right under the convoy. In these cases, the underwater Asdic searches were almost useless, and the old-fashioned lookouts were as useful as the modern electronics. It was only later in 1943, that the advent of good shipborne radar in almost all escorts and air cover made these surface attacks too chancy, drove the U-boats below, and gave the by then experienced Asdic teams their opportunity to shine.

The fitting of the yachts with their A/S sets began in early June, and the few yachts that were ready before their sets were available were sent on patrol anyway to gain sea experience for their RCNVR crews and to gain practice in naval operations for the already sea experienced RCNRs. At least they provided some appearances of protection to the merchantmen, technically weak as it might be. Lieutenant F.W.R. Angus, RCNVR, was placed in charge of fitting the sets in both the yachts and the new construction corvettes and minesweepers now on the builders' ways, the first ships ready getting the first sets. As it turned out, the yachts proved satisfactory in their jobs, so retained theirs, and sets were made available separately for the new construction. Shortly the sets were being made in Canada too, so the backlog was never too serious to provide at least an elementary Asdic for all ships requiring one. As the war progressed, the sets were upgraded in quality, first converting to the electric gyro compass, then with depth predictors (the 127 "Sword" set), and with longer range main sets. Eventually *Elk* and *Sans Peur* were fitted with much the same modern sets as the later frigates, and were able to be used in the last year and a half of the war as advanced A/S training ships at the huge base (HMCS *Cornwallis*) at Deep Brook, Nova Scotia, on the Bay of Fundy.

So in various dockyards, at Halifax, Montreal, Pictou, and on the west coast at Esquimalt, the vessels that had once been beautiful white-hulled pleasure yachts had their foredeck dining saloons torn off, their decks strengthened, some mahogany panelling removed, small cabins knocked into larger mess decks, and electrical equipment replaced. They had steel-walled ammunition magazines built below, a 3-foot hole cut in the hulls for the Asdic dome, the hut added above an often remodelled bridge, and then the whole given a coat of Admiralty grey paint. (Camouflage in a disruptive pattern was tried in different configurations as war experience and results of interrogation of U-boat survivors indicated which colours and designs made the ships harder to see through periscopes. Samples can be seen in the photographs of *Renard* and *Vison*).

Each yacht was given an identifying number, at first starting with S, although this changed two or three times during the war, not always consistently or uniformly. And except for *Ambler* and *Sans Peur*, each was then given a new name. Some orderly bureacratic mind, or perhaps an early Ships Names Committee decreed that the names should all be of one type for ease of identification, and the animal classification was the happy choice. This carried on a longstanding Naval tradition that names were better if they had a history of naval use, in this case, of course, in the Royal Navy, from which the Canadian Navy had evolved. Of the fourteen animal names chosen, eight had appeared previously in the Royal Navy's ship lists, with histories going back as far as the Dutch Wars of 1656, often for smaller ships. *Wolf* had been used on twenty occasions; *Renard* on ten; *Beaver*, eleven, and even *Caribou* and *Moose* each once before. The battle honours associated with the ships of those names rings like a bugle call through history. Battles like Barfleur in 1692; Louisburg, 1758; Copenhagen in 1801, and the Dardanelles in 1915, at all of which vessels with these names had fought. But in most cases this was far too esoteric an interest for the ex-merchant seamen of the RCNR crews. And for the newly arriving 'V.R.s, it was all so strange and different from any experience they had ever had that such matters as the choice of names for their ships seemed a very trivial matter. But such small items all contributed, often unknowingly, to that mystical but invaluable source of pride and fighting spirit, the naval tradition, that makes a seaman go on with his job when all his senses tell him to quit. Oddly the 'V.R.'s and the 'N.R.'s were to become immensely proud and a part of this naval tradition, which has stayed with them to this day.

The yachts sent up-river for their refits were commissioned as HMC Ships for their voyages, and flew the White Ensign. Those taken into the dockyards at Halifax and Esquimalt were not commissioned as naval ships until they were ready for service. Hence the records of commissioning dates are not a reliable measure of when the ships first reported for duty. *Sans Peur*, because she required little work to make her fit for service, and was the first in naval hands, was commissioned at Esquimalt on March 3, 1940, ready for work, a gun forward and depth charges aft. *Ambler* was next; she was fitted with neither gun nor Asdic, and was commissioned for patrols on the St. Lawrence on May 6. These were follwed by *Raccoon*, *Caribou* and *Renard*, but only for their trips to dockyards —

Raccoon to Pictou Foundry & Machine Company at Pictou, and the other two, in company, up-river to Morton Shipbuilding at Quebec. The rest followed as crews could be found, and reliable officers appointed who at least had merchant ship experience or were ex-yachtsmen who had been tested for a minimal knowledge of navigation and leadership. Contracts were being signed, and Lambert and German were acting as the overseers of the whole project.

The last yacht was out of dockyard hands and ready for duty by October 5, 1940, when *Vison* commissioned at Pictou. Ready for duty was open to some variable interpretations. There were bitter comments by some naval dockyard staff at the ships' home ports when they arrived with what the Navy considered major defects still uncorrected. This was by no means all sour grapes. In the rush and unfamiliarity of the civilian and even naval dockyards with their new projects, problems were overlooked, in some cases; this was even admitted by Lambert and German to be partly due to relatively inexperienced supervisors from their firm, as the new construction put tremendous demands on the small band of experienced and qualified naval architects and supervisors available in Canada. Soon all the yachts were "on their war stations" and at work, even poor old *Grizzly*, immobile in the harbour approaches at Prince Rupert, acting as a guard vessel.

Charles H. Sheppard.

Ambler as C.H. Sheppard's yacht at his home in Waubashene, Ont., dressed for his daughter's wedding.

CHAPTER 7

KEEPING THE FOE AT BAY

The west coast, until the opening of the war with Japan in December 1941, was never more than a peacetime training area. Naval authorities quite rightly anticipated that the Germans would not be able to spare or support U-boats for attacks on that coast, and while there could be potential attacks by surface warships or raiders, this was highly unlikely without considerable warning in advance.

For political reasons, however, the British Columbians had to be shown that the government, and its navy, were seriously interested, nay concerned, about their safety. So some armed patrol vessels were maintained on that coast, to lend credibility to that concern. Here the armed yachts played a useful role, as did some new construction warships, when they began to come off the building ways in late 1940 and in 1941.

After Pearl Harbor, the defence of this coast became a more serious matter, and armed merchant cruisers and anti-submarine corvettes were more in evidence, although this was still more of a gesture to public pressures. The Canadian Navy had no vessels that could counter a serious Japanese surface fleet attack on the installations at Victoria and Vancouver. Anyway, it was expected that the USN would be quite prepared to counter any west coast attacks on Canada's behalf. So the yachts were useful for their anti-submarine role, which was not only anticipated, but occurred.

To look at the easiest story first, at least as far as anything of interest happening to an armed yacht throughout the war, we turn to *Grizzly* on the west coast. With no engines, and hence no ability to defend the coast against marauding submarines or possibly Japanese battleships, *Grizzly* was anchored fore and aft off one of the passages into Prince Rupert, both as an offshore deterrent, and as an "examination vessel." Many of the armed yachts performed this latter role sooner or later, and although there was not much danger from the enemy, it was no easy job in foul weather, and downright dangerous in dense fog or on a pitch black night in those days before any ships had radar.

Every inbound merchant ship (and even coasters if not recognized) had to be stopped, or at least queried by light as she approached a harbour entrance and her name, cargo and destination determined. If the examination vessel had been given a list of anticipated arrivals, the matter was soon cleared, and with no more than a pause, the ship carried on to her destined berth. But if due to stress of weather, breakdown, re-routing, or due to some administrative foul-up, the little examination vessel had no forwarning of a ship's arrival, then she must get in touch with harbour authorities to find out whether the newcomer was genuine, and if so, where she was to go. It might be that incoming ships were not fully aware of the underwater mine defences of the harbour, and blundering inward over the corner of a minefield could, and did on occasion, lead to disastrous results. Hence the need for the little examination vessels offshore. The ships were not always armed (*Grizzly*, with a few .303 rifles and a revolver or two, could hardly be called "armed"), but they had some armament, on the theory that this lent credence to any orders they might be issuing to inbound, and usually much larger ships.

Grizzly effectively blocked one passage between Dundas Island and the mainland, through which mostly passed small ocean fishing boats, while another mobile naval craft patrolled the other channel leading directly up to Prince Rupert. Both passages, as was usual in all the harbour approaches, were defended as well by army-manned medium guns of 6″ or 4.5″ calibre in concrete emplacements along the shorelines. Water and supplies were brought out to the ship every week or so, and the crew granted some leave once a

HMCS *Grizzly*, ex-*Machigonne*, at Esquimalt, B.C., in September, 1942.

week, via a small supply vessel into Prince Rupert. About every six months, the ship was towed up to Prince Rupert for docking and examination, and for a short overhaul of her diesel generators, which had to be run continually for light, heat in the winter and her radio and pumps. They were in port on one of these brief overhauls when the Japanese attacked Pearl Harbor. Crew member Fred Vance tells how *Grizzly*'s crew were prepared for this new offshore war:

"Since it was a day of excitement in that area, and we were going out to sea (what a laugh!), the Naval Officer In Charge Prince Rupert, Commander Reid, RCNR, came down and gave us a little pep talk, and his finishing remarks were 'that when we were back on station, our captain would send us ashore, and we were to cut ourselves a stout cudgel and take it back to the ship with us, to be used in case of attack'."

The crew at first consisted of two or three sub-lieutenants (later reduced to one, and sometimes to no officer on board at all), one chief motor mechanic, three stokers (a hold-over term from the days when coal was to be shovelled into boilers, but in this case referred to as "Stokers (M)" for their being trained in motors and engines instead), two radiomen, a visual signalman, a leading seaman as senior hand, and about four seamen. The numbers varied, depending on shortages of men for the fleet at sea, *Grizzly* being well down the list of priorities. About the time of Pearl Harbor, *Grizzly* was equipped with two Lewis machine guns which were kept securely locked up, but could be mounted on pedestals on the roofs of the two upper deck cabins in an emergency. Fortunately, they were never required for more than the occasional practice shot.

In mid-1942, the north passage into Prince Rupert was permanently closed by a log boom, to give easier control of entry into the port, particularly as there was considerable nervousness at the height of the Japanese supremacy in the Pacific that they might try to infiltrate small "spy" craft into this busy harbour. *Grizzly* was then moored in the south passage, and remained there doing her examination vessel and guard ship job until June 1944, when she was found to be too deteriorated in the hull plates to leave at sea, so was paid off as no longer required. She was sold in late December 1944, being taken over by

Capital Iron and Metal Company of Victoria for scrapping on March 25, 1945. As recently as 1980 her ship's wheel was still to be seen on the wall of that firm's main office, the only visible memento of that little warship.

Cougar was also a yacht that spent her whole time on the west coast, on patrols mostly in the Strait of Juan de Fuca. She was mobile, with two good Winton diesel engines that rarely caused any problem, so was given a 6-pounder gun on her foc's'le, one machine gun, and eventually sixteen depth charges, and was equipped with the original basic Asdic 123 type set, hand operated. This was later up-graded to have a range recorder added, so that if a submarine was detected on a bearing, there would at least be an indication of its distance away, a rather fundamental shortcoming of the earlier sets. Also, late in the war, a Canadian-made radar was added, making life on patrol in the Strait much easier in fog and at night, although the Canadian "Swick" set was notorious for its unreliability, tending to break down at the slightest jar from heavy seas, and certainly from the concussion of firing the 6-pounder! Being rather too small for carrying extra crew for training purposes, as many of the yachts did, *Cougar* remained on offshore and harbour entrance patrols until no longer required in early 1945, and was available for sale on December 4th 1945.

Based on Esquimalt dockyard for much of the time, patrols consisted of being out for four of five days, patrolling between Vancouver Island and the U.S. shore of Washington State, out to Cape Flattery and the open Pacific.

The misnamed Pacific was not always a kindly place for these small ex-pleasure yachts. One report describes *Cougar*'s condition after a gale on December 13 - 14, off Vancouver Island:

> "Deck strained, skylights broken away, and ventilators. Asdic room flooded. Windows of pilot house broken. Fire after fire in pilot house, due to wiring short circuits, and all lights out for over 4 hours. Galley and crew's quarters flooded. 4½ feet of water in bilges.

Often they patrolled with ships of the USN, which was popular, for they were better supplied than the Canadians with extras such as chocolate bars and good quality jockey shorts. Canadian naval underwear was always terrible, right to the end of the war, and all RCN ships appreciated the chance of being partners with the Americans, if only for the opportunity to buy or trade for better supplies, so they too looked forward to the exchanges that took place, not necessarily officially. It was a thick-headed commanding officer that did not look the other way at some times, if it improved his crew's welfare.

On one occasion *Cougar* borrowed some fresh bread from USS *Amherst*, her patrol partner. This was sliced and wrapped when received, something new for the Canadians. When it came time to return the loan, the Canadian ship provided their standard fare, unwrapped, unsliced, in boxes. They were thanked by the Americans, who then steamed on their way. As Leading Stoker Murray Doucette tells it, "A half hour later we saw a hell of a bunch of seagulls following their ship. We sure knew where our bread went!" On occasion *Cougar* was sent up to Prince Rupert, and even out to the Queen Charlotte Islands, 250 miles northwest of Vancouver Island, when an extra patrol was required, usually as a result of a suspicious ship or possibly submarine sighted. She, like *Grizzly*, did the job required, killed no submarines, but made the protection of the coast visible and believable, and formed a reasonable training ground for her crews when they later went on to the more dangerous and vital duties in the raging Battle of the Atlantic. They were, at least, no longer green farm and factory hands with no sea experience, and took no little umbrage if their east coast compatriots were patronizing. A patrol off Flattery was just as arduous and hard as one off Sydney.

HMCS *Cougar*, ex-*Breezin' Thru*, with the Asdic hut perched atop the bridge, in the Strait of Juan de Fuca, December 1940.

HMCS *Wolf* was the third of the four west coast armed yachts. Like *Cougar* and *Grizzly*, she had been in the USN in the First World War, but was a little larger, at 172 feet, so was armed with a 12-pounder, 3″ gun, depth charges and machine guns, and later an anti-aircraft 1″ pom-pom for the training of gunnery ratings for a day or so at sea as part of their courses. She too was used for patrols in the Strait of Juan de Fuca, but being a bit larger than *Cougar*, and with more reliable guns, took out classes more frequently for their "sea time."

After the outbreak of war with Japan, *Wolf* and the other yachts were on patrols off the Fraser River mouth, as the population was very apprehensive of the large number of Japanese, both native and immigrant, in British Columbia, and there were rumours of arms caches along unfrequented areas of the coast, all unfounded of course, but none the less very worrisome at the time. Command of these patrols came under COAV — Commanding Officer Auxiliary Vessels — at Victoria. On Christmas Eve, 1941, Sub-Lieutenant D. Lukin Johnston, a newly commissioned officer, was aboard *Wolf*, while all the others were ashore celebrating. A message arrived from COAV asking: "Can you sail? We have heard there may be a Japanese attack on Esquimalt."

Johnston called together his little band of chiefs and petty officers, had the engines warmed over and their lines singled up ready for letting go on the instant. With their little 4″ gun they were ready for the foe. Maybe fortunately nothing came of it, but the spirit was willing!

On patrol, like all careful watchers, the Asdic operator would detect a possible submarine echo, and several depth charges would be dropped, detonating at 50 to 100 feet with a heavy thud against the hull, followed a moment after by a plume of spray thrown up, well astern. No submarines were ever verified, and on most occasions there were hundreds of fish soon lying dead or stunned on the surface. If the echo had by then disappeared, or been classified in retrospect as "non-sub" by the operator or the Asdic control officer (in most cases because the echo had been returned in the first place from the school of fish, but one could never be sure at the beginning), the ship would frequently lower a boat to pick up some fresh fish for the next meal for all on board, a welcome relief from the normal meals. By August 1945, *Wolf* was no longer required. She was put up for sale, and bought by the Gulf Lines of Vancouver as a coastal ferry. Her life as such was short and tragic, as will be seen in a later chapter.

By far the best known of the west coast yachts was the Duke of Sutherland's *Sans Peur*. Requiring little stiffening for guns or depth charge rails due to her strong construction only six years before, she was ready for patrols by March 1940, and set off for the Strait on March 11, proceeding up to Alert Bay and eventually to Price Rupert on a shakedown cruise, for her new ship's company. She was fitted with a 4″ ex-destroyer's gun, and a 1″ pom-pom, a somewhat better than normal Asdic set and twenty-five depth charges. A year later radar was even added. Being quite a formidable little warship, she was considered as a normal war vessel as far as supplies and the provision of confidential books was concerned, and even later provided with a code and cypher machine.

Due to the added top-hamper of radar, guns, and later an anti-submarine mortar weapon, the "Hedgehog," her heavy mahogany motor launches had to be left ashore. Also fuel was always to be left in tanks number 3, 6, and 7; if used, water had to be taken in, an unpopular move for her engineers, for then the tanks had to be laboriously flushed out again to remove all traces of water. It was only later in the war that it was found that water could be added to tanks containing fuel, particularly gasoline, so long as arrangements were made to draw the fuel off the top of the tank: also, as the tank filled up with its replacement water, there had to be careful controls that water was not sucked into the lines. In this way, the danger of explosion from fumes of the empty fuel oil tanks was avoided, and ships' stability was maintained as well.

In addition to patrols off the coast as required, *Sans Peur* took out anti-submarine training classes, gunnery classes for anti-aircraft shooting, and by 1943 radar classes, as

HMCS *Wolf*, ex-*Blue Water*, at Nanoose Bay, Vancouver Island, September, 1940.

well, for their sea training time. As she had quite commodious living spaces, beyond that required strictly for her crew, she was also used to transport trainees to bases up the coast, and on occasion to take prisoners of war and internees captured from German merchantmen in the Pacific, from Victoria to Vancouver for onward transport to their internment camps. A maid of all work, a "Warrior for the working day."

On June 20, 1942 there was high excitement on the west coast, when a Japanese submarine surfaced and shelled the lighthouse and wireless station at Estevan, halfway up Vancouver Island. While no damage was done to the installations, and only a few trees set afire, it was the first attack on Canada since the days of the Fenian Raids in the 1860's, and occurred on the same day as a British freighter was hit off the Strait of Juan de Fuca by another submarine's torpedo, although not sunk. *Sans Peur*, on patrol off the Island, received a genuine operation message: "HMCS *Timmins* reports a submarine sighted by aircraft 052° 03′N, 130° 06′W at 0918 PDT. Proceed with all despatch assist HMCS *Timmins* search."

Although the two ships searched diligently for some time, apparently the intruder had decamped hurriedly to the west and home, for there were no more insults to Canadian sovereignty from the sea on that coast. Some years later a few incendiary bombs were wafted over the west coast by balloon from the northern Japanese islands, but the yachts could do little about that, and they caused but a brief panic.

As the active war in the Pacific began to retreat westward in late 1943, and it became obvious that the Japanese had been forced onto the defensive by their losses to the USN in the battles of the South Pacific area, it was decided to send *Sans Peur* around to the main theatre of both war and training on the east coast. She sailed from Esquimalt dockyard, in company with a newly built frigate, *New Glasgow*, on January 24, 1944, via the Panama Canal, arriving in Halifax on February 6 for a brief refit, before being sent around to HMCS *Cornwallis*, the huge seaman training base in Annapolis Basin, opening off the Bay of Fundy. There she joined seven other armed yachts already assigned to that base for seaman and specialist training.

HMCS *Sans Peur*, one of the two to retain her pre-war name, at Esquimalt, May 1941.

CHAPTER 8

FACING THE U-BOATS

On the east coast meanwhile, twelve yachts had been commissioned for various duties: *Ambler*, *Beaver*, *Caribou*, *Elk*, *Husky*, *Lynx*, *Moose*, *Otter*, *Raccoon*, *Reindeer*, *Renard* and *Vison*. Until late 1942 they were extremely busy, in a hundred small yet important duties that "miscellaneous" vessels are put to when regular warships are in short supply.

In May and June 1940, the U-boats were moving out into the open Atlantic because of increasingly successful attacks on them in the restricted areas around the British Isles. In July 1940, they were able to reach even father into the mid-Atlantic as a result of the German seizure of the French Atlantic ports and the final fall of Dunkirk. They established submarine bases within a few weeks at St. Nazaire, Lorient, Brest, Bordeaux, and a few other minor ports, six hundred miles west of their former German bases — this saving two days steaming.

It was not until late in 1940 that the Asdics and the operators became a skilled enough combination to cause any real concern to the marauding U-boats, and radar only began to arrive on board the escort vessels in December 1940.

Yet in 1939 alone, 527 ships had Canadian escorts, such as they were, and during 1940 this rose to 3,497 ships out of Halifax and another 556 out of Sydney, Nova Scotia. To look ahead, these figures had risen to 5,050 during 1941, and gives an idea of the magnitude of the problem to be faced and the urgent need, for a Navy with no ocean escorts when the war began.

Ambler, as soon as commissioned for service on June 26, 1940, was sent on patrols and escort duty in the lower Gulf of St. Lawrence, with her base at Gaspé. She was manned by four officers and twenty-nine petty officers and men when at full strength, which was not always the case. She was on the move almost continually, between Quebec City, Rivière-du-Loup, Ile-aux-Coudres, Anticosti Island, Gaspé and Sydney. At the time, the naval policy for protection in this area was to have ships patrolling more or less continually. If possible, merchant ships would sail together and the Navy would provide some escorting vessels, such as *Ambler* and other large but unarmed motor launches (with such un-naval names as *Anna Mildred* or *Cleopatra*) to patrol around them, keeping an eye open for U-boat periscopes or conning towers. Although *Ambler* had no underwater detection gear, and could only rely on her lookouts and bridge personnel, she did have four depth charges, and of course a few rifles, four heavy .455 revolvers, and an ancient .303 Vickers machine gun. In fact, these would have been enough to deter or at least cause considerable difficulties for any U-boat operating in her vicinity, since submarine captains were understandably nervous and usually apprehensive at working in the constricted and relatively shallow water of gulfs and river estuaries, where, if detected, escape was much more difficult than in the open ocean. In fact, the first U-boat attacks in the Gulf of St. Lawrence were not actually to take place until May 11, 1942, when two ships were sunk off the Gaspé coast.

These patrols under the command of Captain Donald, RCN, with his base at HMCS *Fort Ramsay*, at Gaspé. When there were enough escort ships available between Anticosti Island and the Quebec north shore, and a third running down-river, northeasterly along the north shore to Seven Islands, thence across the Gulf to the south shore and back to Gaspé, a fourth ship would be storing and resting at Gaspé, or under repairs at Quebec.

As Admiral Murray had said, the waters of the Gulf are "a very unfriendly part of the

Five of the armed yachts together, at Sydney, N.S. in 1941. From out-board: *Husky, Caribou, Reindeer, Raccoon,* taken from *Elk*.

HMCS *Ambler*, the only Canadian yacht, and the only one without a gun.

ocean," so in mid-December *Ambler* was withdrawn from patrols for the winter of 1940-1941 to Morton Engineering at Quebec City for a refit and further modifications and repairs. Similarly in the winter of 1941-42 she went to Halifax as a tender on October 29, for use by the training school at the base there, HMCS *Stadacona*. Although the open Atlantic off Halifax was all too often not very friendly as well, she could at least go up to the sheltered Bedford Basin at the head of the harbour for the initial sea experience for the new entries on board.

In October 1940, Lieutenant Commander Harold Beament, who had had a brief experience in the armed yacht *Stadacona* as a RNCVR midshipman during the First World War, took command of *Ambler*. He was already an accomplished artist and art teacher, and in postwar years was to become one of Canada's most prestigious landscape artists. One of his crew at the time, Chief ERA J.W. Pierce, recalls that while patrolling it was not unusual "for the ship to be manoeuvred to get the proper light effects, and the C.O. would get out his easle and start painting!" The crew were quite a mixed bag, with six stokers who had bunks, and twelve seamen who had to sling hammocks in two mess deck spaces. The chief ERA reports that his assistant for electrics on board was a regular force RCN "3 badge AB," meaning he had three badges on his arm for over thirteen years good conduct service, but his motor mechanics were RCNVRs and had only filling station experience, if that. "They were young, full of hell, but were a great crowd of boys who made first class men in every way. *Ambler*'s ballast was lead, in 80 pound 'pigs', a great source of grog money (when smuggled ashore and sold to lead-short dealers for booze)." Later, in mid-1943 *Ambler* badly failed her stability test, which had never been good anyway. A considerable weight of iron ingots had to be added to her keel. No doubt the naval engineers thought she should always have had more ballast!

Commander Beament gives a good idea of the life and problems of those river patrols:

> The intention was, by dashing from one spot to another, to give the impression that the river was effectively defended. Our worst enemy turned out to be the autumnal fogs which were frequent and often thick. Much too often we would find ourseles in the path of an onward rushing ocean vessel which would suddenly appear without warning from the fog. My First Lieutenant was a French Canadian 'NR who had been captain of a river steamer. He knew the St. Lawrence very well, which was a great help.

Cooking was done on a small coal stove in the galley. A relief from the patrols was going up to Quebec twice a month for supplies and pay. And there was the added excitement when the armed patrol ship *Bras d'Or* caught the Italian liner *Capo Noli* trying to escape down river and forced her to run herself ashore at Bic Island. Shortly after, that next winter, the little *Bras d'Or* was lost will all hands in the western Atlantic, presumably overwhelmed by the weight of ice during a winter storm at sea. In September 1941, *Ambler* took ashore Air Commodore the Duke of Kent from his passenger liner in Quebec. It was not a major event, but more interesting than rolling around in the rough seas of the lower Gulf.

By December 1941, the first of the wartime purpose-built warships were becoming available, such as the corvettes and Bangor Class minesweepers, most of which were sent right off to the Battle of the Atlantic for convoy escort, and the 112-foot wooden Fairmile design motor launches which began replacing the collection of odd vessels at Gaspé. So *Ambler* went again to Halifax to act as a sea training ship for the school there, and then, in March 1943, to the huge new training base on Annapolis Basin on the opposite side of Nova Scotia, HMCS *Cornwallis*. Sea training consisted of taking a class of ten seamen or stokers out on patrols off Halifax, or along the coast to Sheet Harbour to the northeast or to St. Margaret's Bay or to Lunenburg on the Eastern Shore for two weeks, after these trainees had completed their six-week technical courses. On return they were considered trained, and sent off to war in other ships, or to other jobs throughout the country.

HMCS *Beaver*, ex-*Aztec*, looking a bit care-worn from patrol duties. The longest of the armed yachts.

HMCS *Beaver*, ex-*Aztec*, the oldest and largest ex-yacht, was not commissioned at Halifax until September 1940 due to shortages of equipment and the press of more urgent work in the shipyard there. She was the only one of the yachts with steam triple expansion engines, almost exactly the same as the corvettes, rather than the diesel motors of other and smaller yachts. She was at once put on anti-submarine patrols off Halifax, and between there and Sydney, Cape Breton, and to Cornerbrook and St. John's, Newfoundland. Sometimes she escorted single ships joining convoys passing up from New York or Boston, or those leaving Halifax and Sydney. Or she met, or at least searched for, stragglers who had been forced to leave convoys due to mechanical problems, collisions, or an inability to keep up to convoy speed.

Hardly a week went by when there was not a ship or a small group to be shepherded somewhere, gales and fog notwithstanding, or a lost ship to be searched for, often only because of faulty radio equipment, misunderstood orders, bad or inadequate navigation or a thousand reasons. In 1941 there were 6,974 ships in convoys in the North Atlantic alone. If only 5 per cent had any problems, and half of those on the Canadian side of the ocean, that is 175 ships in trouble, or one every other day. During winter gales that figure could triple, and if there were heavy U-boat attacks, that contributed another quota of damaged, lost, panicked or otherwise worrisome vessels. The weather was always a factor, often decisive for the yachts, designed for peacetime fair weather cruising, and it was always more of a danger than the U-boats!

> TO: NOIC SYDNEY CB
>
> FROM: BEAVER
>
> Hove to for 13 hours. Deck leaking badly and mess deck very wet.

Or again, the "Report of Proceedings" rendered by *Beaver* in November, 1942, in part:

> Convoy assembled off Governor's island 1030P/13 following route as per convoy instructions. Average speed to point of detachments, seven and three quarter knots.

Wind and sea increased to gale force and convoy became detached at approximately 2123P/13 in position 48° 06′N, 59° 37′W.

Efforts made to contact convoy by closing inshore, HMCS *Beaver* being stationed to seaward of convoy, but due to SE gale and high confused sea HMCS *Beaver* was laboring heavily and search had to be abandoned at 0117P/14 for safety of HMCS *Beaver*. At 0200P/14 W/T (the ship's wireless) went out of commission. Convoy was lost due to the possibility of S/S *Keydon* and S/S *Cedarton* deviating from track.

The weather was not the only danger, for sometimes senior officers were not overly sympathetic with the yacht's shortcomings. Witness the following paragraphs from a report by Captain R. Schwert, RCN, the naval officer in charge at Sydney, to his senior officer at Halifax, Rear Admiral Murray:

2. HMCS *Beaver* arrived at Sydney at 1830Z/14 without her convoy and it was not until 2030Z/16 that anxiety regarding the safety of her convoy was allayed by the receipt of a message from NCSO St. John's, stating that these two ships had sheltered in St. George's Bay.

3. I am not personally acquainted with the sea-going qualities of the *Beaver*, but I am inclined to think that it would have been possible for her to proceed to St. George's Bay to look for her convoy, this being the only anchorage south of Port Au Port in which any ship could shelter.

4. The Commanding Officer of HMCS *Beaver* is aware of my opinion ...

Fortunately, and quite typically of that great seaman, Admiral Murray was a little more sympathetic with the sea-going qualities of the thirty-five year-old *Beaver*, and "... felt he was probably justified."

An extract from a Report of Proceedings only a month later, again for a convoy between Sydney and St. John's, illustrated very clearly the problems all escorts faced, with no radar in winter in the North Atlantic. Fortunately German U-boats didn't even enter into the picture.

... Visibility became very bad before the convoy completed forming up, 2100/16.

During the night of 16th - 17th, kept in touch with ships which, it was presumed, were in starboard column.

At dawn on the 17th visibility was fair between snow flurries, but only two ships of the convoy were in sight: *Primo* and *Moyra* ...

Weather became very bad during the night of 17th - 18th, westerly gale with 35 ft. seas. At 1730/18th *Prima* and *Moyra* hove to. Considered it was dangerous to bring *Beaver* about, and ran before the storm.

At 1330/18th, when 20 miles south of Cape Race, a high cross-sea struck the *Beaver* doing considerable damage. At 2310/18th, storm moderated and course was set for St. John's, Nfld. Arrived St. John's at 1915/19th.

Between 1900/17th and 2100/18th, due to high seas, Asdic was almost useless. The remainder of the passage, Asdic conditions were good. At 1300/18th W/T was damaged by sea and was out of commission for remainder of passage.

Entered Naval Dockyard at 2235/19th for repairs. Completed at 1630/23rd ...

Beaver, due to her size, was one of the first Canadian warships to be equipped with radar for its early trials. It was still a very closely guarded secret device, and remained so until well into 1945. In mid-1944, when the author was taking his Sub-Lieutenant's courses, he was told almost nothing about the sets and their operation. All the notes taken during the one-week course were turned in at the end and burned, and these new officers, off to sea, were told, "If you need to know more, you'll be told in your ships when you get there." In *Beaver*, if any watchkeeper entered the chartroom where the test set was fitted, the civilian operators at once turned on the lights (so the glowing trace on the face of the scan tube could not be seen), and stood in front of the set. The antenna at the masthead was turned by hand by a long bicycle chain.

On one occasion, patrolling off Halifax, dawn found *Beaver* surrounded by cruisers, aircraft carriers and destroyers of the USN's Atlantic Fleet. Not having been told anything of this arrival, Lieutenant- Commander George Griffiths' duties were clear, despite his ancient 4″ gun. He issued the daily challenge signal to this "unidentified" danger to Halifax! Fortunately he received not only the correct reply for the day, but the added compliment, "WELL DONE CANADA" and "the whole bunch then steamed into Halifax for refuelling." That 4″ gun was rather much, even for her construction, for when it was fired it was inclined to break the non-standard and non-naval style of glass windows in her cabins, and the deck under it was always leaking due to the strain of the concussion.

On another occasion, the ship was slowed almost to a stop to examine an oil slick they came across at sea, and to pick up a sample. Just as they passed through the slick, the officer on the bridge gave a hand motion for the sailor back aft to drop the container to recover the sample. Another sailor, on duty by the depth charges, and knowing nothing of the reason for slowing down, mistook the signal and dropped a depth charge, set to explode at about 150 ft., which was never done at less than 12 knots, to avoid the upheaval of the explosion. As one seaman participant said, "We took quite a nose dive, but learned the hard way that at least old *Beaver*'s plates were good!"

In the same vein, in the words of Leading Telegraphist A.D. Chisholm of Moncton, "One night around midnight we were just carrying a little headway on patrol in a pea soup fog when all of a sudden we felt this great crash, and *Beaver* was laid right over on her side. One of our minesweepers that was also doing patrols but should have been somewhere else at that time had rammed us right square amidships. We both naturally went into Halifax for examination. The minesweeper damaged her bows so badly all her forward quarters were flooded, and she was in port for repairs for over a month. The *Beaver* went back to sea the next morning with just a small dent in her heavily plated side."

On another day at sea, *Beaver* came across a ship's lifeboat adrift after a storm or a torpedoing. The ship was eased alongside, and the boat hoisted aboard — waste not, want not. The first lieutenant had Chisholm look into a small compartment under the after seat, where he found two black quart bottles. The captain, who was watching from the bridge above asked "What is that, Mr. Childs?" "Engine oil, sir" replied the first lieutenant. On closer examination it turned out to be over-proof dark rum but the C.O. was never told, since he was known to be a strict temperance advocate. As a lot of time in fog was spent almost stopped, some of the crew purchased lines and jiggers "and got themselves some very fine cod and haddock, and along with some real good fun, we had some great fish meals. This was the advantage of having Nova Scotia ex-fishermen and Newfoundlanders in your ship's company."

They also acquired a small ship's kitten, who unfortunately suffered from seasickness. So the victualling assistant, Charles Therrien, made up a small hammock for it. After that, whenever it got rough, "Castor" (French for *Beaver*) rode out the storm in fine style.

Beaver was hauled out for a short refit and repairs in January to March, 1941, and again, as the first warship to be refitted at Liverpool, N.S., in November 1941. In August she had another minor collision with S/S *Roshern*, and in August 1942, was operating out of Saint John, N.B., "for local patrols," where once more she was involved in a collision with the tug *Ocean Hawk I* in a dense fog in the harbour. Her message to her shore authority tells a not untypical story:

> Regret to report a collision occurred 17 September in harbour in dense fog with harbour tug *Ocean Hawk*. Inclined to think we are at fault. Owing to ripe condition of this old tug's hull planking, damage extensive, $2,000 - $3,000. *Beaver* not damaged.

Life wasn't easy, and a lot of the officers and crew in these auxiliary ships were pretty raw amateurs, or had little ship-handling or lookout experience, and can be excused if their sea sense and instant reactions were not honed to their later wartime sharpness. A few watchkeeping officers never acquired that sharpness or natural ship-handling ability. But most of them did very well after a few months or a year in these handy little yachts, and many developed a sixth sense of pending trouble or danger, not explainable in any text or classroom. There are a multitude of stories of a ship being stopped or turned aside, for no visible reason, by the officer of the watch, just before another vessel or a shoreline appeared out of the fog or the black of a moonless night. Even they could rarely explain — "I just thought I heard something," or "I got the feeling we were a bit out of station." It saved many lives.

In the spring of 1943, *Beaver* was also sent around to HMCS *Cornwallis* for sea training duties, to join other yachts removed from patrols.

After HMCS *Caribou* was brought into Halifax on her arrival from the United States, she was actually commissioned twice, for she sailed from Halifax for fitting out at Morton's Shipbuilding at Quebec City on May 25, 1940, as HMCS *Elfreda*, in company with HMCS *Winchester*, Vanderbilt's yacht that became *Renard*. *Caribou* recommissioned by that name was on station by November 10 at Halifax, where she spent two years on patrol and on convoy escort, back and forth to Sydney and St. John's. *Caribou*'s gun was an elderly 12-pounder, which had come from the First World War minesweeping trawlers. She had six .303 rifles, four revolvers, and a stripped Lewis First War machine gun. She carried sixteen depth charges, and later was provided with two throwers for them, as well as the stern racks.

Caribou's engines, like many of the others, were Winton diesels, which in her case were not too reliable, at one stage throwing a rod through the engine-casing, entailing long and

HMCS *Caribou*, ex-*Elfreda*, in April 1943. The depth charge chute arrangement can be easily seen.

costly repairs in late 1941. There were always problems obtaining spare parts for these, and even requirements for making missing parts from scratch. These Wintons had air-blast starting and reversing, whereby the engines had to be turned over by a blast of air first, and switched to running in reverse the same way, the required air being stored at 2,000 pounds per square inch in high-pressure air bottles. If the air ran out, you anchored or at least stopped until it could be built up again by compressors run off electric motors driven from the ship's batteries. On one occasion, at Sydney, a pilot brought *Caribou* in quite fast from the harbour entrance gate, and on arrival near her berth ordered "Full astern," only to find he had used up all the air but a puff or so in previous manoeuvring. Lieutenant J.C. Fritz, her C.O. tells us, "A destroyer's anchor fluke projecting outboard tore into *Caribou*'s deckhouse as she swept past. 'Now look what you've done!' I said to the pilot. Everyone was very worried about the official outcome, and I said I'd have to put it in my report." The pilot persuaded him not to, and had the damage repaired by his friends in the base carpentry shop at *Protector II*, one of the few advantages of a wooden superstructure.

> The slow convoys out of Sydney were of all ages of ships, of all types and nationalities ... lakers, whalers, and small coasters, all were pressed into service to replace sunk tonnage. Many were ships that had proved not able to keep up with the "fast," i.e. over 9 knot, or 11 mile an hour convoys. It was a red letter day when no ships remained in harbour after a convoy sailed, as running repairs to old and ill-found ships strained facilities to the utmost. Crew troubles added to the delays, although it was extremely rare that crews objected to sailing. It was usually shortages of key seamen or radio operators. But the convoys sailed on schedule, whether ocean convoy escorts were available or not. In one case neither Convoy Commodore nor escort could be found, but to the credit of the Merchant Navy, the ships sailed on time. Ships were sailed that would never have received a seaworthy ticket in peacetime.*

As late as December 1942, despite wolf-pack attacks by U-boats for over a year, on some convoys to Newfoundland masters were very uncooperative with the commanding officers of the escorts, and some refused to take any orders from them at all! This only added to the already difficult job of the 'NR and 'VR watchkeepers.

After the tough winter of 1941 - '42, *Caribou* was reported as being "unfit for patrols," so was sent around to Saint John, N.B., to serve as an examination vessel, for port area patrols, and shortly thereafter over to *Cornwallis* across the Bay of Fundy with the other yachts as a seaman training ship.

HMCS *Elk* was one of the larger yachts at 188 feet, and had a reasonably modern 4″ gun. After fitting out at Pictou, Nova Scotia, she too was employed on patrols off Halifax, Sydney, Port Aux Basques, etc., from September 8, 1940. But in her case there was a happy change, for in December 1940 she was loaned to the Royal Navy for five months, with *Husky* and *Vison*, to strengthen their polyglot and weak anti-submarine escort forces in the West Indies, operating out of Port of Spain, Trinidad, especially in protection of the vital oil tanker routes. It was a time for summer white uniforms, fair weather most of the time, and apart from escorting the valuable tankers and the bauxite carriers out into the Atlantic, not hard to take; and a far cry from the miserable North Atlantic winters through which counterparts were suffering off Sydney. There were runs ashore, and rum was cheap and available. At first there were almost no U-boats that far south, since their pickings on the North Atlantic routes were still easy and more productive, and until the next year the United States was neutral.

* N.C.S.O. Sydney, June 1945, "A history of Naval Control Service at Sydney, N.S.", quoted in Dr. G.N. Tucker's *Naval Service of Canada* (Ottawa: King's Printer, 1952).

HMCS *Elk*, at *Cornwallis* Naval Base in 1944, with a flag indicating a submarine contact, for training, at her foremast head.

Elk's rather fancy prewar motor launch, retained for naval service.

On return in the spring, the British commander-in-chief, America and West Indies, sent this message to Ottawa: "HMCS *Vison* and HMCS *Elk* sailed today 10th May to return to you. Very many thanks for their cooperation which has been of great assistance to me. I only wish we could have refitted one or both for you."

Lucky *Elk* was involved in the same routine the next winter, and again in 1942. So she spent her summers off Halifax or Sydney, had a period in dock for repairs and for leave for her crew, and then spent the winters largely in the West Indies. Admittedly the U-boat menace increased in late 1941, but she neither attacked or even saw one for certain, although some depth charges were dropped on suspicious sounds occasionally, just to take some positive action. This was after all her role, codified in the escort instructions — "The safe and timely arrival of her convoy" — not dashing about killing submarines.

On her way back from the West Indies in 1942, at Bermuda, they encountered a freighter there, immobilized because she had lost her rudder, but loaded with valuable manganese ore. Although there had arrived a huge Dutch tug, the *Zuider Zee*, her master would not tow the cripple to Norfolk, Virginia, her destination, because of the danger of U-boats and no escort but little *Elk*. So an American Moran Towing Company tug was called in, half the size of the Dutch one, and it took them five days to reach Norfolk at 3 or 4 knots. Seaman Norm Harris remembers: "Ships were sunk all around us, but we didn't see a thing but wreckage, and plenty of it. The U.S. coast was littered with wrecks by this time."

In between these idyllic days in the south, life in the North Atlantic was much the same for *Elk* as for the others when she was serving there. A typical episode occurred on December 11, 1942: "HMCS *Elk* en route Cornerbrook via St. Pierre. HMCS *Elk* and USS tug *Buttercup* in collision en route. Minor damage to HMCS *Elk*, no damage to USS tug *Buttercup*." Apparently *Elk*'s electric power steering had failed when she was running parallel to *Buttercup*, and the warship had sheared into the tug. The official notification to Ottawa continued: "The primary steering had been defective for some time, and it had been the practice to switch to hand control when navigating in close water. The C.O. however appears to have been unaware of this, as it was his second day in command and his first at sea in *Elk*."

Problems like this were not unusual — the ships were too busy to be withdrawn for minor repairs; spare parts not easily available anyway for a sixteen-year-old American-built ship, and a continuous turnover of officers and crews.

Among the crew, *Elk* is primarily remembered for one of her officers, Lieutenant John Farrow, RCNVR, an established and respected Hollywood producer (he was later to direct part of "Around the World in 80 Days"), and married to the actress Maureen O'Sullivan. Being of English birth, John had volunteered for the Navy when the war broke out, and was eventually posted to *Elk* as one of her watchkeepers, before being recalled to Ottawa later in the war for publicity duties. When in Bermuda, Miss O'Sullivan and their infant son Michael came aboard for a visit, to everyone's delight and pride. The engineer officer was Commissioned Engineer Lou Somers, ex-RCMP Marine Division, as were several of the yachts' officers and petty officers. In his pre-war role he had at one time fired on a rum-smuggling schooner in which was serving the man who became his assistant engineer in *Elk*, and a close friend. Added to these notables, the first lieutenant wrote poetry, albeit a bit laboriously!

By late 1942 the wartime building program was catching up with the inshore and coastal escort ship requirements, and the problems of keeping these pleasure yachts at sea as convoy escorts were causing concern, and there were frequent breakdowns. In December, 1941, the first five wooden Fairmile motor launches specifically built in the inland boat yards such as Taylor's in Toronto and at Grew Marine in Midland, Ontario, for use on coastal anti-submarine patrols had arrived. And the corvettes and Bangors were appearing on the scene, some of them to be used off the east coast ports as well as in transatlantic convoys. The yachts held on for some time yet for the slow convoy sections out of Sydney, as escorts for coastwise shipping, and as examination vessels off the seaports. But on October 23, 1942, Ottawa signalled to the Flag Office Atlantic Coast: "All A/S Yachts are to be declassified to XV or training vessels as soon as they can be spared." But it was to be some time before they could all be spared.

HMCS *Husky* had an interesting first two years, starting with patrols off Halifax on July 23, 1940, fitted with the usual 4″ QF gun, twenty depth charges and two throwers for them. By September she was at Sydney escorting the early SC convoys from that port, most of whose ships had come down the St. Lawrence River or from northeastern ports to join the next ocean convoy bound for England. Sometimes a couple of these yachts were all the local ocean escort that could be provided. Other times there might be a lone Canadian destroyer such as *Ottawa*, or a British sloop like *Deptford*, and even on occasion an elderly cruiser such as *Caradoc*, a holdover from the First World War.

The shortage of suitable escorts was acute and continuing. Except on the rare occasions when a destroyer or sloop could be present, the others would have been scant and not very effective protection against even a modestly pressed-home U-boat attack. The allies were very fortunate that the Germans had so few ocean-going boats that none could be spared in the early days to roam the Canadian coastline. Another ten or fifteen boats at sea in those days off the coast would have been a disaster. When America entered the war in December 1941, and U-boats pressed their early advantage, the Canadians had two years of experience under their belts, plus more and more suitable anti-submarine escorts.

The routine in the early days was unchanging, and not very interesting. *Husky*, for instance, and another yacht or ex-government or RCMP vessel, if available, would sail from Sydney the night before the convoy was to leave, and patrol off the boom to ensure no U-boats were awaiting its exit. In the forenoon of the following day, the merchantmen would start to leave harbour, in single line ahead as they passed out the gate in the boom. Once in the open ocean beyond the headlands, each ship would move to take up her prearranged and numbered position, in columns and parallel to each other in a rectangular

HMCS *Husky*, ex-*Wild Duck*, "a warrior for the working day."

box-like shape, its extent depending on the number of ships. If there were only four or five, there would be two columns. But there could be as many as twenty to forty ships, as the Naval Control of Shipping Organization became better able to schedule shipping and organize for fewer but larger convoys, which were easier to defend than small convoys with one one or two escorts. After the ships were formed up, the two or three escorts would take up screening positions on either bow of the convoy, or ahead. Approximately 24 hours later the main convoy from Halifax, or Boston, or New York, would be sighted, and messages exchanged with its senior officer. He often sailed in an armed merchant cruiser in the early days, as defence in the mid-Atlantic area against the German pocket battleships and their merchantmen-disguised heavily armed raiders. Having shepherded the Sydney section in astern of the Halifax contingent, the yachts would receive permission to return home, where they would arrive the next day. Since the Sydney approaches tended to freeze over in the winter *Husky*, as with *Elk* was loaned to the West Indies station, with *Vison* as a running mate. There the three carried out vital patrols in the passages through the island chains. While *Elk* and *Vison* were required back in Canada by early May 1941, the Commander-in-Chief specifically asked that *Husky* be allowed to remain until mid-June.

In the meantime, in February 1941, *Husky* and *Vison* had been involved in an opéra bouffé episode, with a cast of the C-in-C, a Dutch gunnery training ship, and two Danish tankers chartered by Standard Oil of New Jersey. The two 9,000-ton tankers had been loaded for European delivery, since Denmark was under German pressures, and in early 1941 the United States was still neutral. But clandestine arrangements had been made with Standard Oil's Marine Superintendent, Captain Ryan, for the ships to be stopped on the high seas and "seized," with the assumption that the Danish crew would offer only token resistance (although some of them might still be anxious to return to their homes).

The operational orders contained a built-in contingency plan. The tankers *Christian Holm* and *Skandia* were to be seized by the cruiser *Caradoc*. If she did not appear, the interception was to be carried out by the Dutch ship *Van Kinsbergen*. If this ship failed to make contact with the tankers, the last line of defence was to be *Husky* and *Vison*, who would be expected to stop the ships and escort them back to Trinidad.

On February 5, Lieutenant Harry "The Horse" Freeland, the captain of *Husky*, reported sighting the tankers steaming toward the Venezualan coast. He promptly signalled their position to *Van Kinsbergen*. The ships were at that time about five miles outside territorial waters. Lieutenant Freeland accordingly ordered the ships to stop. As *Van Kinsbergen* was nowhere in sight, he decided to board and seize the ships to prevent evasive or destructive action by the crew, and a boarding party was sent out under Skipper H.D.G. Bould.

Chief Petty Officer Warren Cope, a shipwright from *Husky*, who had five years experience in Imperial Oil Company tankers (which had been equipped with 5,000 hp diesel engines) was part of Skipper Bould's boarding party due to this experience, and was given a .455 revolver which he had never seen before. The boarding party were not exactly experts. On the way over in the small ship's boat, he asked a seaman with a .303 rifle "Is that thing loaded?" The lad replied "No." "What's the use of that? You'd better put something in it." At which the seaman replied "But Warren, I don't know how." So Cope loaded it, and then said, "Now the gun's loaded, but for God's sake don't point it at me!", for the lad was detailed to cover the engineer when he went down to the tanker's engine room. Already, just as they left Husky, someone had let off a burst of Bren machine gun fire by accident, and that was enough to make all of them apprehensive.

To continue, and quoting from Skipper Bould's report to Lieutenant Freeland:

> 2. ... The sea boat left *Husky* at approximately 0615 and I arrived on board the *Christian Holm* approximately 0630.

3. Being that I had been instructed by you that the Danish flag was not to be struck unless it was necessary in the case of resistance being offered on arrival aboard the ship, I detailed one engineer and one rating to the engineroom to see that no moves were made toward scuttling the ship; one rating was sent to the lower bridge with orders to look aft so he could see all movements of the crew. I instructed the wireless operator that he was to leave his cabin, and not to use his set for transmissions, then I carried on to the bridge.

4. On arrival on the bridge, I instructed the Captain that he was to proceed to Port of Spain, then asked him all the necessary details such as number of crew, where he was from ...

5. At approximately 0630 I sent the following message to you by flashing light from the *Christian Holm*: "THE OTHER SHIP HAS STARTED IN AHEAD. MAY I FOLLOW NOW?" When the answer came in the affirmative, I asked the captain of the ship to proceed at full speed, and follow astern of *Skandia*, which he did.

6. After we had been under way for approximately ten minutes, I sighted *Van Kinsbergen* coming toward us ... As he approached, it could be seen that he had a signal up to stop. Both engines were stopped immediately, and then I saw they were sending a boarding party over to the ship. As their boat arrived alongside, I met the officer in charge of the party, and informed him that I had already a boarding party on board and had everything straightened up with the captain of the ship. But he had passed right by me and had ignored me completely, and went up on the bridge, and after he had his men placed he decided to speak to me, and asked me if I had searched the ship for arms and ammunition. I told him that being that my party was so limited, I had not had the chance to do so, but now he was on board if he would grant me permission to take a few of his men I would do so now. Permission was granted, and the search carried out ... I reported to the officer that there were no arms in the ship but two revolvers that the Captain held, and produced them to the Officer in charge ...

8. When I returned on deck from searching the cabins I was surprised to see that the Netherlands ensign was flying, and found out on my return to the bridge that it was flying under protest of the ship's Captain.

9. As soon as the engineers from the *Van Kinsbergen* had arrived in the engineroom, they informed my engineer that he was not needed any more, and that he could go back on deck. But he had been placed there, and stated that he would not leave there until he had received orders from his officer, which were given to him later by me.

10. I was asked by the Captain of the *Christian Holm* why the British flag was not flying instead of the Netherlands one, as I had been on board some fifty minutes before the *Van Kinsbergen* had arrived on the scene, and I informed him that we would not strike his flag, being that we were not at war with his country ...

12. After the ship had been anchored, we went to the Captain's quarters, and there the officer from the *Vans Kinsbergen* informed us that that was now ten ships that his ship had seized, much to the surprise of the ship's Captain and myself ...

In the *Skandia* much the same confrontation took place, to the extent that the boarding officer there, Lieutenant J.E. Harrington also saw the comic side when about 60 Dutch seamen boarded, complete with hand grenades, automatics, and so forth, quite ready to fight a pitched battle. In that ship Harrington's force of eight had hoisted the Canadian Navy's White Ensign, which the Dutch summarily struck and replaced with their own red, white and blue. Harrington then signalled by light to Freeland: "WHAT DO I DO NOW, FIGHT THE DUTCH?" Fortunately moderation prevailed, and Freeland replied: "LEAVE IT. WE'LL ARGUE IN HARBOUR."

As Freeland continued in his report:

> 4. ... On being informed by my officer in charge of the boarding party on board the S/S *Skandia* that the ships were being seized in the name of the Netherlands Government, and seeing the Netherlands ensign hoisted I made to *Van Kinsbergen* "DID YOU ORDER THE NETHERLANDS ENSIGN HOISTED?" Reply was received "I DID." I then made to *Van Kinsbergen* "*SUBMIT THESE ARE BRITISH PRIZES.*

On return to Port of Spain, tempers were, as Harrington says, "a little high, and the boys of *Husky* and *Vison* (probably forty in all) were all for taking on several hundred Dutchmen in the local pub. The senior naval officer was a perfect diplomat. He sailed the *Van Kinsbergen* forthwith and we enjoyed a night in harbour without any brawls! An aftermath, which could have been tragedy, occurred in *Husky*'s wardroom, when a .455 revolver, believed empty, was jubilantly fired and the slug buried in the wall about three inches from the Chief's head. This, of course, called for another drink!"

So this contretemps ended peacefully, and as the official historian says, "The important thing was that two valuable tankers had been added to the Allied merchant fleet." Everyone's sensibilities were hurt, and the C-in-C's report of March 5 to his superiors at the Admiralty, probably strikes the right final note:

> 2. I consider that *Husky* had reason to put boarding parties on board in view of the close proximity of the ships to Venezuelan territorial waters, though the *Van Kinsbergen* expected him to "report" only.
>
> 3. *Van Kinsbergen*'s anxiety was evidently to claim the prizes as so many more German ships to his own credit, and not with any view to claiming the ships as Dutch prizes ...
>
> 4. The whole operation was under order of *Van Kinsbergen* and the mutual friction and boorishness of the Dutch officers was very unfortunate.
>
> 5. With the exception of the flag incident, I consider that *Husky* acted correctly, although somewhat in excess of his actual orders, and that he showed initiative in boarding at the time he did; he could not risk one or both ships getting into foreign territorial waters.
>
> 6. I am informing the Commanding Officer HMCS *Husky* of my views and propose to regard the incident as closed.

Husky arrived back in Halifax on June 26, 1941, and went straight into refit at Lunenburg until August, thence onto A/S patrols there, and then around to Saint John for five months as an examination vessel. She alternated every three days with another vessel, stopping all inbound ships to ensure their legitimacy so their reception on arrival could be organized at their correct and appropriate berth.

U-boats were getting closer by the end of 1941, and in January 1942 they sank the first ship inside U.S. territorial waters, just off Cape Cod, the first of 360 merchantmen sunk off that coast in the six months after the United States had entered the war. The importance of establishing local convoys for protection seems obvious now, in that only 11 of those 360 ships were lost while being convoyed, a detail the USN could not cope with at first. Despite two years of Canadian expertise, and even proffered advice, the Americans' shortage of escorts was so acute that they were forced to requisition fishing vessels and even sailing yachts to serve as armed auxiliaries, most without anti-submarine Asdic, and only had ten of these in hand when they declared war on Germany. Even the Royal Navy, whose own resources were stretched to the breaking point, had to lend the USN thirty-two escorts to protect the east coast until American destroyers could be put into large-scale production. The USN also instituted, under Commodore Alfred Stanford of the Cruising Club of America, a patrol of sailing vessels, manned by the Coast Guard Reserve, and armed only with rifles and sometimes two or three light depth charges. These ships cooperated with the unarmed small private aircraft of the Civil Air Patrol and a few Navy "Blimp" airships. It grated on the USN's senior officers' sensibilities to suggest that they could learn from the British or Canadian experience only one hundred or so miles to the north before their war started, so all the Canadian hard-won lessons had to be relearned in the school of experience on their own.

After her West Indies tours, *Husky* still had her adventures at Halifax. While alongside at Jetty 4 in the dockyard at lunchtime one day, with a Dutch training submarine secured alongside, the elderly ex-American destroyer *Hamilton* was lying right ahead of them, warming through her engines. Someone opened the main steam valve in the destroyer, admitting steam to the engines, and the ship surged astern, parted all her lines, and rammed between *Husky* and the submarine, jamming the latter up against the next jetty and putting a large hole in her side, whereupon the submarine sank. Fortunately there was no loss of life, since her crew were all ashore at lunch.

In the summer of 1942, *Husky* was again escorting convoys, this time from Saint John. The ships sailing from here were bound as joiners to Halifax-Boston or reverse coastal convoys, or for ports to the south like New York, Bermuda or to the West Indies,. American escorts were still so short that in many cases they could only provide escort during the day, and the merchantmen had to anchor in protected bays at night, which in effect meant a 50 per cent blockade or reduction in traffic. What with fogs, gales, late sailings and changes in times of departure, the rendezvous were not always made, and *Husky* would be left to sort out what to do with her southbound charges, at sea by herself. Queries by radio were discouraged as attracting potential listening U-boats. Ending up once again as an examination vessel off Saint John, she too was sent across the Bay of Fundy as a tender for seamen training at *Cornwallis* in mid-1943.

HMCS *Lynx*, ex-*Ramona*, was a rather elderly vessel of 180 feet, having been built in 1922. She cost the Navy over $196,500 to purchase and to convert, and was only used sporadically until late 1942. In July 1943 she was sold for conversion to a merchant vessel. She had the usual 4″ gun, Asdic, fifteen depth charges, rails and throwers, and an old Lewis machine fun. Her crew consisted of four or five officers, and provision for up to thirty-five men.

First assigned as a training vessel at Halifax for the seamen school there, she was sent in September 1940 to Sydney, but broke an engine crankshaft on the way. It was almost impossible to obtain spares for her 18-year-old engines, so after some delay she returned to Halifax on one engine for repairs, which could not be completed until July 1941, as there were other priorities demanding the dockyard and civilian ship-repairers' attention, and an elderly ex-yacht was not high on the list. *Lynx* was then despatched to Gaspé for

HMCS *Lynx*, ex-*Ramona*, fitting out at George T. Davies' yard at Levis, Quebec. Note the absence of a deck gun at this point.

river patrols for two months, and she again broke a shaft off Rimouski. After repairs this time, the river was closed, so she went to Shelburne for A/S patrols off the southeast Nova Scotian coast, and for use an an examination vessel. In January 1942, she performed her one valuable service by rescuing the entire crew of the S/S *Empire Kingfisher* which had struck an object at sea off Cape Sable, and although anchored when *Lynx* arrived, sank shortly after.

Before the end of that January, she was hunting a submarine which had torpedoed the Norwegian tanker *Alexander Hoegh*, also off Cape Sable. The crew had been rescued this time by an American schooner. Due to further damages caused by shallow-set depth charges when hunting the submarine, she was plagued by further engine troubles and an inability to obtain spares, so was finally condemned for further sea service in April 1942. *Lynx* lay alongside at Halifax awaiting disposal, and at one time it was even proposed that she be expended as a gunnery target. She was eventually sold to W.D. Branson of Toronto, for $7,500 for conversion at Boston to a fruit carrier. Not a real success story, although the *Kingfisher* survivors might disagree!

HMCS *Moose* was a smart, small (130 foot), reasonably new (1930) yacht, that caused no problems and served most of her time at Sydney as an examination vessel or on local patrols right to the end of the war. Her gun was removed during 1942, as it was felt there would be little need to use it on the inbound Allied merchantmen, although depth charges were left in her racks in case U-boats came that close to Sydney, as they later did. Due to her smaller size and the added weight of her armament, she was not used in the open Atlantic as a convoy escort.

As HMCS *Moose*, but not yet commissioned, in 1940, Note the Red Ensign rather than the naval White Ensign. On commissioning trials, ready for war.

As an examination vessel, when a freighter was stopped, the examination officer, one of the yacht's normal serving officers, would go over the side into one of the dories manned, usually, by two Newfoundland seamen. It was considered that they made the world's best small boatmen in the rolling seas of the open Atlantic. In the seas often running high, in snow, gales, fog and on pitch black nights, and with no lights allowed, they took considerable risks. When they arrived alongside the wall-sided freighters, surging up and down as much as twenty feet beside their rough steel hulls, it took considerable small-boat handling skills to get just close enough for the officer and usually one other armed seaman to jump for the rope and rung "jumping ladder" suspended over the side from far above without being caught between the 300-pound dory and the hull, or dropped into the often freezing sea. It was no sinecure for these new Reserve seamen, often completely unfamiliar with this ocean until their first draft to sea in little ships like *Moose*. But all her men returned safely, although frequently wet, and with the occasional scraped fingers or bruised knee or hip.

Aboard *Moose*, and in other yachts, in gales, when green seas washed aboard, and even in heavy rains, wires would be shorted, lights would go out, and the men would get strong electrical shocks when they touched any metal fittings. The electrical artificers were kept busy tracing faults, and even running new wiring temporarily. *Moose*'s engine room chief was also an ex-RCMP Marine Division Engineer, and his two motor mechanics were ex-fishermen rumrunners of the RCNR. The cook, too, was an ex-fisherman, but reportedly a good one, and he is remembered fondly for his ability to serve up something hot even in the worst of bad weather. Better a fisherman, used to the sea, who could produce some good plain cooking, than a gourmet cook who could not cope with the rolling and pitching, often wet, galley.

Reindeer was very much the average armed yacht — she did her job, got into the odd scrape, served for a few months off Halifax as an ocean escort, then out of Sydney, and then in 1941 was sent on Gulf patrols out of HMCS *Fort Ramsey* at Gaspé. A timetable kept by Seaman W.R. Craig gives a clear picture of the typical routine of these yachts at Sydney and Gaspé:

> Sailed for Sydney: 5 June; Patrols: 5 - 9 June
> At Sydney: 9 - 11 June; Patrols: 12 - 23 June
> At Sydney: 23 June; Patrols: 24 - 28 June
> At Sydney: 29 June - 1 July; Patrols: 2 - 4 July
> At Sydney: 5 - 6 July; Sailed for Gaspé: 7 - 8 July
> At Gaspé: 8 July; Sailed on passage: 9 July
> At Port Daniel, Que. 10 July; Patrols: 11 - 12 July
> Anchored Miscou Bay: 13 July; Patrols: 12 - 15 July
> At Gaspé: 15 July; Patrols: 16 - 18 July
> Anchored 7 Islands: 18 July; Patrols: 19 - 20 July
> At Gaspé: 20 July ... etc., etc., etc.

In August *Reindeer* was at Rimouski, Gaspé, Mingan, Clark City, Gaspé, and then went into mid-Gulf to the Magdalene Islands, and thence to all the ports once again. It was a great chance for ship handling and learning pilotage, but one certainly was hardly "seeing the world"! When going through the Strait of Canso one night, between the Nova Scotia mainland and Cape Breton Island (and in the days before the causeway and locks that exist now), the ship was run hard aground. As Craig tells it:

> "We were in our bunks at the time. *Reindeer* had bunks made of iron pipe frames and canvas, with pipes secured to the deck and the deckhead, our hammocks spread out on them. It was a blinding snowstorm; not blowing snow, as it was very quiet, but a soft wet snow. There was a heavy bump, and the leading hand hit the deck, saying "Jesus, they've run us ashore!" Then "All hands on deck" was piped. On deck there was no panic, although one ERA was below packing his kit ... he wasn't going to leave his personal belongings behind.
>
> The first thing I saw was the bank of earth in front, about twice the height of our ship. The navigating officer assured us everything was O.K. He said the ship was in reverse and the tide was on the rise, so in a while you could feel her come loose. The Asdic did not fit so well after that, as the dome was twisted to the side.

Life, though, had its ups as well as downs:

> They would stop engines, I imagine on a cod bank, and jig for cod. When one of the Newfoundland seamen on board figured they had enough for a chowder, we would move on. That night he would borrow the use of the galley and made up a pot of cod chowder, with potatoes, celery, Carnation milk, peppercorns, onions, and a big blob of butter. I can still taste it!

Convoy escorting was often difficult, as a quotation from *Reindeer*'s commanding officer's report of September 23, 1942, shows all too clearly:

> (E) At 0850Z/20 Sept. assumed station DE #1 and zigzagged 40° each side of mean course until gale force winds abeam rendered it impossible. At 1520Z/20 secured alongside Bowater's Wharf at Cornerbrook.
> (F) S/S *Surewater* (a tanker) caused considerable trouble, panicking at the slightest excuse, keeping bad station, and making smoke, etc.

HMCS *Reindeer*, ex-*Mascotte*, at *Cornwallis* in December, 1944, as a seamen's training ship.

Results from a favourite pastime — O/S Coates of *Reindeer* and a caught cod.

> (G) Neither of these two ships could read Morse and had to be contacted at sea alongside by megaphone, a distasteful operation when rough sea, high swell and darkness were present. It is submitted that the officers on these small lake vessels should be required to learn enough Morse to allow them to read the two-letter groups and signals contained in MERSIGS before being allowed to obtain convoy.

Reindeer too eventually ended up as a training vessel at *Cornwallis* for A/S classes by mid-1943.

Apart from *Sans Peur*, HMCS *Renard* was the most spectacular of the armed yachts. Built along World War I destroyer lines, with two funnels and equipped with high-speed turbines, she was the only yacht to be fitted with torpedo tubes, which had been retained from the early interwar destroyers *Patriot* and *Patrician*. In her case she sailed under the Navy's White Ensign from Halifax to Quebec to be fitted out, referred to as HMC YACHT *Winchester*. After recommissioning as HMCS *Renard*, she was on duty out of Halifax by September 1940, as a convoy escort out to a point south of Newfoundland. Due to *Renard*'s age (at over twenty-four years, and having already served in one war, in the USN), and her narrow beam, there were often problems of breakdowns, and she was a poor sea boat in bad weather, even though she could still do 30 knots if pressed. She was also employed about twice a week for a day on torpedo-firing trials for the original torpedo and anti-submarine school in the dockyard at Halifax. And on more than one occasion she was used as a high-speed target-towing vessel. During 1941 and 1942 she was employed continually up and down the Nova Scotian coastline.

With such relentless time at sea, by the winter of 1943-1944 *Renard* needed an extensive refit, and a costly one. This included opening up her turbines and renewing some blades, which might or might not be available. And when chipping off old paint, seaman found that their chipping hammers sometimes went right through her thin and now rusty plates. So by February *Renard* lay alongside a jetty at Halifax under only a small "care and maintenance" party, and later was towed to a small cove in the upper harbour, while the Navy pondered if there was any further use for her at a cost that was reasonable, and at an expenditure of dockyard time that could be spared. In August, 1944 *Renard* was declared surplus to the Navy's requirements, and placed with War Assets for disposal in November. In January 1945, she was sold to Wentworth MacDonald of Sydney, who hoped at least to use her engines.

HMCS *Vison* was a bit of a rarity among the yachts. She was relatively new, being only nine years old, and was a very handsome vessel, even in naval colours, with a fine raked bow, a short, solid, oval funnel, and a good turn of speed which she maintained right to the war's end. Perhaps all this should be taken with a grain of salt, as *Vison* was the author's first ship as an ordinary seaman, and that always causes great pride, or sometimes great hatred. She was fitted with only a 12-pounder, 3″ gun, but on either wing of her bridge had two pairs of .5″ Browning modern water-cooled machine guns, great if she were ever attacked by aircraft, which she never was! When fired they made the most appalling noise, and promptly filled the small space in their area with empty cartridge cases. They were used from time to time at *Cornwallis* by trainees from the gunnery school to fire at targets towed by Beaufighter aircraft.

One of her early commanding officers, Lieutenant W.E. Nicholson, an experienced ex-merchant seaman, wrote to Colonel Jones who had brought her up from the United States:

For the first year she operated out of Sydney on the Newfoundland, west Atlantic and St. Lawrence on convoy and patrol. A dreadful winter and we were 86% of the time at sea. Out five days and in one night and away again. Not once was the ship unable to proceed. Bad weather or not, *Vison* could make it. Her quickness and efficiency gave us quite a lot of amusement. *Vison* is always away from the jetty and heading out to sea in a matter of minutes, while other ships require several hours notice.

She gets more manoeuvring in a week than a normal yacht would in a year. I poke her around corners and into all sorts of awkward places, even in a full gale. When getting underway we scorn tugs as they only get in the way. 'Round comes the stern on the engines without going ahead a bit. Or we stick that wonderful bow against the jetty and play her around. The bow and her shallow draft are her trump cards ... She has no inertia, and her engines are finger tip control (from the bridge). Behaviour at sea is excellent. She can go full speed into a moderate gale and never ships a sea. The designer attained the impossible: the bow wave breaks well aft, the entry is perfect. Down she goes; the flare and sheer get her at once, and up she comes like a gull. The bow never goes under. (This is a bit of an exaggeration, for there is a photo of *Vison* with ice over the top of her A/S hut above the bridge due to flying spray.) It is just for pounding that I ease her down, and I can make good headway in a heavy gale at "Slow both". I have dropped a lot of depth charges, and barring a few light bulbs, no damage at all. The secret is the shallow draft and the quick get-away. Most ships avoid a 50 foot setting on the charges. *Vison* can let go a pattern at that depth and it just gives her a kick in the pants, and on she goes all the faster ...

Vison did also drop her depth charges in anger. Her attack on a U-boat occurred in October 1942 when on escort duty with two lakers from Cornerbrook to Sydney.

When almost within sight of Cape Breton, the laker *Waterton* was hit by one or possibly two torpedoes, even with *Vison* patrolling ahead of the ships, and an RCAF Canso flying boat right overhead. Despite chasing down the bearing from which the torpedoes appeared to come, and dropping two charges at once to scare off the attacker or at least drive the U-boat deeper and thus blind, and later attacking with a six-charge and a five-charge pattern, no firm contact was gained with the U-boat. So *Vison* returned to protect *Omaha*, the other laker, who, although the convoy speed up to then had been a difficult 6½ knots, suddenly found she could make 9 knots, to Nicholson's annoyance. *Omaha* reached safety, but *Waterton* sank very quickly, leaving her deck cargo of rolls of newsprint littering the sea, looking, according to Sub-Lieutenent J.B. Fotheringham, "for all the world like rolls of toilet paper. It was most frustrating to realise that despite ideal weather conditions, as well as the presence of aircraft, that we were unable to prevent such an event."

Operating conditions in the mouth of the St. Lawrence river estuary were always difficult for Asdic, as the mixture of fresh and salt water caused distortions of the Asdic beam, and the usually choppy waves hid any periscope "feather" or wake. In November 1942, *Vison* again dropped charges on a possible U-boat contact, but then decided maybe it wasn't. The same had occurred back in July in the Gulf. Altogether a busy five months, actually attacking U-boats.

Her first patrols had been in the Gulf, and then she was sent together with *Elk* and *Husky*, to the West Indies for patrols in the winter of 1940-'41 and again in 1941-'42. On the way down in December 1940, just to demonstrate all too tragically that the only enemy was not German U-boats, an able seaman was lost overboard in heavy weather. Returning from Trinidad in early 1942, *Vison* stopped at Bermuda to bring back some trainees for the RCAF. She had left Trinidad with eleven days fuel supply, which should have been ample for the four or five-day trip. So as to avoid depleting the stocks in Bermuda, she took on no extra there. Only four hours out of Bermuda for Halifax she ran

HMCS *Vison*, ex-*Avalon*, still looking very yacht-like, at Cornwallis, in 1944.

Vison's foc's'le after a winter crossing of the Bay of Fundy.

Vison's Asdic hut and bridge, completely covered in ice from the spray thrown up.

Success — a boat-load of survivors from S.S. *Waterton* coming alongside *Vison*, October, 1942, in the Cabot Strait.

And failure — the tanker *Camden* sinking off the Oregon coast, when *Sans Peur*'s towing was unsuccessful.

into gales and then snowstorms. The wireless shorted out and was useless, and there were no sun or star sights for three days. Finally the navigator briefly caught a morning star sight, and they reached Halifax late one afternoon, eleven days out of Trinidad. The C.O., then Commander W. Geoff Shedden, hastened to report to Captain (D) in the dockyard, Captain G.C. Jones, and following exchange ensued:

> Capt. Jones: "Where have you been? I've been worried!"
> Shedden: "You've been worried, sir? How do you think I felt?"

On another occasion, when in a small Gulf harbour for a day, Lieutenant Nicholson, took several ratings ashore, armed with "pike poles." Able Seaman A.J. Wigmore describes their foray:

> "We proceeded down the beach some distance, where Mr. Nicholson instructed us to drive these poles into the soft sandy beach, and continue to do this at intervals of about five feet, moving them up and down vigorously until we got a hard bottom and a "bonging" noise. When this happened, several other ratings were to dig until they found what made this peculiar noise. Much to our surprise, but not to his, we unburied a number of wooden rum kegs full of contraband, and took them back aboard. Needless to say, in *Vison* we "Spliced the Main Brace" more often than most of HMC ships!"

Reindeer ploughing into heavy seas in the Gulf — normal routine.

Many hours were spent patrolling off Sydney, enough for severe boredom to set in. This could be a temptation for a young, adventurous, sub of the watch. Sub Lieutenant Fotheringham describes how a dull afternoon could be alleviated:

> "I did a standing Middle and Afternoon Watch, and S/LT Graham Ferguson, the other Sub, did a standing Forenoon and First Watch. One forenoon I joined him on the bridge to pass the time of day, and found him relieving his boredom by seeing how close he could come to the buoys which marked the turning points of our patrol. These were large buoys, with an iron ring which must have been five feet in diameter protecting the light mounted atop the massive buoy. I was duly impressed with Graham's skill as we approached, when the buoy, disturbed by our bow wave, swung away from the ship and back again in time for the protecting ring to contact our ship's boat swung outboard on the port side. The ring went through the forward half of the boat like the proverbial knife through butter, leaving the bottom half of the boat dangling most forlornly. I succeeded in vacating the bridge before "Nick" made it up the ladder and hence added nothing to my nautical vocabulary that day!
>
> Nick, for a Reservist, was very sensitive about the sanctity of the quarterdeck, but had a much greater "thing" about the wardroom table. Nothing was allowed ever to be placed on that beautiful mahogany table except a meal. With only four officers in the ship, Graham and I had to stand watch-and-watch in harbour, which failed to endear John Bovey, the other Sub, to us, who declined to join the group, understandably as he had a wife in Sydney. On very special occasions, when Graham and I wished to double date, Nick would come aboard in the evening to allow us a run ashore together. On one such night he came into the wardroom to find on the table — horrors — an unopened package of cigars which Graham had just received from his father, as well as two bundles of Bovey's laundry. In response to an angry outburst from Nick, Graham picked up his cigars and stepped out onto the quarterdeck and dropped them over the side. He calmly returned, picked up the largest of the laundry bundles and repeated the process. Nick watched with speechless rage as Graham picked up the second bundle of laundry. The final outcome is lost to memory, but is was some weeks before the two Subs had another run ashore together!"

Obviously Ferguson's life in *Vison*, despite its problems, created a love for the Navy in this wartime 'VR officer, for Fotheringham's letter continued:

> Graham Ferguson aspired to being a playwright, and moved to the U.S. after the War. While Captain in command of *Shearwater*, 1967-1970, I received a copy of his will, requesting that a sum of money which he had left should be used for providing officers and men of the RCN no better purpose than a convivial glass. I was glad to partake, but was saddened that his end came so early from a cause which he must have anticipated.

Captain "Pop" Fortheringham remained in the Navy until the late 1970's, latterly in NATO postings at Richmond, Virginia, and John Bovey also later rose to become a Captain, RCN, and Director of Naval Intelligence. "Nick" Nicholson returned the merchant navy after the war, where Captain Fotheringham encountered him again when in command of the destroyer *St. Laurent* at Alert Bay, Vancouver Island. It was by Captain Fotheringham's report, a wonderful reunion.

Like the others, *Vison* went around to the Annapolis Basin and *Cornwallis* for use as a sea training ship for seamen and A/S ratings.

Conseco, arriving at Halifax, after her purchase from John Hubbard by Philip S. Ross of Montreal. Lost by fire off Halifax within a year, no war-time photograph exists of *Otter*.

CHAPTER 9

NAVAL SERVICE HEADQUARTERS REGRETS ...

The only yachts to be lost on active service were *Otter*, in March 1941 off Halifax, and *Raccoon* in September 1942 in the Gulf of St. Lawrence. In both cases, there was heavy loss of life; in *Raccoon*'s case there being no survivors.

Otter was commissioned for service at Halifax on October 4th, 1940, as a tender to the sea training school there, and alternated on that job with anti-submarine patrols off the port. She was not the first *Otter* on patrols off Halifax, for HMS *Otter* was stationed at Halifax in 1755-56 during the wars with France over Fort Louisbourg and Quebec. It was a severe winter in 1940, and our *Otter* had already experienced a minor short-circuit fire in her twenty-year-old wiring during a storm on her way up to Montreal for conversion. After several escort trips with convoys outbound from Halifax and slow convoys from Sydney, and more short circuits, she was taken into the dockyard at Halifax in January 1941 to have some of the wiring replaced. Escorts were too scarce and too valuable to be spared, and those serving just had to make do with things as they were. Many yachts were only modified just sufficiently to take the extra seamen, with cabins on the foredeck cut away to make room for a gun, and racks mounted on the afterdeck for depth charges. The equipment that came with the yachts was not always appreciated. Witness a memory of Petty Officer T.C. Carey of Dartmouth:

> When we took *Otter* over everything was the same as it was with the original owner. I had to sign for everything, including the medical kit. The box was like a large trunk. When I opened it, I quickly padlocked it again, and turned it over to the Medical Officer ashore. I wanted no part of that stuff. I was issued a proper kit.

Obviously Carey wanted only the "proper" service-issued medical outfits, not something fancy from rich American peacetime cruising.

On one early trip with a convoy to Newfoundland, a storm blew up, and due to wiring problems — old wire cut off but not removed, and shorts — *Otter* was "a blue flashing light" in the dark and the senior officer chased them home. Few of these minor fires were reported, partly, no doubt, because the C.O. did not want his ship withdrawn from service, and partly because in view of the harsher realities of torpedoings taking place in the eastern and central Atlantic, a few fires in temporary warships would not be given much weight by harried naval commands ashore. The problem with *Otter* was that apart from her steel hull, her decks and cabins were of wood, and not the steel of regular warships, so the risk of fire was rather more crucial. And being ex-pleasure yachts they were not as strong as all-steel warships, hence subject to unusual "working" strains in heavy seas. One officer was convinced she had broken a vital strengthener in her hull that winter.

On March 26, 1941, *Otter* was sent out from Halifax to the vicinity of the Sambro Light vessel, about seven miles off Chebucto Head, the entrance to the harbour, to meet and escort the British submarine *Tailsman* into Halifax. A strong southwest wind was blowing, with intermittent rain, and there was a choppy sea with a heavy swell, causing *Otter* to roll and plunge considerably as she idled very slowly through the seas. At 0830 *Otter*'s C.O., Lieutenant D.D. Mossman, RCNR, who had gone to his cabin only a few minutes earlier, heard the ship's fire alarm ringing, and shortly after shouts of "Fire!" Rushing to the bridge, he discovered flames already coming up through the bridge deck. Masses of black smoke were belching from the engine room. The chief motor mechanic reported that the engine room was completely enveloped in flames. The cause of the fire was never definitely established, as none of the engine room staff who were on duty as the time survived. The fire apparently started with the electric generator, but it may once again have been due to faulty wiring nearby. Since the generator itself was on fire, the electric pumps could not be operated, and in a short time all the hand extinguishers had been emptied, and the sand thrown on the fire was ineffective. The fire spread rapidly to the wooden Captain's cabin above, and to the wireless office. There were no hand-pump facilities on board and the fire soon raged so fiercely it was not considered feasible to form a bucket party.

The commanding officer gave the order for the magazine, containing the shells for the gun and rifle ammuniation, to be flooded, and a distress message to be sent out. Unfortunately only part of the message got away before the radio batteries caught fire. This was doubly unfortunate, as the inquiry afterward revealed that the only merchantmen that appeared soon on the scene had an inoperative wireless, and the Sambro light vessel, within sight of the whole affair, presumed an alarm message had already been sent by the *Otter* or the merchantman. After the confidential books had been locked in weighted bags and thrown overboard, the order to "Abandon Ship" was given at 0855. The ship's crew got away from the vessel in an orderly manner, depite the thick smoke and flames, the crew of forty-one distributed between two small sea boats and a life raft. The waves were 15 feet high, it was still raining, and a strong wind was blowing. The lifeboats were quickly swept a considerable distance from the ship. Then it was seen that Lieutenant Mossman was still on board, ensuring no one had been left behind, in the best tradition of the sea. So the port lifeboat put back to his rescue. The number of men crowded into that boat, however, handicapped her crew severely, and one of the ratings, as they laboriously rowed back past the life raft, volunteered to take his chances with those clinging to the raft so as to relieve the overcrowding and allow the remainder more room to row. Two others followed him and thus the lifeboat was able to reach the ship and take the captain on board. The three who gave up their places in the relative safety of the boat, going into the water that was only a few degrees above freezing, to join others they could see were up to their chests in water, were Able Seaman T.K. Guildford, Ordinary Seamen J.J. Slavin and Wallace O'Hara. O'Hara did not survive his ordeal on the raft. These three received a "Mentioned In Despatches" for their selfless sacrifice of place, a modest reward indeed for such a courageous action.

It was two hours before the survivors began to be plucked from the sea. In the meantime the heavy seas were continually sweeping over the men on the raft until most of them had died from exposure. Then the in-bound Polish merchantman S/S *Wisla* appeared, as did the submarine *Talisman*, who set about rescuing the survivors, a most difficult and dangerous business in the seas running. While the starboard lifeboat was coming alongside the merchant ship, it was capsized, throwing the occupants into the heavy sea. All except three were carried beyond reach of the ship. These three were hauled on board by lines and rope ladders, but it was twenty minutes before the ship could regain her position to attempt the rescue of the remaining men who had contrived to make their way back to the water-filled boat. The merchant captain attempted to lower two of his lifeboats to expedite the rescue work, but the ship being light and with high sides, each was smashed against the ship's side before this could be accomplished. In this part of the rescue operation, the board of inquiry particularly noted the gallantry of one of *Wilsa*'s seamen who risked his own life to try to bring aboard numbed and dying seamen from the lifeboat. Two died after being hauled aboard.

It was even more difficult for *Talisman* to rescue those in the water, and in the end, she was only able to pick up four. A submarine lies very low in the water, with wide "saddle tanks'' projecting out to either side, smooth and rounded, into which air is forced to bring her to or keep her on the surface. Men of her crew, all in lifejackets, and fastened to fittings on the narrow ''casing'' running along the centre of her exposed hull, would only be able to throw lines to those washed up against her sides, and on one occasion the life raft she brought alongside was caught by the tanks when the submarine rose to a sea and capsized. A fifth survivor was lost in this way and could not be recovered. The first lieutenant of *Talisman* was also commended for his particular efforts to rescue survivors. *Otter* herself sank at 1115, just as rescue operations were being completed.

In all, of the crew of forty-one on the *Otter*, nineteen lost their lives — two officers, one chief petty officer, and sixteen seamen and stokers. Apart from the three who gave up their places in the lifeboat, three others were also Mentioned in Despathces, two of them posthumously. It was a sad and heavy loss, not to the danger of the enemy they felt they faced, but to the ever-present danger of the ''steep Atlantic stream.'' *Otter*, in fact, was to be the only ship to be lost by fire of the twenty-four Canadian warships lost during the war.

Raccoon's loss was more directly attributable to the U-boat war. She was one of the first yachts in service, few changes other than the essential ones being made internally. As one seaman described her accommodation: ''Posh was the word!'' By June 22, 1940, *Raccoon* was serving as an examination vessel off Halifax, three days out and three in. There was always something of a swell running, even on sunny summer days, frequently with fog or haze, particularly in the Halifax approaches; the nights were usually very black, and in those days at sea no ships dared show any lights. On one occasion a large pilot boat rammed *Raccoon* amidships, almost rolling her on her side, but putting only a large dent in her solid steel side. More serious was a near miss, in daylight but in very hazy weather, by the battleship HMS *Royal Sovereign*, which would have been the end of *Raccoon* if she had been hit by the 26-thousand-ton monster used for protecting convoys.

By August 22 *Raccoon* too was off protecting convoys. She carried a Scottish chief motor mechanic who was also a piper, and he would play up and down the boat deck when troopships were leaving harbour. In December, when offshore weather was at its worst, she was withdrawn for a refit for two months at Pictou, and another fourteen months later, in February 1942, at Liverpool, N.S. In the spring of 1941 she was on patrols, usually from Chebucto Head off Halifax southwesterly to Egg Island.If duties, time or the weather allowed, she would take shelter, and the crew would jig for cod. On one occasion, after anchoring for several hours, when a rating was sent below to call the engine room crew to start up again, the lower spaces were found to be flooding as the sea poured in through a valve that had given way. While the valve could be isolated and closed, the ship's pumps soon clogged up with loaves of bread that were floating about from the flooded victualling stores, so that the area had to be bailed out in the ancient manner by buckets and a chain of seamen. And when the anchor was eventually to be raised, it was found to be firmly wedged under some obstruction on the bottom; the anchor winch burned out, and the offending anchor could not be raised by hand! Eventually a tug had to be sent around from Halifax to break the ship loose. Not a big success. She then went to sea with A/S classes, as well as patrols. There was a nasty accident, and a court of inquiry, when the ship's cook, Alfie Field, was shot in the arm by a careless jetty sentry at Halifax, costing him his arm. By the spring of 1942, *Raccoon*, like other yachts, was escorting in the Gulf of St. Lawrence, and between Sydney and Newfoundland, leading a busy but normal escort vessel life. But events were beginning to catch up with this erstwhile peaceful and unwarlike existence.

As a result of increasing pressures around the British Isles, the U-boats were moving farther out into the mid-Atlantic, where convoys were weakly defended, the escorts were

HMCS *Raccoon*, ex-*Halonia*, at Sydney, N.S., hustling past in-bound freighter.

less experienced, and pickings were easier if you were a skilled and resolute commander. The seizure of the French Atlantic ports in mid-1940 also meant shorter voyages to the hunting grounds, more time on station and, of more direct concern to Canada, an ability to roam farther afield. By March 1941, the U-boats were instituting "wolf pack" attacks, now coordinated by their shore-based commands in France rather than by the group commander at sea. These were usually on the surface and at night, where they were extremely hard to see. Asdic was of no use, and suface radar was still in its infancy. Losses became staggering for the Allies, but it was not entirely one-sided. Radar was now being fitted in all the escorts as they could be spared to go into dockyard for its fitting, and sets became more reliable. The corvettes and other ocean escorts were arriving in increasing numbers from the builders, and their crews were gaining in hard-won experience at U-boat hunting, lead by the RN and RCN officers who by now at least had their ship-handling down cold, and could concentrate on the A/S tactics as they evolved by trial and error, or were developed in the anti-submarine school at Liverpool under Captain Robertson. Even the Reserves, very shaky at first in both ship-handling and thinking tactically in the midst of a U-boat battle, were catching up when given firm and skilful leadership by the Regular Force and ex-Merchant Marine officers.

By May 1942, the St. Lawrence escort force consisted of a total of three corvettes, five Bangor class escorts, one or two yachts, and three Fairmile motor launches. With the large number of ships passing up and down the St. Lawrence through the Gulf to and from the open ocean or Halifax and Sydney, this force was barely enough for the almost continual demand for escorts.

Then, almost suddenly, war came to Canada's shores. On May 12, U-533, Korvettenkapitan Thurman sank two merchantmen, *Nicoya* and the Dutchman *Leto* less than fifty miles northwest of Gaspé, at Cloridorme, Quebec. No ship had been sunk by enemy action in the inland waters of Canada since 1813. The battle of the St. Lawrence had begun — not a major, decision-making battle, but one all too visible, right on Canada's doorstep. As Joseph Schull puts it in his *Far Distant Ships*, "The battle was no longer a remote tale echoing from the dim reaches of the mid-Atlantic. From the U-boat pens of Kiel, Wilhelmshaven and St. Nazaire it had advanced to within 200 miles of Quebec City." Because the prime minister, Mackenzie King, was concerned that the Canadian populace would be in a panic if they knew, and insist on a major reallocation of forces to protect their homes, and because a release of the news of sinkings within the St. Lawrence basin would help the German U-boat headquarters assess the progress of their marauding wolves, no word of the location of any St. Lawrence attacks was to be released to the press. Tales of U-boat crews coming ashore and found later with theatre tickets in their pockets are unsubstantiated and highly unlikely, but show the freedom the Navy was all too ready to think they enjoyed, partly as a result of the RCN's largely unsuccessful hunts for these submarines in home waters. This was, in reality, still a minor area of war operations, and quite correctly, the Navy refused to be diverted from the main theatres in the open Atlantic.

On July 6, three ships were sunk off Cap Chat, and on the 20th, another off Cap de la Madeleine, with the loss of ten crew members. Despite extensive searches, including from the air, no U-boats were even seriously damaged, again probably due to very poor Asdic operating conditions. In July and August U-boat reinforcements began arriving, under U-517 Kapitanleutnant Hartwig, sinking a ship northwest of Newfoundland and two more in the Strait of Belle Isle on his way down the Labrador coast. From then on, for a year, there was almost always one and sometimes as many as three or four U-boats in the St. Lawrence or its approaches.

On September 2, U-517 fired at a convoy escorted by the corvette *Weyburn* in the outer Gulf, sinking the SS *Donald Stewart*.

On September 3, the war came to *Raccoon*, when at 9:40 p.m. local time she had two torpedoes fired across her bow, just below Matane as she came down river with a convoy.

Next day, *Raccoon*'s Headquarters was able to give a full description of the event to COAC, so that action could be taken, and so that all U-boats were plotted and hunts ordered, if possible:

> Following received from *Raccoon* on arrival: First torpedo passed 25 feet ahead of me. Second torpedo passed under me forward of bridge. Both within 3 seconds, at 0240 3rd and tracks clearly visible due to phosphorescence. My position 1500 yards abreast of leading ship port column, course degrees 240. Course of both torpedoes 285. Fired from my port quarter. Ran up track 6000 yards dropping depth charges but no contact. Afterwards I steered closing course zigzagging and resumed station.

On September 6, *Raccoon* was again up river, to join part of the escort force for convoy QS 33 from Quebec to Sydney. It consisted of eight merchantmen in two columns about 200 yards apart, protected by *Raccoon*, the corvette *Arrowhead* (as senior officer), the Bangor *Truro*, and two Fairmiles, Q065 and Q083. (Most of the material in this section is taken directly from the summary prepared by the Directorate of History after the war.)

They passed Father Point at 4:30 p.m. local time, travelling at 9 knots, (about 10 miles per hour) the speed of the slowest ship, but either aided by current or held back by the flooding tide as time went on. *Arrowhead* was on the port or left beam of the convoy, *Truro* on the starboard beam, ML Q083 right ahead, ML Q065 astern, and *Raccoon* on the port quarter of Q065, behind her and to her left, in the direction it was anticipated an attack might be mounted. That night there was a light swell, and a following wind of about 10 miles an hour. The sky was completely overcast, it was very dark, and *Arrowhead* reported visibility at only half a mile. With the experiences of the last few days, all ships were fully alert and ready for any eventualities.

Despite this readiness, at 10:10 p.m. the leading ship in the left column, the Greek SS *Aneas* was suddenly torpedoed, and shortly afterwards sank. *Arrowhead* saw nothing at that time, and casting back towards the stern of the convoy, illuminated with starshell. She thought she saw the submarine (U-165 Hoffmann), and certainly saw *Raccoon* clearly, in her station on the port quarter, zigzagging and also searching. This was the last time that *Raccoon* was sighted. She carried no radio telephone, contact by Morse radio was laborious, and to use a light to communicate at night would have been suicidal with U-boats about.

The convoy forged ahead without further incident for almost three hours, the ships only occasionally catching the faintest glimpse of a vessel nearby as a slightly darker shape against the black sky and water. All anyone knew was where their ship was supposed to be, the mean course of 72°, at a speed of 9 knots. At about 1:00 a.m. *Arrowhead* temporarily pushed ahead of her station to make a sweep ahead and to port of the convoy, away from the coastline, and in the direction an attack could reasonably be expected. At 1:12 a.m., when about 10 miles northwest of the Martin River light, near Rivière la Madeleine, several ships of the convoy heard two explosions in rapid succession followed by a three-second blast of a ship's siren. At the same time two columns of white water were sighted on the convoy's port quarter against the black night. No special significance was attached to this event other than it was thought that *Raccoon* was carrying out a depth charge attack, and perhaps required assistance. *Arrowhead* immediately put about and swept down the port side of the convoy until well astern of *Raccoon*'s supposed position. No contacts were made and there was nothing to report. Although somewhat concerned or mystified as to what was going on, the commanding officer of *Arrowhead* reasonably thought that,in the dark, he had just missed *Raccoon*, whom he considered quite competent to look after events in her area, and he returned gradually to his own station. However, he did report this turn of events by radio to the area commander at Gaspé, who, still trying to clarify the situation after dawn on the 7th, seven hours later, signalled *Raccoon* to report her present location. There was no reply. *Raccoon* had been blasted out of existence and her remains and entire crew lay at the bottom of the river, a victim of the U-165's torpedoes. Since Hoffman and U-165 did not survive his tour of operations in U-boats, it can only be surmised that he caught a glimpse of *Raccoon* in the dark from his conning tower, and thinking her one of the merchantmen, fired at least two torpedoes at this passing shape, set to run shallower than those she had fired four days before.

The convoy and the remaining escorts pressed on, but by 5 p.m. the next afternoon had lost three more merchantmen to torpedoes within a minute, off Cap de Rosiers, in the approaches to Gaspé itself. In all it was a 50 per cent decimation of the convoy, plus the loss of one of the escorts, one of the worst records of the war, although not on a par with the sheer numbers of ships lost in some of the mid-Atlantic convoy battles.

Four corvettes searched back the track of QS 33 over the next two days, as well as RCAF aircraft, and carried out extensive searches, without result. Their final signal was a sad one:

> TO: NOIC Gaspé, NCSO Rimouski
>
> FROM: *Weyburn*
>
> Arrival Rimouski HMCS *Weyburn* and HMCS *Chedabucto*. No sign of *Raccoon* encountered.

The only concrete evidence of *Raccoon*'s fate was found later on the shore of Ellis Bay, Anticosti Island, several miles to the northeast. This consisted of a portion of her wooden wheelhouse and a bundle of naval signals. A few days later a life ring was found bearing the name *Halonia*(*Raccoon*'s prewar name), and the body of Lieutenant R.H. McConnell.

That was a sad finale for Russ McConnell, a noted University of McGill football and hockey player, who had been offered a professional contract, but elected to join the Navy instead. No other crewmen were ever found. They lay beneath the grey cold waters of the St. Lawrence, with the remains of their little warship.

A tribute to the torpedoed *Raccoon* in the Halifax "Herald", September, 1942.

CHAPTER 10

TRAINING AT CORNWALLIS

Although after early 1943 most of the yachts were relegated to training and patrol duties at HMCS *Cornwallis*, life there was not necessarily dull. The Annapolis Basin on which *Cornwallis* still fronts is an almost landlocked harbour, some 3 miles wide near its entrance and 12 miles long. It was an excellent site for small-boat work and for training, except for a tremendous tidal range of about 28 feet at spring and fall periods, which created difficult currents for sailing, and even problems in getting away from the up-stream side of the jetty in a pulling or powered boat if the tide was flowing strongly outward. But within the Basin there was more than enough room to moor the eight yachts eventually stationed there. They could only occasionally lie alongside the very long jetty extending out from the base due to insufficient room for them all. Anyway, with the huge rise and fall of the tides, lying alongside the jetty was no sinecure, for either the ship's lines had to be continually eased off as the ship dropped down with a falling tide, or continually hauled in as they became slack on a rising tide. This latter was no easy matter if a strong wind was tending to blow the ship away from the jetty, or the current hold her off, keeping the lines taut, whereby the ship would gradually leave a gap of 10 to 20 feet between her side and the jetty, a major annoyance to returning officers, or to the ship's company who had to be turned out to haul her back alongside again, or were awakened by the noise of the capstan winches that must be run to exert enough pull to do the same job mechanically.

So most of the ships elected to lie at permanent moorings or anchor a hundred yards off the jetty when in port, which was by no means very often. Anyway, the same tide problems occurred in their two other ports, Digby, just inside the Basin entrance, and across the Bay of Fundy at Saint John. In addition to the yachts and to a few smaller tenders, also moored at *Cornwallis* were HMCS *Saguenay*, HMS *Buxton*, sometimes HMCS *Hamilton*, and often one or two submarines for training. *Saguenay* had been torpedoed in the bow early in the war and repaired. Then she was in a collision, rammed by a merchant ship at sea, and so badly damaged in the stern that she was not worth repairing, so was permanently moored at the base for familiarization and gunnery training, since she could carry out all her functions except steam away. *Buxton* and *Hamilton* were two of fifty twenty-year-old ex-American "Town" class destroyers, acquired by Churchill in exchange for U.S. base rights in British colonies in 1940 when the RN was desperate for anti-submarine destroyers. For a year or two, like the yachts, they filled a vital necessity for escorts. But although very fast, they were bad sea boats, being unusually narrow-beamed and inclined to be top-heavy with extra guns, radar and radio gear added for war service. Hence, as soon as they could be spared, they were withdrawn from ocean escorting. *Buxton* was on loan to Canada, but since she could not steam, like *Saguenay*, she was used for static training, mostly for stokers. *Hamilton* had started her Second World War career with the RN, but was returned to Canada in 1942 to join six others that Canada had retained. She was used for sea training, torpedo firing and drills, and coastal escorting, in much the same role as *Renard*, back and forth to Halifax and *Cornwallis*.

An idea of the tides is gained by the fact that on one occasion the author climbed a gangway up to *Hamilton*'s upper deck as she lay alongside the base jetty at high tide, only to step ashore onto the same jetty about six hours later from the wing of her upper bridge at low tide!

Although the Basin was well protected, once a ship passed out the Digby Gut which gave access to the Bay of Fundy half a mile from Digby town, the sea and the weather could be much less hospitable. Like the Bay of Biscay, the Bay of Fundy has a foul reputation for storms, dense fogs, heavy and confused seas, and generally bad conditions. It faces, more or less, the open Atlantic, between the south tip of Nova Scotia and the coast of Maine, 45 miles wide at the mouth, and tapering funnel-like to a river's width at the upper end, 140 miles away. It is this taper that tends to contribute to the enormous tides, and due to this surge of water in and out twice daily, strong contrary winds soon build up choppy, heavy, seas. In the summer this was uncomfortable but not insurmountable. In the winter, even in the Digby Gut, freezing spray and green seas soon caused heavy ice to form. *Hamilton* and some of the less stable yachts such as *Reindeer* tended to roll when there was a modest swell, and a 2 or 3-inch accumulation of ice on their upper works could have been fatal to their stability. One of the goverment patrol vessels, about the same size and age as the yachts, *Bras d'Or*, capsized off Newfoundland with the loss of her whole crew probably due to just this accumulation of ice in heavy weather.

But the bay did provide, when not too rough or foggy, an excellent training ground for new-entry seamen, experiencing their first taste of life in a "warship" (albeit an ex-pleasure yacht), and for classes of a practical nature in gunnery target firing and in submarine hunting. These exercises continued even in poor weather, since sea time was better than having these new entries sitting in their barrack blocks ashore. But if it became very rough, most of the yachts would seek shelter or return, since usually 60 per cent of the ship's company promptly became seasick! The determination of what constituted "rough" often varied widely between the weather-bitten old Merchant Navy C.O.s and the memories of the seventeen to nineteen year-old trainees! The C.O.s tended to feel it had to be dangerously rough before it was worth coming in. The new entries felt that the C.O.s chose the absolutely worst days to go out and delighted in torturing their charges. As one seaman phrased it, "If medals had been given for seasickness, I would have had the Victoria Cross."

Aircraft were periodically provided to tow targets for anti-aircraft firings and radar tracking, and there were occasional reports of submarines off the mouth of the bay that required prompt investigation and hunting. There were no U-boat kills there, but then no ships were sunk within the Bay of Fundy either, so maybe that was in a large part due to the continuous patrolling and exercising by the yachts. One job that was constant throughout most of the war, and usually allocated to the armed yachts, was the escorting of the large CPR steamer *Princess Helene*, the passenger ferry between Saint John and Digby. Since she had a good turn of speed, if times were quiet an escort would not always be provided. But if U-boats were about, and particularly after the sinking of the SS *Caribou*, the ferry plying between Sydney and Port-Aux-Basques, Newfoundland, in 1942, the *Princess Helene* usually had the company of an armed yacht, just in case, combining patrol and training for her crew.

The training program in which the yachts became involved at the base was essentially in two phases. The first was a two-week period at sea for all new entry seamen and stokers as soon as their eight or ten-week basic course was completed. They went off, twenty or so at a time in two or three of the ships, into whichever yacht or destroyer was scheduled to receive them. A new class finished every two weeks, so there was a continuous turnover. Each of these new entry training ships had a small permanent crew of officers, petty officers and key training seamen and technicians. When the trainees joined, the ships would sail, often on a Saturday or Sunday, for patrols, escorting exercises in the Bay of Fundy, and for general sea familiarization around the coastline. There, two yachts might take each other in tow, fire at home-made targets with their 4″ gun or with machine guns, or even have a first chance to fire the ship's rifles and revolvers (a blown-up and tied

Obviously ready for a run ashore, the ship's company of *Elk*.

A ship's company in normal harbour dress, a mixed bag. The crew of *Husky*, Lt. J.P. Kiernan, RCNR, on the left in command.

The 1915 vintage 4″ gun of *Reindeer*.

The same gun, after a winter's patrol off Sydney in 1942.

condom or "safe" made an excellent pistol and rifle target at the end of 100-foot of cod-line). Or they would anchor and hoist anchor, sometimes by hand, referred to as "handraulically"; lower, row and re-hoist the ship's boats; drop the emergency Carley floats, designed to hold the crew if a ship's boats could not be got away in a torpedoing. It was a bit disconcerting one time in *Caribou* to drop the Carley float from its rack and see it plunge into the sea and not resurface! "It gave one to think!" said one seaman, assigned to it as his abandon ship station. There were a multitude of evolutions and exercises to go through in only two weeks that, it was hoped, would stand the trainees in good stead when they shortly went off to other warships and the serious business of the war at sea in the Atlantic, or even farther afield. It was a humdrum but busy and absolutely vital job, that contributed materially to the professionalism that the largely inland-born Canadian sailors soon developed at sea.

Much later, in February 1945, when it was suggested to the commanding officer at *Cornwallis* that maybe he could do with fewer of the vessels, he replied to his admiral at Halifax:

> *Ambler* and *Caribou* are still usefully employed, and used continually for target towing, compass and helm instruction, officers' Divisional Course training, and periodically to accommodate day classes for seamanship training. These ships are quite suitable ... and could not be replaced.

The other role in which the yachts participated was in the field of technical training for the schools located at *Cornwallis* — the anti-submarine school, the gunnery school, and the mechanical training establishment (MTE). In these cases, students under training, seamen, petty officers and even junior officers would be taken to sea, perhaps on two or three occasions during a long course, to practise the theoretical skills learned in class. Hunting the submarines like L23 or *Seawolf*, or the occasional elderly Dutch submarine with the yachts' rather elementary Asdic; target shoots, sometimes even with the luxury of a dockyard-made towed target, or an aircraft-sleeve target towed by a fast Beaufighter for realistic anti-aircraft practice. These exercises might be for only a day, or could go on for a week or more. In fair weather it was a great life, wherein the participants felt that at last they were getting down to serious business after months of classroom study, for many of the students had not seen the inside of a classroom for ten or twenty years. But in winter cold, snow, gales, ice and tremendous seas it was an appalling introduction to the life at sea for greenhorns.

It was then of very little use to the poor Asdic operator, cooped up in his tiny cabinet high above the deck, with headset on, unable to hear a thing over the wash of the sea, wracked by seasickness, and badgered by an unfeeling, unsympathetic, and apparently immune jerk of an officer, who appeared to think this hideous torture was teaching him anything at all. For the gunner, soaked to the skin or half frozen, on a rolling, surging, spray-washed deck, trying to manhandle a 40-pound live shell into a swaying breech, and unable to see any target over mountainous seas, he could only hope that the "real thing" on larger warships would be better, or at least more realistic. It was, maybe, better than being cooped up in a classroom, and it was certainly realistic. And too often it was all the practical training there was available. On the other hand, in the summer and fall, there were glorious, warm, sunny days, with only a slight swell, the submarine could be followed at two miles distance, half the crew were allowed off watch to lie on the upper deck to sun, because the C.O. was having an afternoon snooze, and the nineteen-year-old sub-lieutenant officer of the watch was no more interested in stirring up trouble during his watch than he was in the antics of the A/S training class carried for the day. At the end of the afternoon the yacht would slip into Black's Harbour, or into St. Andrews or a dozen other comfortable hideaways, where the crew could fish, or row ashore to see some real people, or just lie in the evening shadows and play a mouth organ and tell stories of home, or what they hoped to get as their next draft to sea in a warship or even in a soft shore appointment.

By the end of March 1943, *Ambler*, *Caribou*, and *Beaver* were at *Cornwallis* for sea training for new entries; *Vison*, *Elk* and *Reindeer* for A/S school training, and *Husky* for both, as required. Repairs had to be done as they went, or in slips at Saint John, where there was a very large dry dock, dating from the First World War, and capable of taking battleships out of the water, or by going around the coast to Shelburne or Halifax. Sometimes the very high tides of Saint John could be used to advantage. On one occasion, *Husky* ran through some fishermen's nets, entangling them in her propeller shaft. The dry

The problem with massive tides. HMCS *Ambler* alongside at Digby, N.S., at low tide. Six hours later, her hull would tower over the jetty, meaning constant mooring line tending by the Duty Watch.

Two views of HM S/M *Seawolf*. Above in a formal portrait, and exercising with an armed yacht in the Bay of Fundy in 1944, on the surface for a change.

dock was occupied, so she could not be hauled out, and with a fouled prop, the authorities were reluctant to send her around the coast. So she was moored in the Market Slip at Saint John, which dried out entirely at low tide. As the tide dropped, *Husky* settled on the hard sandy bottom of the slip, and then the engineers could walk up to her propeller shaft and cut away the offending rope. A neat and cheap maintenance arrangement, that was to be followed on several occasions when needed.

On another occasion when *Caribou* was sent around to Halifax to escort *Ambler* who had been encountering engine difficulties, the two ships were delayed by several hours with *Ambler*'s engine problems. In the Navy it is considered a heinous crime to be late at port of arrival for a ship's "Estimated Time of Arrival" or ETA. The term "estimated" was considered to be the real time, unless the C.O. had a good reason for being late. Even being early was considered a sign of incompetent navigation calculations. So in mid-1944 when *Caribou* was obviously going to be several hours late on her ETA at Halifax, the C.O. decided to "cut the corner" as they came up toward the marked channel leading the fourteen miles into the harbour. This channel was guaranteed clear of any possible mines, the areas beside it were unknown. So *Caribou* and *Ambler* cut across the open area, to pick up the swept channel further in, and arrive more or less on their ETA. Next day, based on some information, the minesweepers were ordered out to sweep the unknown area through which the two yachts had passed, and there they swept up a considerable number of German mines, to the considerable discomfiture of the ships' companies in retrospect. And the two ships were not even fitted with degaussing cables, designed to protect ships against magnetically detonated mines which were found. Sometimes luck was on their side.

Caribou was adopted by the town of Burnaby's IODE. These associations were always useful, for the civilians would send comforts and small items not provided by the naval service. Warm winter clothing was always most welcome, particularly such items as long-sleeved sweaters, scarves, mitts, woollen hats, and leather or suede wind-proof vests. Some of these items were available from the Navy, but only one per man, so when they became soaked as seas washed over the decks, and even the bridge, spares were always a valuable asset. Cigarettes were nearly always included in each package, bearing in mind that they were quite strictly rationed. Even for the non-smokers these were very welcome as a trading item. For a package or two of cigarettes, one could get a messmate to stand an extra weekend watch out of turn, or obtain an extra chocolate bar or two, a share of the smoker's rum ration, or even the carefully guarded telephone number of a worthwhile date in St. John's or Sydney. Money was fairly scarce (a seaman was paid about $40 a month in basic wage), but barter was a way of life, developed to a fine art. And the packets from the adopting towns and cities gave the officers and men a "normal" association with folks back home. Many of the cities and even villages were very generous in their support of "their" ship, sending or paying for even major appliances such as washing machines and even pianos (although not in the armed yachts!).

Mail censoring was a continuous, dull, time-consuming and nuisance job, done by all the wardroom officers on a rotation basis, which nobody appreciated. In *Husky* one of the better crewmen had an ongoing correspondence with his wife, as well as with a girl in Halifax with whom he had been having an affair. Somehow he mixed up two letters, and his wife got the wrong letter. Of course there was hell to pay, and the man could not be convinced that the censoring officer hadn't deliberately switched letters. Eyeryone was aggrieved. Most letter-writers were careful not to say where they had been, or what their equipment did, or how the war was going in their area. One had to be careful not to give away to the families at home items that might find their way into the local paper, and hence be fed into the German information net, such as the sinkings in the Upper St. Lawrence. No courses were given, or even any serious guidance to the censoring officers, so common sense was the only real guide. And, anyway, the system was forever being circumvented by phrases known only to the writer and the readers. Such comments as "Had a chance to thank Cousin Mae for her Christmas present last weekend. They have a new car" would mean the seaman was in, say, Pictou, Nova Scotia, on a particular day, but the censors did not know what the phrase meant, so it was usually left in.

In this routine of day-after-day training in the same areas, there was always boredom to cope with. On one occasion, Lieutenant John Ewart, the commanding officer of *Reindeer*, decided to relieve the idle hour by experimenting in dropping *Reindeer*'s sea boat at full speed, rather than at the normal 5 or 6 knots. This required very careful handling of the davits and boats' falls (the ropes by which the boat was suspended from the davits) to ensure the boat hit the water smoothly and level. Unfortunately, as *Reindeer* swept along, galloping over the swells, the foremost falls at the bow of the sea boat jammed. In the struggle to clear them, they let go, the bow hit the water, and the boat was torn in half. Consequently the officer in charge in the boat found himself in the Bay of Fundy with an able seaman and six new entry seamen! No one was hurt, but there was some explaining to do, and the base commander was not necessarily told *all* the details of the accident!

Another time *Reindeer* was exercising in the Bay of Fundy when heavy fog rolled in. Their submarine returned to Digby, but *Reindeer* was scheduled to go to Saint John, the entrance to which was a fairly narrow channel, requiring careful navigation, especially since the ship's radar was out of service. But then the *Princess Helene* came along. She travelled that route rain, fog, storm or darkness, regardless of the weather, very rarely even slowing down. She was heard passing by, with her foghorn blasting intermittently. *Reindeer* simply fell in behind the sound and picked up her wash, following it neatly into the safety of Saint John.

Another time *Husky* had been exercising with the submarine *Seawolf*. On return to Digby, *Seawolf* was secured outboard and alongside *Husky*, where a party was soon under way in the wardroom. Soon the X.O. of the submarine invited all the participants, the officers and their girls, aboard his boat "for a small smash." So in the dark of evening they

Reindeer hauled out at the Dartmouth dockyard, winter 1941-1942, when the St. Lawrence was frozen over and there was time for repairs.

C.P.R. ferry *Princess Helene*, which the yachts spent endless days escorting from St. John to Digby, and back again.

all proceeded down the gangway from *Husky* to *Seawolf*. The gangway was narrow, and ended just aft of the conning tower structure, where a "manhole" or deck hatch led to the bowels of the submarine. There was no barrier to stop anyone from walking straight off into the sea. The X.O. led the way, and on arrival on the submarine's deck turned sharp left and down the hatch, with no concern for the girl who was following. She walked on and straight over the side, falling onto the saddle tanks and sliding into the dirty water of Digby harbour. Fortunately she was rescued by a watching submarine crewman.

These submarines, on loan from the Royal Navy or the Dutch Navy, and obviously not commanded by their experienced senior submarine commanders, were not immune to the problems that the armed yachts faced. The elderly submarine L23 in particular ran into, was blown onto, or even scraped along various yachts with which she operated. The records of *Husky*, *Sans Peur* and *Renard* are studded with solemn, time-consuming reports of minor and not quite so minor scrapes and crashes. The officer in charge at Digby reported in one investigation:

> A further unfortunate feature in HMS L23 is that her forward hydroplanes do not fold in as in more modern S/M, and which represent a considerable danger to any ships with which she comes in contact.

To which an unsympathetic director of the operations division in NSHQ replied:

> If L23 is such a menace with her hydroplanes, I suggest it is not very intelligent to berth her alongside a delicate ship like *Sans Peur*. Why ask for trouble?

In June, 1944, *Beaver* was withdrawn from training duties, and until September was used as a Naval transport between Halifax, Sydney and Newfoundland. The days when there were no other ships available and the armed yachts had to carry the load were past. It was noted as well that defects costing over $6,000 to make good and make her fit for

The elderly RN submarine L 23, used for training at Halifax and *Cornwallis*.

service would be required, and seemed unwarranted. So on October 17, 1944, *Beaver* was paid off and removed from service, being towed by tug around to Sydney, Cape Breton.

As the war at sea wound down, during the late winter and early spring of 1945, the armed yachts were used less and less, as fewer new entries arrived, and fewer long courses were started. By early summer, the war in Europe was over and the fleet was fully manned by experienced seamen and officers. Mackenzie King had made a political commitment to release a considerable number of servicemen, and only to provide a few ships for the end of the war in the Pacific. The three seamanship training yachts, *Ambler*, *Caribou* and *Reindeer*, were ordered decommissioned on July 20, 1945. The three technical course training ships, *Elk*, *Husky* and *Vison* followed on August 4. *Renard* had gone before, and initially it was decided that *Sans Peur* would be retained, as she was barely twelve years old, large enough to be useful for weapons training, and in excellent shape.

The end came with a flurry of messages, little honour or ceremony, but with none of the secrecy of their beginnings some five and a half years earlier. Usually alongside a wharf in Sydney harbour, the lines would be made fast by a much reduced and rather quiet crew. The very young or elderly lieutenant in command would speak into the voicepipe to the wheelhouse for the last time "Midships. Ring off main engines. Finished with engines." All hands would be mustered on the upper deck shortly after, and the C.O. would order "Pipe the 'Still'." Plaintively over the water, maybe barely heard above the sound of the heedless traffic and activities nearby, would come the long rise and fall notes of the Bos'n's call, and the White Ensign at the stern, the Blue Canadian Ensign at the jackstaff at the bow, and the long narrow red and white commissioning pennant at the masthead would come slowly down. "Sound the 'Carry On'," and the C.O. would hold out his hand to the signalman for the pennant and the last White Ensign to be flown by "his" yacht. With luck another seaman or officer would get to keep the Blue Ensign, and their absence in the last stores' muster would simply be written off. So HMCS *Elk*, *Vison*, *Husky* and half a dozen others quietly retired from the naval service and Hitler's War.

Sans Peur was kept busy up to and beyond the end of the war. She was continuously exercising with submarines L23, *Seawolf*, *Unseen* and *Upright*, as classes of specialists continued their training. For some time there was an expectation that the war in the Pacific would last for quite some time, so A/S experts would still be required. Canada, or at least the Navy, was not privy to the atomic bomb secrets, and while our governmental commitments for the Pacific were much reduced, we were prepared to make quite a contribution in destroyers and escort carriers and cruisers, one of which was with the British Pacific Fleet already. But the events at Hiroshima and Nagasaki ended all these discussions, and the Pacific war came to almost naught for Canadian ships.

In January 1946, as *Cornwallis* began to close down as a major base, and since two brand new "Castle" class corvettes were allocated there for training duties, *Sans Peur* was sent around to Halifax, to be a tender for the Reserve Division there, HMCS *Scotian*. In early 1946 she was down the coast at St. Margaret's Bay, exercising with the submarine *Token*, and doing bathythermograph water temperature trials. She spent some of her time, as all the yachts had, in difficulties! She had a small hole punched in one plate by the ever-dangerous L23 at Reed's Point, N.B. She provided accommodation for the crew of the surrendered German U-boat U-190, and was used for experimental and ex post facto researches as a commissioned ship in the Royal Canadian Navy.

In November, 1946, *Sans Peur* was sent off to escort the RN submarine *Token* as far as Bermuda. Despite the fact that war was over, a couple of messages from *Token* brought sharply into focus the concept that the only enemy in the Atlantic in the long run was the sea itself:

> My position, course and speed: 38° 15′N, 64° 43′W, hove to. *Sans Peur* in company. Intend remaining hove to until weather eased to prevent any further damage to *Sans Peur*.

A day later *Sans Peur* herself reported in; life was ending rather as it had begun, and had been for five years of war: "2 boats badly damaged, one rating slightly injured. Situation in hand. Proceeding on passage."

On November 9, 1945, the Duke of Sutherland asked if *Sans Peur* would be available for repurchase but naval service headquarters replied that she would be retained permanently. Permanently turned out to be a very short time, as is often the case with such governmental remarks. On February 14, 1947, the Department of National Defence was told she was surplus to requirements. The postwar financial pinch was already being felt, and only valuable and useful warships could be afforded in the small peacetime fleet. The Navy suggested that the Duke of Sutherland be asked if he was still interested in repurchasing his former yacht. In a few days he replied that he was not — he had already gone elsewhere.

So, like all her contemporaries that had survived, *Sans Peur* was offered for sale, and was sold for $90,000 on June 6, 1947, the last yacht to be given up.

It had been a tough war, and they had been called upon to do far more than their designers or their builders had expected of them, or allowed for. One might legitimately apply to them the remarks of E.J. Chambers, writing in his history of the Dominion Marine Fleet, and referring to the few little ships of the Provincial Marine on the Great Lakes at the outbreak there of the War of 1812.

> Its work had, perhaps, not been very brilliant. But military operations absolutely depended on its preservation. During the critical months, the Candian Marine Militia offered a pretty fair security for the Army's water transport. It probably saved Upper Canada.

If one were to substitute 1940-41 for 1812-13, and the armed yachts for the Marine Militia, a better and more honourable tribute would be hard to pay.

Sans Peur, renamed *Trenora*, her first name, at Monte Carlo in 1971, once again a yacht, but available for commerical charter.

CHAPTER 11

AFTERMATH AGAIN; SALE AND DISPOSAL

Apart from the loss of the two yachts *Otter* and *Raccoon* to enemy action and wartime misadventure, four yachts were decommissioned from naval service before the war ended, as already mentioned. They were *Lynx*, *Grizzly*, *Renard* and *Beaver*. Then, as the war reached its last stages, the other surviving ex-yachts were declared surplus to requirements and sold off whenever buyers could be found. So we shall follow these gallant little ships as they passed from their naval grey paint to, in some cases, rather bizarre peacetime existences. For convenience we will follow each ship to its end, in the order of its release from the Navy.

The first to be declared unfit for naval patrols and the North Atlantic and be decommissioned was HMCS *Lynx*, on April 23, 1942. And her disposal provides a ludicrous example of how not to accomplish a simple job — dispose of a vessel no longer needed.

At first it was presumed at the coast that she would be destroyed, any valuable parts removed, and the hulk sunk offshore. So all movable stores and fittings were removed: steering gear, engineroom auxiliary machinery, telegraphs, heating systems, toilets, anchors and cables and so on. This slow process, having no priority in an extremely busy dockyard, generated a spate of complaints from the Navy to the Treasury Office salvage officer that the elderly and useless vessel was taking up valuable dock space. Then on November 3, John Simon of Halifax offered $100 for her, delivered to his iron and metal scrapyard in the harbour. The low bid, he said, was because she was of little scrap value, and men and cutting gases were in very short supply.

Commodore C.R.H. Taylor, NOIC Halifax, wrote the supervising stores officer (who technically owned the wreck): "I am very anxious to get rid of *Lynx*, but there appears to be something fishy about this offer ... It looks to me as if he (Simon) was using the Navy to establish a right to the foreshore" (his plant was in fact across a public beach and a railway track from the water).

There followed considerable waffling about the low price, and then Ottawa sent this message to the Commanding Officer Atlantic Coast:

> Do you recommend *Lynx* be used for a full calibre shoot? Alternatively, recommend a not too conspicuous place where she could be beached.

It was eventually agreed to expend her in a gunnery target practice shoot, but before this could be organized in the press of more urgent events, J.P. Porter and Company of Halifax offered $3,000 for her; they intended to cannibalise her for another of their vessels. Then, to everyone's joy, William D. Branson of Toronto offered $7,500 for her, at the dockyard. The amount was tendered in full on July 14, 1943 and *Lynx* turned over on July 22. Mr. Branson had to pay another $1,509 for the stripped supplies and stores to be reacquired and put back aboard.

With the tremendous losses of merchant ships due to the war, and almost all shipbuilding committed to warships or deep-sea replacements, any ship was valuable, and was snapped up by those businessmen who needed ships for their trade, which they must try to continue. Mr. Branson was in the fruit and vegetable importing business, and as soon as *Lynx* could be given a complete overhaul and made relatively seaworthy again, she was put into the banana-carrying trade between Mexico and Toronto. Despite this seemingly innocent pastime, at one stage, while in a Caribbean port, she was embroiled in the trade war between the famous United Fruit Company and their equally tough competitor Standard Fruit. Someone "person or persons unknown" opened poor old *Lynx*'s sea cocks and flooded her engine room, sending her to the bottom in the shallow water alongside her dock. She was raised and returned to fruit trading again. For a few years after 1951 her use was sporadic, and she passed to various owners, under such names as *Elena*, and *Samana Queen*, owned by Captain N.G. Manessis of the United States. By 1953 she had become the *Rican Star*, owned under the name of the Rican Star Line and registered in Puerto Lima, Costa Rica, although the line's head office was in Dallas, Texas. She was no longer in Lloyd's Register, nor in the American Bureau book for some years. She then reappeared in 1958, now owned by the Northland Navigation Company of Vancouver, who applied for Canadian registration and certification, for trading up and down the British Columbian coast. Quite naturally, the shipping authority in Ottawa had some searching questions about her reliability and seaworthiness, since she was now almost 40 years old. Northland could not satisfy the authorities and she was refused registration. She was then sold to the Canrica Trading Company and in 1962 was resold to Australian interests.

From hearsay evidence only, it seems old *Lynx* was then used in the fresh shrimp trade between Australia and her Pacific customers. At long last, in 1967, she was finally lost at sea, two hundred miles southeast of Sydney. She had seen a great deal of the world from the initial construction as a leisure yacht for Mr. Schiff, the New York banker in 1922.

As noted before, HMCS *Grizzly*, decommissioned on June 17, 1944, was sold for only her scrap value on March 3, 1945, to the Victoria firm of Capital Iron and Metals, and broken up for whatever value could be recovered.

The next group of disposals fell to the lot of a rather unusual Cape Bretoner, Wentworth Neil Macdonald of Sydney, Nova Scotia. He was a well-known enterpreneur in the area, and a description of him from the Sydney marine historian Captin John P. Parker, MBE, gives as clear a picture as any:

> His main occupations were coal mines, which were always in difficulties, and buying yachts, which he converted at small expense to operate along the coast. You can imagine that a great deal of his effort was spent in persuading the Government to provide subsidies, especially as he lived and died a red-eyed Tory.

Another local, a Catholic priest, remembers that "most of his boats disintegrated in Sydney Harbour, to the great disgust of the city fathers. Two or three were an eyesore to the patients in St. Rita Hospital, until they sank in the end." As recently as 1979, alongside the disintegrating remains of Went Macdonald's old wooden pier, running quite a distance out into Upper Sydney Harbour, behind the modern Wandlyn Inn, could be seen the funnel and upper bridge of two of his postwar purchases, settled onto the bottom. They are not ex-armed yachts, but apparently much the same happened to some of them too. In all, after the war he bought fifteen warships from the government. Macdonald picked up the venerable yacht *Renard*, surplus to naval requirements in August 1944, and bought by him on February 6, 1945, the first of seven armed yachts he was to acquire. He had planned to use her as a power plant, as her turbines were still serviceable and powerful, at one of the coal mines he controlled at Mabou Mines, on the Gulf of St. Lawrence side of Cape Breton. His idea was to convert *Renard*'s boilers to burn pulverized coal from the mine, and use her turbines driven thereby to drive electric motors to provide power to run the mine's machinery. But on closer study, local fishermen convinced Macdonald that the exposed harbour at Mabou, open to strong gales off the turbulent Gulf, would make the plan unfeasible, as *Renard*'s hull was in such poor shape.

In fact, Macdonald nearly did not get her in the first place. The terms of her release from the naval service to Crown Assets Disposal Corporation stipulated that she must first be made available to any other government service if wanted. The RCAF advised that they wanted her as a bombing target, rather the way the Navy itself had wanted to use *Lynx* as a gunnery target two years before. But the financial wing of the Treasury decided that her sale to Went Macdonald at a scrap value of $5,000 outweighed her use as a destructable target. So she never left Sydney, and apparently just rusted out alongside. Until 1955 she was still listed in Lloyd's Register of Yachts; but in that year she was removed, under the section describing vessels broken up or lost. So *Renard* had, in fact, been of last use to the Navy.

Another vessel released in October 1944 and bought by Went Macdonald's Margaree Steamship Company on January 7, 1946, for $5,000 was HMCS *Beaver*, the largest and oldest of the yachts. Despite her age and rundown appearance, she was still operational, and large enough to be of some practical use to Macdonald in his shipping business. She was sufficiently converted to make a few commercial "package freight" and passenger ferry trips to western Newfoundland. She was not continuously in use, as his endeavours waxed and waned, and eventually was reported as sold, undoubtedly for scrapping, in 1956.

Macdonald also bought *Reindeer* on October 30, 1945, and her very simple bill of sale is included in the exhibits at the back of this book. Apparently he made almost no use of her beyond a few passenger-carrying trips around the Gulf and over to western Newfoundland. *Reindeer*'s register simply runs out in the early fifties, apparently abandoned or scrapped by Macdonald.

HMCS *Wolf*, who spent her entire naval life patrolling on the west coast of Canada, was in very good shape at the end of the war when declared surplus on May 16, 1945, only eight days after the end of the war inEurope. True, the Japanese had by no means given up in the Pacific, but their Navy was mostly on the bottom, or more than fully involved in trying to prevent the USN and the British Pacific Fleet breaking further into their once vaunted "co-prosperity sphere." There was no longer a threat to Canada's west coast. So, on July 15th, 1946, *Wolf* was sold for $7,500 to Gulf Lines of Vancouver, for conversion and use in their passenger and small freight trade up the Pacific coast. Many of the small ports and habitations up that rough and isolated coastline are on islands, or on inlets from the sea, and many are not even served by roads because of the mountain chains running within a few miles of the sea. For access to the smaller ports, and with no great mass of passengers or freight to move, *Wolf* should have been ideal, and served for many useful years. But through a tragic accident she only lasted a year.

Gulf Lines took her in hand, and had her fitted with new diesel engines, to replace the ones originally fitted thirty-five years before, which had carried her through two wars. She was certified to carry 202 passengers, and a crew of sixteen. These were of course day passengers, and only a small number could be accommodated in the few cabins available in a 336-ton, 146-foot vessel. She carried about one ton of general cargo for distribution up the coast.

For what turned out to be her last trip up the coast, there were only fifteen passengers, five officers, a crew of sixteen and "one janitor." At 1.30 p.m. on October 11, 1947, *Gulf Stream*, as *Wolf* was now renamed, sailed from her home port of Vancouver on her normal route up through the Strait of Georgia, between Vancouver Island and the mainland, as far as Cortez Island, about half way up the Vancouver Island shoreline. She stopped to drop some passengers at Westview, the port for Powell River, and sailed at 7.30 p.m., in the dark, with a gentle rain falling, turned north, up the coast for her next port of call. There had been considerable drinking going on among the passengers during the afternoon's voyage up to Westview, and investigation later revealed that the first mate, the ship's senior crewman, the bos'n, and the chief steward had been participating with them, to the extent that they were of no use in running the ship. After leaving the harbour, the master turned over the watch to the twenty-three-year-old second mate and a young helmsman, and went below. The visibility was poor, and unknown to the mate, currents were setting the ship farther towards the shore than he anticipated. When he missed an expected light about 7.45, and with a following sea and wind and variable but poor visibility, the mate became slightly worried. But when he saw a line of surf about 75 yards ahead for a moment he thought it to be just a breaking wave. He couldn't have been more wrong. At 14 knots on a black night, time had already run out.

At this location the channel is a little over a mile wide. About 350 yards out from the starboard side of the channel lies Dinner Rock, about 500 feet in diameter, and sloping gradually out of the sea to a height of some 65 feet. The scene is well set in the words of the unfortunate second mate, then in command on the bridge of *Gulf Stream*, as reported at the inquiry shortly afterwards:

The end of *Wolf*, on her side on Dinner Rock, off Powell River, British Columbia, in October, 1947.

> After I didn't pick up the light, I figured we were either quite a little too close or there must have been a squall ahead that obliterated the light, or it was not burning. I carried on for a while and still no light. It must have been five or six minutes afterwards when I spotted the rock straight ahead, at about 50 or 75 yards. It looked like a white patch across the bow and I could not figure out what it was for a couple of seconds.
>
> Just as that time the helmsman must have glanced up and seen it and said "What is that?" At the same time I realized it was a rock and gave him an order hard to port, which he did. She was swinging around on that, with helm hard to port when we struck and bounced up onto the ledge and bounced again and went right up onto the rock, and capsized right over to port, with the bottom up in the air.

In fact, *Gulf Stream*'s fore part was high on the rock, and her after part completely under water. And it was in this after part that five passengers were drowned, two ladies and three children. The rest of the passengers and the crew from the capsized vessel were able to clamber onto Dinner Rock. An SOS signal was then flashed by flashlight to a passing fish-packer, the *Betty L*. Her skipper, Robier York, noticed the flashing signals, stood in close to the rock and played his searchlight on the wreck, greatly assisting the master to get his surviving passengers and the crew safely onto Dinner Rock. A small boat was launched from the *Betty L* and took aboard that ship the surviving women and the injured. Later she went around to the lee of the rock and embarked all the remaining survivors, and then left for Powell River, where hospital services were provided.

As a result of this sad affair, the master lost his certificate for six months for not ensuring that the mate was keeping a better watch, and for incaution in setting a course that led the ship onto Dinner Rock by only the set of the current. The second mate also lost his certification for a period, and the first mate was severely reprimanded for being intoxicated and of no use in the safe navigation of *Gulf Stream*, although commended for his assistance in saving lives when the ship stranded. Four of the five bodies were recovered the next day from the saloon across the after part of the ship, which was not particularly badly damaged, due to the smoothness of the rock. But then a storm blew up, and *Gulf Stream* slipped back off the ledge and into 130 feet of water. At this point the ship was abandoned as a total loss. In the 1960's a salvage group rolled her further over with explosives to recover her valuable brass propellers. In the last few years sport divers have gone down to the ship where she still lies at the foot of Dinner Rock. So *Wolf* still exists, but much removed from the ordinary and interested viewer.

Ambler, the lone Canadian yacht, was also declared surplus to naval requirements in July 1945, and on November 3, 1945, was technically resold to her original owner, Charles Sheppard, for the original one dollar he had received when he gave her to the Navy in 1940. After an assessment, Mr. Sheppard decided she could not be reconverted usefully for his purposes. Anyway, he had realized she was too large for the restricted waters of Georgian Bay, and he had pretty well retired from the lumbering business which had been her only real use before the war. So, without recovering her from her final berth at Sydney, he sold her to a Toronto investment dealer, who a year later arranged to sell her to our old friend Wentworth Macdonald of Sydney, on December 28, 1946. He in turn was not prepared to spend the money necessary to convert her for useful passenger service, so sold her to Greek interests in November 1947. At that stage *Ambler* disappears from the scene. She could have been put to use ferrying in the Mediterranean, but being over twenty-five years old, could just as easily have been scrapped.

HMCS *Caribou* was also one of the yachts bought by Went Macdonald. She may have been used for a few local passenger and freighting trips around to the local fishing villages, but she was never formally registered again. She was on Lloyd's Register's books until 1952 and then just disappears, like so many other of Macdonald's purchases, presumably for scrap, or even to the harbour bottom as a rusted hulk.

HMCS *Moose*, the neat little yacht built in 1930 for A.C. Murphy of New York, being in relatively good shape at the end of the war, was the only one to revert to her former role as a luxury yacht. Forty miles outside the city of Montreal, at Sorel, on the south shore of the St. Lawrence, lies a large shipbuilding, repairing and servicing enterprise, Marine Industries, essentially owned by the Simard family. They had built many of Canada's warships during the war, so not unnaturally they bought up quite a few after the war at bargain prices, either as a source of parts, for scrap steel, or for useful reconversion into peacetime shipping. In fact, MIL bought sixteen vessels, including *Moose*, and such esoteric craft as three submarines (for scrap, and their powerful diesel engines), two naval tankers, and the Fairmile mother ship *Preserver*.

In July 1945, *Moose* was declared surplus to naval requirements like her compatriots, and in January 1946 she was bought by Marine Industries for $9,000. Her sale price excluded, it turned out after considerable back and forth correspondence, her two motor launches, which had simply "disappeared"! After a short delay, she was reconverted in their yards into a luxury yacht for the use of M. Joseph Simard, the president, who not only made business trips to the cities of Montreal and Quebec in the comfort of his own fast yacht by river, but had a summer residence at Cacouna on the south shore below Quebec. Since this is the only instance of any of the yachts being reconverted to their

Wentworth N. Macdonald of Sydney, who bought seven yachts after the war.

Renard and *Caribou's* last berth, at Sydney, N.S. awaiting a sale that never came.

Moose at Marine Industries yard in 1946, after a hard war, lying alongside a large trawler minesweeper. Awaiting re-conversion.

prewar private purpose there was obviously just no demand for such large pleasure vessels. Everyone had turned to busy business lives, and long distance travel was undertaken by trans-ocean aircraft. It so happened that M. Simard had the facilities easily at hand in his case, and could use her for both business and pleasure. But her sale price was not much for the Navy's initial expenditure of $239,000 to convert her into a warship.

Renamed *Fraternité*, she was used by the Simards for ten years, until October 1956, when she was sold to Mr. W. E. Pennick of New Orleans, who, in turn named her *Ottelia*, and promptly transferred her to A.H. Schaupeter, a consulting engineer from Detroit, who retained her in the Mexican Gulf for his use when down there. In 1974, he sold her to a firm by the name of Green Seas of Gibraltar. Still named *Ottelia*, she was registered in Southampton, England, and with a home port of Monaco, is no doubt being used for charter cruising in the Mediterranean, apparently still going strong after forty-nine years.

Like *Moose*, *Husky* is also still afloat. Bought in January 1946 by Went Macdonald, he was able to sell her almost at once to the Port of New Orleans Board of Commissioners, renamed for her trip south down the inland passage with her prewar name of *Wild Duck*. On the Mississippi at her new home port, she was rehabilitated, given two new 450-horsepower diesels, her fine panelling renewed, and the grey naval paint replaced by powder blue for the hull, with white trim and the traditional small buff funnel, bearing the seal of the Port of New Orleans. For twenty years she remained the port inspection vessel, now bearing the name of *Good Neighbor*, and taking out visiting dignitaries such as General de Gaulle of France, the King and Queen of Greece, and even visiting Japanese teachers and the 1960 "Miss Louisiana" contestants.

Having eventually outlived her usefulness in that role and being thirty-seven years old, the port sold her in February 1967 to the W.S. Young Construction Company, also of New Orleans, who fell on financial hard times, for they had to give her up in 1968, when she was bought at a U.S. Marshal's sale by Twinkling Star Inc., usually the sign of a ship that is being sold for bills that are owing. For a short time, still named *Good Neighbor*, she was used as a cruise yacht, and then sold again to Mr. Vernon Allen's sport diving company, as *Aquarius No. 2*, being employed as a diving tender off the Louisiana and Texas coasts. In 1972 she was taken down to Honduras and registered there, under the Honduran flag. She was based on the bay island of Guanaja, Honduras. For the ten years in this business, she acted as a support base for divers in various locations, with no time lost between dives, since she had on board the air compression services they needed. She would cruise from place to place where diving was spectacular or interesting, stopping to anchor in inlets and bays, to let her passengers drop to the bottom in those crystal clear and warm waters. In the mid 1970's she made an emergency trip up to New Orleans again to pick up relief supplies after a disastrous hurricane had caused considerable damage and loss in Honduras.

However, being owned by Mr. Allen of distant Morgan City, Louisiana, meant that there was little direct control of the enterprise, and by 1979 there was insufficient profit to continue, especially as *Good Neighbor* was by now, not too surprisingly, having increasing maintenance problems. She was then sold and steamed up to New Orleans again, where her new owner, in 1981, took most of the insides out of her, including the two large diesel engines, and turned her into a floating restaurant in that city. So *Husky* survives to this day, immobile, but afloat, more or less.

Elk, one of the larger yachts, also passed into commercial use after her wartime service. She was bought on November 6, 1945, by H.B. Gault of Saint John, New Brunswick, for his Eastern Canada Coastal Steamships, and taken in hand for reconversion. Two new General Motors 900-horsepower diesels were installed, and the accommodation rebuilt

Elk as the passenger ferry *Grand Manan III*, running between St. John, N.B. and the island of Grand Manan.

to take passengers on short trips. On completion, her name was changed to *Grand Manan III*, and now technically owned by Saint John Marine Transport, she was for twenty-two years the ferry from Black's Harbour and from Saint John to the island of Grand Manan, located in the Bay of Fundy about 50 miles southeast of St. John. For years old *Elk* was the reliable transportation between the offshore islands (there was also a Little Manan Island, with a few people on it) and the Canadian mainland, only being replaced when in need of an overhaul during the winter. The Bay of Fundy is known to be one of the roughest bodies of water in the world, so *Grand Manan III* was not always on time at her destination, nor on some days, did she arrive at all. Eventually, becoming too outdated and unreliable for that vital service, in July 1968, at the age of forty-two years, she was sold to an American buyer who shortly afterwards scrapped her. She had performed very well in her three varied careers.

Vison, the second newest of all the yachts when she was purchased in 1940, is one of Wentworth Macdonald's paradoxes. At the end of the war she was still only fourteen years old, and in excellent shape when he bought her in January of 1946. Her engines were still reliable, and even parts were still available. She had not been extensively modified, not having been fitted with a large saloon forward, and should have been a useful postwar ship for some purpose. Yet there is no indication that Macdonald ever used her, for she did not appear on the Canadian merchant shipping or yacht registers, nor did he appear to sell her to anyone else, for there can be found no details of any transfer to other ownership. Maybe, like his other ships, she just rusted out alongside his pier. At any rate, *Vison* has no postwar history that can be discovered.

Cougar, the west coast yacht, was planned to be put to use after the war. She was not released by the Navy until November 23, 1945, being used to transport returning soldiers and sailors to their outport homes up the British Columbian coast. Then, on October 9, 1946, she was sold to Jack Gilmore of Vancouver, for $8,000, who promptly resold her to a Mr. Bearl Sprott, who while listing a Vancouver address for his business, was in fact a

Pasadena, California, businessman. In February 1948, after using the yacht, which he had renamed by her prewar appellation of *Breezin' Thru*, for some cruises up and down the Pacific coast, she was transferred to U.S. registry and moved to Pasadena.

Mr. Sprott then arranged to sell her to someone mysteriously referred to as "the Duke" in his correspondence with the purchaser's agent in London, in mid-1950. Some of the crew who were taken on to deliver the ship to Europe had a suspicion that the new owner might be Spanish, since their eventual delivery port might be in Spain or the United Kingdom. It was all kept very vague and thus intriguing. At any rate, *Breezin' Thru* sailed from California on July 22, 1950, and the ship eventually reached the Panama Canal Zone on August 9, a rather lengthy time for a fairly modest distance. Since she, and her engines, were by this time thirty-four years old, and she had seen service in two wars in both Canadian and American naval hands, it is not too surprising that the voyage was a series of machinery problems, breakdowns and so on. Even the funnel fitting leaked in rainstorms, allowing water into the engine room, which then caused electrical short circuits with the equipment. While the captain was a retired Coast Guard Lieutenant Commander, and the senior two engineers were paid and competent, the crew were almost all university students, unpaid, using the trip as a cheap way to reach Europe on a holiday. So when the ship had to put into Manzanillo and Acapulco, Mexico, and again into Punta Arenas, Costa Rica, the captain had some difficulty getting his crew together to leave port as soon as repairs were made. To quote him (in a letter to the Agents, explaining the delays in arrival):

> Sailed at 0100 of the 30th, after some slight difficulty assembling my high spirited volunteer crew (seven young fellows just out of college) who did not feel the weight of the yoke attached to a pay cheque, since they are unpaid, and had to be rounded up from the fleshpots of Manzanillo by appeals to their sportsmanship.
>
> In case my policy of granting liberty in these ports is deemed to be over generous, I might say that the problem of keeping a crowd of young volunteers working satisfactorily can only be solved by extra consideration in matters of this sort. These chaps are out for a lark in order to see Europe and way ports, and are perfectly capable of swimming ashore to see a place if not permitted to go officially.

At any rate, on the way down the ship had apparently struck a whale with one of her propellers. So when she had passed through the Canal, she lay off the city of Colon, awaiting a chance to get into a drydock there so her shaft could be examined, as there was considerable vibration when running at any speed. After a week or so, the shaft was straightened, and the ship set off to Kingston, Jamaica, where she was to await the arrival by air of quite a list of spare parts needed to correct faults before an ocean crossing could be attempted. While lying in the harbour at Kingston, hurricane Charlie struck and poor old *Breezin' Thru* sank in the harbour. At that point, Mr. Sprott, or whoever was to be her new owner gave up, and she was abandoned to her insurers, and only salvaged for the value of what scrap could be easily recovered.

The last yacht in naval hands, *Sans Peur*, it was hoped could be retained as a useful vessel in the postwar Navy, as the Duke of Sutherland was told. But financial restrictions caused a rethinking of these plans, and on January 31, 1947, *Sans Peur* was paid off for the last time, and soon put up for sale. On July 11, 1948, she was bought by Maple Leaf Steamships of Montreal for $90,000, not very much considering the $329,000 she had cost the Navy only five years before. Then, on December 31, 1948, she was sold again to a Panamanian firm, and her name changed back to her original one of *Trenora*. She then sailed for the Mediterranean, now owned by Jose M. Bash and the Equipment & Supply Company of New York, although registered in Panama. Shortly after arrival in Gibraltar *Trenora* was taken in hand by her original builders, Thorneycrofts of Southampton for a modest refit, to make her once more a luxury yacht. She then passed into the hands of the Genoese shipping family named Ravano, although still registered in Panama and still flying the Panamanian quartered flag.

While essentially a family yacht, *Trenora* was available for selected parties to charter, and indeed was used from time to time by such notables as the Duke and Duchess of Windsor, Henry Ford and Count Marzotto of Italy. She was crewed by Italian officers, and in reality was not used too much, being noticed in and around Gibraltar and Monaco for the most part. Then in late 1972 the senior Ravano died, and the family, owning other large motor yachts of their own, arranged to sell *Trenora* through an agent to Japanese buyers, who were searching for large motor yachts for charter use in and around Japan. The new owners contracted with Captain Ian Walker, who had already brought a previously purchased yacht out to Japan, to pick up *Trenora* and bring her out as well. One unusual condition of the sale was that the name was to be changed. Captain Walker, being a traditionalist, was reluctant to adopt just any name. So he travelled back to Scotland to see the Duchess of Sutherland, to ask her if the ship could reassume the earlier name of *Sans Peur*, from the Sutherland family motto. The duchess was pleased to be asked, and in fact came out to Monte Carlo for the renaming. The acceptance survey for the sale was quickly passed and favourable, since *Sans Peur* had been beautifully kept up, and she set off for the Far East via the Panama Canal and Honolulu, taking forty-nine days for the passage, arriving at the end of May, 1973.

She was immediately put to chartering, and some idea of how her new owners approached their project is given from a brochure of the day on the ship, translated from the Japanese:

> Use the ship's interior for displays of all types, cruising all around Japan. Stop overs at various harbours for exhibitions and demonstrations will make a great impact, this guaranteeing 100% success.
>
> Important meetings involve a certain amount of secrecy. Out at sea unneccessary worry is eliminated and you can concentrate on matters at hand. After such meetings there is the cruise to be enjoyed.
>
> For your comfort, meals and all services are by France International. A *Sans Peur* charter is more than ordinary. Forget all your worries and relax in soothing atmosphere.

Unfortunately the president of the firm died shortly after *Sans Peur*'s arrival, and the new executive did not have his abilities to make a profit from the charter business. Due to overspending on stores, and skimping on up-keep, which resulted in breakdowns and delays, the enterprise soon went bankrupt, and *Sans Peur* was sold to another Japanese firm, Hatsubaichi Kanko of Hiroshima. She was used as a VIP hotel ship in Okinawa in mid-1975 during that island's Ocean Olympics show. Since then she mostly swung to her moorings in the harbour at Hiroshima, looking a bit the worse for wear, paint somewhat grey and in places rust-streaked. To pass her it could be seen that she was not being kept up; even minor maintenance was slipping and the varnish on her teak rails peeling. Maybe she will be taken in hand with an upturn in Japan's economy. With a ship of such interesting, even proud heritage, one would hope so.

So, with this *Sans Peur*, we have followed the armed yachts from the earliest built, the old *Stadacona* of 1899 to the three that are known to still exist — *Husky*, *Moose*, and *Sans Peur*. They will not pass this way again, for two reasons: there are almost no yachts available of that size and type, even if Canada were again to need some small warships for temporary defence of our coasts, and future wars are likely to require something more sophisticated even at the outset than a 130-foot steel yacht, fitted with one modest gun and a simple, lighweight Asdic set.

Looking at our preparedness today, it seems reasonable that we will need some panic buying of ships in any certain war condition. And, as an American admiral has said, "the next war will be a come-as-you-are war, with no time to leisurely build up supplies." No time to scrounge around the continent looking for suitable vessels. And no significant stock of surplus large motor yachts to be found. Canada will have to look elsewhere, and the story of the armed anti-submarine yacht would seem closed for ever.

FOR SALE: Former twin-screw oil burning steam yacht *Aztec*, now called *Beaver*, 260′ x 216′ x 31′ x 15′. Two triple expansion engines, four-cylinder, 1100 h.p. each. Used as Canadian patrol vessel during the war. Photo shows her when she was used as a yacht. Changes have been made in her accommodations. Suitable for commercial purposes.

FOR SALE: Twin-screw Diesel yacht *Reindeer*, ex *Mascotte*. 140′ x 132′ x 24′ 2″ x 9′. Steel construction, built in 1926. Two 400 h.p. Winton Diesel motors installed 1931, six cylinders. Speed 12–13 knots. Cruising radius about 4000 miles. Was used as Canadian patrol vessel. Photo shows her as a yacht. Changes were made for patrol duty. Suitable for commercial purposes.

FOR SALE: Twin-screw Diesel yacht *Ambler*, 129′ x 112′ 6″ x 23′ x 6′ 6″. Steel construction. Built 1922. Two 250 h.p. Winton Diesel motors; six cylinders, speed 12–13 m.p.h. Was used as a Canadian patrol vessel. Photo shows her as a yacht before purchased by Canadian Government. Changes were made for patrol duty.

FOR SALE: Twin-screw Diesel yacht *Caribou*, formerly *Elfreda*, 141′ 8″ x 130′ 5″ x 23′ 2″ x 9′. Steel construction, built 1928. Two 425 h.p. Cooper-Bessemer Diesel motors, eight cylinders each. Speed 15–17 m.p.h., cruising radius about 4000 miles. Was used as Canadian patrol vessel. Photo shows her as a yacht before purchased by Canadian Government. Changes were made for patrol duty. Suitable for commercial purposes.

A typical advertisement, this one from "Yachting" Magazine, from New York, announcing the disposal of the armed yachts. Few were sold this way.

GLOSSARY OF ABBREVIATIONS

AB — Able seaman, the first step up the promotion ladder
A/S — Anti-submarine
Asdic — An underwater transmitting and listening device; from the letters of the Anti-Submarine Detection Investigation Committee.
ASCO — Anti-Submarine Control Officer
BANGOR — A class of minesweeping ships, named after the first ship of the class, HMS *Bangor*.
Captain (D) — Originally, the captain in charge of destroyers; later of all operational ships in a major Canadian port.
CB — Confidential (secret) Book; or Cape Breton, Nova Scotia.
CDR — Commander, a rank immediately below Captain
CNLO — Canadian Naval Liaison Officer in a foreign port
CNS — The Chief of the Naval Staff, the navy's senior officer
C.O. — Commanding Officer (not always, in fact rarely, a captain in rank)
COAC — Commanding Officer Atlantic Coast, the officer in over-all command at Halifax
CPO — Chief petty officer, the senior non-commissioned rank
ERA — Engineroom artificer, or mechanic
ETA — Estimated time of arrival at a destination
First Lieutenant — In a small ship, the second-in-command. Also called the XO
FONF — Flag Officer Newfoundland Force
Galley — The ship's kitchen
HX convoys — Halifax outbound fast (9 knots and over) convoys
Knot — A rate of speed, about 1.14 miles an hour. Thus 9 knots = 10¼ m.p.h.
NCSO — Naval Control of (merchant) Shipping Officer
NOIC — Naval Officer in Charge of a minor port or base
'NR — See RCNR (below)
NSHQ — Naval Service Headquarters in Ottawa
OOW — Officer-of-the-Watch, the current duty officer
PO — Petty officer
QF — A quick-firing gun, whose breech closed automatically
RCNR — Royal Canadian Naval Reserve; men with merchant ship experience
RCNVR — Royal Canadian Naval Volunteer Reserve, or the "Wavy Navy" (from the stripes on the officers' sleeve); those with, intially, little sea or ship-handling experience
RN — The Royal Navy
RNCVR — Royal Navy Canadian Volunteer Reserve, the RCNVR of the 1913 to 1922 period.
SC convoys — Sydney outbound slow convoys, 6 to 9 knots, sometimes less!
S.O. Patrols — Senior officer in charge of local defence patrols
Sub, or S/LT — Sub-lieutenant, the junior commissioned officers' rank
'VR — RCNVR (above)
Wardroom — The officers' "living room" on board or ashore
W/T — Wireless telegraphy, the ship's radio equipment
X/O — Executive officer, or second in command of a ship
XV — Examination vessel, off a port entrance
2123P — "Papa" time was local, civilian, time in Nova Scotia
0340Z — "Zulu" time was Greenwich Mean Time, world wide, and 5 or 6 hours ahead of "Papa" time

BIBLIOGRAPHY

College, J.J. & Dittmar, F.J. — *British Warships 1914-1919* London, 1972

Colledge. J.J. & Lenton, H.T. — *Warships of World War II, Part 4* London, n.d.

Crabtree, R. — *The Luxury Yacht From Steam to Diesel*

Hoffman, Erik — *The Steam Yachts* London, 1970

Keenleyside, Dr. H. — *Article, Weekend Magazine* Toronto, March 1974

Lenton, H.T. — *Royal Netherlands Navy* London, 1968

Ludham, Harry & Lund, Paul — *Night of the U-Boats* London, 1974

Manning, CAPT, T.D. & Walker, CDR. C.F. — *British Warship Names* London, 1972

Schull, Joseph — *The Far Distant Ships* Ottawa, 1950

Silverstone, Paul H. — *U.S. Warships of World War I* New York, 1970

Tucker, G.N. — *The Naval Service of Canada,* 2 Vols., Ottawa, 1952

The Navy Lists London, 1915-1919

The Canadian Navy Lists Ottawa, 1939-1945

Jane's Fighting Ships London, 1919, 1941, 1944-45

Who's Who In America 1900-1950

Who's Who In Canada 1910-1970

Lloyd's Register of Merchant Ships 1919, 1947-73

Lloyd's Register of American & Canadian Yachts 1923-1960

Department of National Defence

Naval Service

IN REPLY PLEASE QUOTE

NO.

194

THIS IS TO ACKNOWLEDGE RECEIPT

OF

H.M.C.S. "REINDEER"

RECEIVED AT SYDNEY AT 1600 HOURS

30TH NOVEMBER, 1945.

SIGNED W.M. MACDONALD

INDEX

Note: All ships are listed by name at the end of the general Index. Ranks are those at the time of this history

SHIPS

PHOTOGRAPH CREDITS:

The author much appreciates the assistance of the following people and organizations for the use of their photographs, in particular the Norman MacKenzie Art Gallery for Arthur Lismer's painting of *Grilse* on the dust cover.

Mrs. Margaret Bell: pp. 104, 105
W.R. Craig: pp. 130 bottom, 135, 147 top
Mrs. A.H. Crockett: p. 161 top left
G.H. Duggan: p. 66 center
Eaton's of Canada: p. 21 left
Capt. J.B. Fotheringham: p. 134 top
R.H.I. Goddard: p. 56 top
N. Harris: pp. 113 top, 120 bottom
LCDR. C.K. Hurst: p. 146
D.L. Johnston: p. 110
Col. F.H.M. Jones: p. 65 bottom
E.W.I. Keenleyside: p. 68 bottom
André Labanerc: p. 155
Jerry L'Aventure: p. 163
Mrs. M.S. Lorriman: pp. 66 bottom, 73 lower
Mrs. J.I. Maclaren: pp. 79 bottom, 81
K.R. Macpherson: p.85
W.M. McCrae: pp.5, 78 top & bottom, 140
B.P. McCurdy: p.89
Herb Miller: p. 146 top
S.T. Molson: p. 65 center
T.H.P. Molson: p. 56 bottom
D.C. Oland: p. 79 top
Mrs. Ann Porter: p. 65 top
A.C. Rogers: p. 159
R.B. Seager: p. 147 lower
R.E. Sheppard: p. 83 top
Mrs. L.R. Thomson: p. 58
Clarence Wallace: pp. 31 bottom, 69 top
Author: pp 113. lower, 143, 149 center, 152, 153, 161 top

Bath Iron Works, ME: p. 5 top
Cox & Stevens: pp. 72 bottom, 73 top
Dept. Of National Defence, Historical Section: pp. 24 top, 26, 27, 30 top, 31 bottom, 41 top, 99 bottom, 109, 115, 118, 122, 128, 133 top
T. Eaton Co., Historical Section: pp. 17, 21 bottom
W. Gardner & Co.: pp. 64 bottom, 66 top, 72 top, 79 center
Marine Industries Ltd.: p. 161 bottom
Mariners' Museum of Newport News, VA: pp. 13, 23
Maritime Museum of the Atlantic, McBride Collection: p. 149 bottom
Maritime Museum of B.C.: W. Duston Collection: p. 134 bottom
Norman MacKenzie Art Gallery, Regina: p. 7 & dust cover
Public Archives of Canada: pp. 24 bottom, 30 bottom, 31 top, 41 bottom, 44 top, 55, 82, 83 bottom, 99 top, 107, 111, 113 bottom, 120 top, 127, 130 top, 136, 149 top
Royal Canadian Yacht Club: pp. 44 top right, 68
Royal Nova Scotia Yacht Squadron: p. 64 top
Rutherford B. Hayes Library: p 44 bottom
Sea Magazine: p. 87
Solomon R. Guggenheim Foundation, NY: p. 8
U.S. Naval Historical Center: pp. 70, 98
Who's Who & Why: p. 21 right
Yachting Magazine: pp. 95, 166

S06